Becoming the Evidence-Based Manager

BECOMING THE EVIDENCE-BASED MANAGER

MAKING THE
SCIENCE OF MANAGEMENT WORK
FOR YOU

Second Edition

GARY P. LATHAM

SOCIETY FOR HUMAN
RESOURCE MANAGEMENT

NICHOLAS BREALEY
PUBLISHING

BOSTON · LONDON

First edition published in 2009 by Davies-Black, an imprint of Nicholas Brealey Publishing
This new edition published by Nicholas Brealey Publishing in 2018
An imprint of John Murray Press

An Hachette UK company

23 22 21 20 19 18   1 2 3 4 5 6 7 8 9 10

A CIP catalogue record for this title is available from the British Library

Library of Congress Control Number: 2018935972

ISBN 978-1-47367-697-8
US eBook 978-0-89106-373-5
UK eBook ISBN 978-1-47364-352-9

Printed and bound in the United States of America

John Murray Press policy is to use papers that are natural, renewable and recyclable products
and made from wood grown in sustainable forests. The logging and manufacturing processes
are expected to conform to the environmental regulations of the country of origin.

John Murray Press Ltd   Nicholas Brealey Publishing
Carmelite House   Hachette Book Group
50 Victoria Embankment   Market Place Center, 53 State Street
London EC4Y 0DZ   Boston, MA 02109, USA
Tel: 020 3122 6000   Tel: (617) 263 1834

www.nicholasbrealey.com

CONTENTS

ACKNOWLEDGMENTS

The following people were invaluable to me in writing this book. The managers in my executive MBA class ensured that I dotted every *i* and crossed every *t*. More important, they ensured that what I wrote was practical—helpful to them as leaders in the workplace. After I'd followed their suggestions, three governors on the board of the Center for Creative Leadership, with whom I served two terms— Joseph B. Anderson, chairman and CEO of TAG Holdings, LLC; Naomi Marrow, former VP of HR at Reader's Digest; and Marc Noel, chairman of the Noel Group, LLC—gave me invaluable feedback. Dr. David Altman, chief operating officer at the center, was also very helpful, as were my research assistants, Coreen Hrabluik and Amanda Shantz, who are now Drs. Hrabluik and Shantz. Lastly, I am indebted to my editor, Laura Lawson, for the ideas and laughter we shared in producing the final copy of the original edition of this book, and my current editor, Alison Hankey, who provided me advice and encouragement for the revision.

INTRODUCTION

Think back to when you first became a manager. Whether it was two weeks or twenty years ago, most likely the thrill and exhilaration of the promotion quickly gave way to the sinking realization that leading people is a lot harder than it looks. In fact, it is so hard to be an effective manager that a third or more of new managers fail in their job in less than two years.[1] And while management gets easier as one learns the ropes, it never gets easy—I've spent a good deal of my working life with senior managers who still struggle with people problems. So, though experience helps, becoming an effective manager isn't simply a matter of years on the job. What, then, does make for effective management? Effective management is both an art and a science: It results from using solid, proven, tested techniques (the science of management) in an inspiring and engaging way (the art of management). The principles of management science can be taught. They are replicable. The art is in how you apply them.

Most books on management focus only on the art. Although the techniques presented in those books often appear factual and promise results if you use a given step-by-step methodology, the techniques themselves are not well researched or grounded in science. Instead, they are based on the authors' personal experiences as managers, their particular best practices, or plain old-fashioned intuition. Sometimes these methods are transferable to you, the reader; typically they are not. In sum, the advice is hit or miss. Why? Because art and intuition are usually unique to an individual. What works for one manager in one environment (experience and best practices) may not work in another environment, let alone for another manager.

The bottom line is that most management books just have too much art and too little science. Though the art and intuition of management do have value, they can seldom be taught or transferred. In contrast, the science of management *can* be taught and transferred. So it makes a lot more sense—and gives you more return for your time—to focus on tips and techniques for managing others to high performance that are grounded in empirical research.

*The art of management can seldom be taught. The science of management **can be** taught.*

This book was written to underscore the scientific aspect of effective management— what is called *evidence-based management*—in an artful way. Here, I aim to

- Share management techniques that have been proven by valid and reliable research studies to work

- Share this information in an engaging way that makes sense to you, the manager

My goal is to share with you everything I've learned about evidence-based management over the past half century as an organizational psychologist with one foot planted in the real world of the private and public sectors and the other in the academic arena.

As an organizational psychologist, I have conducted countless studies on ways to improve management practices. In my work as a corporate staff psychologist and consultant, I have accumulated years of experience applying the results of psychological research in the workplace. As an HR consultant, I serve as a translator of sorts to help everyday managers become high performers by using evidence-based management practices. In this book, I've worked to share the most effective methods for hiring, inspiring, training, motivating, and appraising employees. These methods have been *shown by years of research* to deliver high performance. As a result, instead of being hit or miss—working for some managers but not others, working in some fields but not others—this book will be right on target for you. It provides you management techniques that really deliver, whether you're in the private or public sector and no matter what your level of management skill or experience.

Historically, managers have not clamored for practices based on evidence, in spite of the quantity of research about which management techniques work well and which do not. This is not because you and other managers don't want to be great at what you do, and it is not because research isn't valued. It is just that most managers are simply too busy to keep up-to-date on the latest studies. Sadly, even if you had the time to read the research, you'd find that scientists are rarely good at translating their results into practical recommendations.

Yet an emphasis on evidence-based practices is sweeping through the fields of medicine, clinical psychology, education, and architecture. Few of us would expect a neurosurgeon to remove a brain tumor or an architect to design a bridge by drawing on intuition alone. Instead, we expect these professionals to ground their work in practices that have been proven in the past to work. We should expect the same evidence-based standards and guidelines for managers.

Evidence-based practices ensure high performance and job satisfaction.

Evidence-based practices ensure high performance and job satisfaction. They're incredibly useful in providing hands-on guidance to people who want to engage effectively in their job.

My hope is that this book will further the evidence-based movement in management—that it will stoke your desire to learn about this approach as you discover that evidence-based management practices work. More important, though, I hope that this book will serve as a handbook on evidence-based management techniques for the entire employee life cycle—hiring, inspiring, training, motivating, and appraising employees—a handbook you can return to time and again.

Specifically, this book will give you the essential information you need to become an evidence-based manager from the hiring stage to the retention stage—from A to Z. This information will be presented within the following ten general lessons of management, plus an eleventh chapter on two evidence-based managers in action—one in the United States and the second in Iran.

Lesson 1: Use the right tools to identify and hire high-performing employees.

Lesson 2: Inspire your employees to effectively execute strategy.

Lesson 3: Develop and train employees to create a high-performing team.

Lesson 4: Motivate your employees to become high performers.

Lesson 5: Engage your employees.

Lesson 6: Ensure career success.

Lesson 7: Create a psychologically healthy workplace.

Lesson 8: Instill resilience in the face of setbacks.

Lesson 9: Make good decisions.

Lesson 10: Appraise and coach your employees to be high performers.

Because of the accumulation of practical everyday knowledge in the behavioral sciences, in the second edition I have added information in chapter 1 on the importance of emotional intelligence. In addition, I have added four new chapters, namely chapter 5 on ways to engage your employees in their work, 6 on ways to ensure your career success, 7 on how to create a psychologically healthy workplace, and 9 on the pitfalls to avoid when making decisions.

In themselves, these lessons are not novel. You already know, for example, that you should use valid tools to hire the right people. Yet most line managers don't know which tools have been proven, through research, to be effective. This book gives that information. Similarly, most managers want to make sure that their team is well trained and prepared for high performance, but they may not have access to training techniques shown by research to be most effective for ensuring that this occurs.

In this book, I explain, synthesize, and translate management research results into practical guidelines for handling the difficult areas of management that many managers deal with daily. Some of this research has not seen the light of day in mainstream business writing. In other cases, you are likely to recognize the evidence-based management techniques—such as coaching—but for the first time will understand why coaching is so effective and how to employ coaching as a technique for developing employees to become high performers. It's the first time, to my knowledge, that someone has attempted to compile a broad overview of the management research of the past half century into a compact, readable, evidence-based handbook for line managers.

With employees inspired and engaged, managers don't have to battle to get desired results.

In my work, I have continually received "Aha!" feedback from managers, employees, audiences, and MBA students when I share these evidence-based management techniques. They make sense, they are simple to understand, and they work in the private and public sectors. Armed with these new tools, managers have been able to boost employee performance significantly and execute desired strategies for their teams with noteworthy success. Good management always requires a lot of hard work and sustained effort, but once evidence-based techniques are mastered, it also can become fun, because employees respond so well to this approach. With employees inspired and engaged, managers don't have to battle to get desired results; they just happen. Managers can actually enjoy the process of leading others because they know what they're supposed to be doing and because their efforts bring tangible results.

Here's to your growth as an evidence-based manager and to using management techniques that truly work!

Becoming the Evidence-Based Manager

USE THE RIGHT TOOLS TO HIRE HIGH-PERFORMING EMPLOYEES

It's an understatement to say that hiring the right employees is integral to executing strategy effectively. In fact, as Larry Bossidy, retired CEO of AlliedSignal, says, "In the race, you bet on people, not strategies."[1] Without the right people, any strategy—no matter how promising or well-designed—will be rendered useless. With the right people, however, goals get met, strategy gets executed, and organizations soar.

For example, in the service industry, it isn't the CEO's vision that brings repeat business—it's the friendliness and helpfulness of the wait staff, desk agents, and parking valets. Bob Ford, a management professor at the University of Central Florida, is fond of saying that at the moment a service is delivered, that one person, that single server, *is* the organization for the customer. If the car rental clerk loses your reservation, you don't just blame that clerk, you conclude that the entire company is, at best, mediocre. If that car rental clerk is working for you, then people may conclude that you too accept mediocrity. Consequently, you must pick *winners*—the kind of people who are able to take decisive action consistent with your team's vision and goals. These high performers are the ones who do great work despite the ambiguity, complexity, and chaos inherent in organizational life.

This chapter focuses on evidence-based methods for selecting high-performing employees who are best suited to the needs of your team. On the basis of empirical research, I recommend four hiring tools, all of which are reliable and valid:[2]

- Situational interviews (SI)
- Patterned behavioral description interviews (PBDI)
- Job simulations
- Realistic job previews

The first three tools are useful in predicting which job applicants will perform at high levels and which will not. The fourth enables people who are offered a job to decide if it is right for them. Managers who adopt these four tools will select winners.

There are two additional tools I am often asked about—cognitive ability tests and personality tests. They do have some uses, which I explain later, but are less easy to adopt as they require the assistance of a psychologist to administer and score them. I also want to say a few words about emotional intelligence.

WHAT DOESN'T WORK, IN BRIEF

The most commonly used interview technique in organizations today—a free-flowing conversation, or what researchers call an *unstructured interview*—is, ironically, the least effective. The unstructured interview often goes something like this:

"Tell me about yourself."

"Where did you go to school?"

"How much do you know about our organization?"

"Why are you interested in this job opening?"

"Do you have any questions for me?"

If you correlate how people perform in an unstructured interview with how they perform on the job, you'll realize you might as well resort to astrology charts.

Many studies, including one in the *Journal of Occupational Psychology*, show that the correlation between how people are assessed in an unstructured interview and how they are assessed on the job is very low.[3] This is because in an unstructured interview for a given job

- Different applicants are typically asked different questions

- The questions are often not directly related to the job

- Interviewers are often unable to agree among themselves what constitutes a great response versus a not-so-great response

If you were to sit in on any hiring panel in the midst of debating possibly acceptable candidates—whether in the banking world, the healthcare industry, or the automotive industry—you would find that the difference of opinion on what constitutes great answers (and great candidates) as revealed by the unstructured interview is tremendous. Hence, the unstructured interview is not very effective for selecting winners. Even though it's a favorite in most organizations, you don't want to use this interview technique—you have much better alternatives.

WHAT WORKS, IN BRIEF

So throw out the unstructured job interview and replace it with the following research-supported tools for hiring top performers. This combination of tools represents the very best of what research shows about making good hiring decisions.

The *situational interview*, as the name implies, presents people with situations they will encounter on the job. Hence it is extremely effective at predicting how people will perform in given situations. What people say they will do on the job and how they actually behave on the job turn out to have a significant correlation.

Research has also shown that the *patterned behavioral interview*, where you ask applicants how they behaved in the past, is a good predictor of how they will behave in the future. This is because a person's past behavior predicts future behavior.

Job simulations test applicants right now, in real time, to see what they can actually do. Simulations have also been backed by many research studies that show them to be effective in predicting job performance (that is, current behavior in a simulated environment predicts subsequent behavior in similar on-the-job situations). One kind of simulation, the assessment center simulation, has been successful in predicting the job promotions and salary progression of people over a twenty-five-year career.

Last, research has revealed the value of a *realistic job preview*.[4] The preview is called realistic because you explain what will be great for an applicant if that person accepts your job offer, and you also explain what job incumbents have found not to be as great. No matter how good your other tools, candidates will always know things about themselves that your selection techniques will not identify. A realistic preview enables candidates to decide whether accepting a job offer is the right decision for them.

EFFECTIVE HIRING TOOLS IN PRACTICE

These first four tools provide a reliable and valid evidence-based package for identifying and then hiring high-performing employees. The following sections offer practical information on how to use these tools so that you can create a winning team.

The Situational Interview

The situational interview assesses an applicant's intentions for dealing with situations likely to arise on the job.[5] Given the clear relationship between intentions and subsequent behavior at work, the situational interview should be a staple of every evidence-based manager's hiring practices.

A situational interview is structured so that every candidate answers the same job-related questions. In addition, a behavioral scoring guide made up of illustrative answers is used to assess each applicant's answer to a question. This type of interview ensures that

- Managers get good job-related information from the candidates

- Managers have a frame of reference that helps them reliably assess the quality of an interviewee's response

Most important, each question presents a dilemma, as shown below. It is this dilemma that "forces" applicants to state what they believe they would actually do on the job (that is, their intentions) rather than telling interviewers what they believe the interviewers are hoping to hear. The situational interview should be conducted by two or more people. The interview panel should include the responsible manager and someone from Human Resources.

The dilemma in each question forces applicants to state what they would actually do on the job.

For example, the Weyerhaeuser Company needed to staff a pulp mill. As staff psychologist, I held a focus group with supervisors to describe critical situations that hourly workers deal with in such a mill. We turned these situations into "What would you do in this situation?" questions, and we then generated answers that we agreed were highly acceptable, acceptable, or unacceptable. These illustrative answers became our scoring guide. We correlated the scores we gave job applicants' responses to each situational question with the scores the successful applicants received one year later on the job. Eureka! What they said in the interview correlated with what they did on the job.

Creating a Situational Interview

To create a situational interview, take these three steps:

1. Conduct a job analysis.

2. Create situational interview questions that contain a dilemma.

3. Develop a scoring guide.

1. Conduct a job analysis. A job analysis identifies important situations that an applicant will likely encounter on the job. These situations typically revolve around your team's vision, goals, and strategy. From this analysis, you will be able to develop a series of questions that will help you assess how a candidate will respond to a given challenge. For example, a job analysis for a purchasing manager position might reveal that a purchasing manager has to choose between competing suppliers, minimizing costs, and maximizing a department's bottom line.

The best way to do a job analysis for developing a situational interview is to use the *critical-incident technique*, where managers interview job incumbents to identify the incidents that make the difference between highly effective and not-so-effective performers.[6]

This job analysis focuses on observable behaviors that job incumbents (the subject matter experts) have seen make the difference between a poor employee and an outstanding one. The critical incident technique allows you to ignore situations that occur routinely. It helps you zero in on situations that can have a significant impact on your team's vision, goals, and strategy execution, such as dealing with an eleventh-hour maintenance issue on the production line or quickly finding a replacement for a team member who calls in sick.

2. Create situational interview questions that contain a dilemma. Once your job analysis identifies critical incidents, you can design a series of situational questions to assess how job candidates intend to handle such challenges. I typically recommend creating at least ten questions in total.

In the case of the job of purchasing manager, you might design questions that assess candidates' technical knowledge, leadership ability, ethical behavior, and team-building skills. Built into each situational interview question is a dilemma that "forces" applicants to state their intentions rather than merely respond with what they believe the interview panel wants to hear. For example, the question in the box below requires the candidate to decide whether to emphasize maximizing the bottom line, keeping a strong relationship with the supplier, or behaving ethically by adhering to the organization's policy.

A SITUATIONAL INTERVIEW QUESTION

You, as the purchasing manager, often negotiate and mingle with suppliers. You frequently speak with Pat, the sales manager of one of your largest suppliers. In fact, you both share a common interest in sports. In one particular conversation, Pat has invited you to an athletic event next week. In the same breath, Pat asks about the offers that were submitted to you last week by other suppliers as part of a sealed-bid process. More specifically, you are asked what the price must be to win the bid. Pat's company has been able to supply parts with very good quality to you in the past. Giving this information to Pat will enable you to drive down your costs, one of your primary mandates as a purchasing manager. What would you do in this situation?

---

3. Develop a scoring guide. Once you have a list of questions, you will be ready to develop a scoring guide for each one—before you conduct the interview. The scoring guide will help you avoid one of the pitfalls of the unstructured interview: argument among interviewers about what constitutes a good or bad answer. In addition, a scoring guide minimizes any bias a member of the interview panel may have about an interviewee's age, race, sex, religion, national origin, sexual orientation, or physical disability. What's more, this scoring guide will make future hiring discussions more efficient,

FURTHER EVIDENCE

Both the legal community and organizational psychologists look for evidence of *content validity*—the extent to which a selection process assesses a representative sample of what a person must do on the job. In looking for this evidence, they look at what has been identified as important by the job analysis and whether that knowledge, skill, or ability is assessed by your method for selecting employees. An interview with fewer than 10 questions is unlikely to be viewed as content valid. The book by Dr. Robert Guion, a past president of the Society for Industrial and Organizational Psychology, referenced in note 2, is a definitive source of this information.

because it forces you and your colleagues to confront your differences regarding what constitutes a highly acceptable, acceptable, or unacceptable answer at the outset, rather than waiting until a particular candidate is being discussed.

The scoring guide for each question typically consists of a five-point scale of illustrative answers, from most to least acceptable. You should solicit these illustrations from the team who did the job analysis by first asking them to think of an employee they have observed to be outstanding on this particular dimension (for example, ethics) and then asking themselves, "How would that person respond to this question?" (a five-point response). The same question should be repeated with regard to an employee who is considered minimally acceptable (a three-point response) and then for an employee considered to be unacceptable (a one-point response). Through discussion of the proposed answers, the interviewing team chooses a behavioral example or illustration of a highly acceptable answer, an acceptable one, or one that is completely unacceptable. These benchmark answers will assist the interview panel in objectively evaluating an interviewee's responses to each situational question.

A SCORING GUIDE

The behavioral scoring guide to the question about the purchasing manager and the sales manager is as follows:

Five points = highly acceptable. I would politely explain to Pat why I can't release the bid information, nor accept an invitation to attend the athletic event, because of the policy of my organization and the logic behind that policy. I would also explain how much I value the relationship between our two organizations.

Three points = acceptable. I would tell Pat that I am unable to provide the information or attend the athletic event. (No explanation is given.)

One point = unacceptable. I would release the information and attend the event. Success in this job is all about personal relationships that increase my bottom line.

Hiring a Middle Manager at Weyerhaeuser

At Weyerhaeuser, in conducting a job analysis for the position of middle manager, I asked current job incumbents, "Thinking back over the past six months to a year, do you recall witnessing an incident that demonstrated ethical or unethical behavior?" Ethical behavior is emphasized by the Weyerhaeuser Company's senior management to all employees because they see it as a competitive advantage in the marketplace (that is, "You can trust Weyerhaeuser to do the right thing"). Then I said, "Once you have an incident in mind, please answer these three questions":

1. "What were the circumstances?" In other words, what was the context? This question is important because what is appropriate in one setting may not be appropriate in another.

2. "What exactly did the person do?" This question is asked to identify observable behavior.

3. "What was the outcome?" This is the "so-what" question. It helps you assess what the impact was. It can be useful to

ask follow-up questions: "Why is the answer to question two important? How does it illustrate ethical behavior?"

In response, a Weyerhaeuser manager responded: "Company policy stipulates that employees are not to accept gifts from suppliers. A high-level manager accepted a wristwatch from a good friend who was also a supplier. The manager was terminated because of the signal that it would have sent throughout the company if senior management had winked at this ethics violation."

It's relatively easy to turn a critical incident into a situational question. In this instance, Weyerhaeuser subsequently presented job applicants with the following ethical problem:

Your boss has emphasized the necessity of having a strong financial fourth quarter. You have heard rumors from people whom you trust that a customer who contributes at least 15 percent to your bottom line may be taking her business to a competitor. As you sit contemplating whether to discuss this issue with this customer, she calls to invite you and your subordinates to attend a fishing trip hosted at her organization's retreat. Your company's written policy on such matters states that you are to say no, but this policy is seldom discussed by anyone. You suspect that the policy may have been overlooked in some cases in the past. You can tell that the customer sounds impatient; you sense that she wants an answer immediately. Your boss is away on vacation. Accepting this invitation may be your best chance for salvaging this business relationship. Given the necessity for a strong fourth quarter, what would you do in this situation?

Weyerhaeuser used the following illustrative answers as behavioral benchmarks to assess candidates' answers to this ethics question:

- **Five points.** I would explain to the customer the organization's policy, the logic behind it, and how appreciative I am that she invited me. I would then suggest that we get together as soon as she returns.

- **Three points**. I would explain that the organization prohibits me from accepting her offer.
- **One point**. This is not a big deal in the larger scheme of things. It is in my organization's best interest that I say yes.

Note that what constitutes a five-point answer in your organization may constitute only a three-point answer in another organization. In the above Weyerhaeuser story, another organization might give a high score to the person who accepts the customer's invitation. The scoring guide for evaluating an applicant's answers should reflect the values and culture of your organization.

Pilot Test

Before using situational questions to make a hire, you should do a pilot test. Try the questions with some of your present employees to see whether there is variability in the answers to each question and to see whether the interviewers can agree on the scoring of each answer (an issue discussed in the research as *interobserver reliability*). If nearly every person who is asked a question gets the same score, delete the question. It won't differentiate between losers and winners. If the scoring guide does not yield agreement among the interview panel, either modify the scoring guide or discard the question.

If nearly every person gets the same score, delete the question.

Another reason to do a pilot study is to assess whether the wording of each question is clear to the interviewee. If people repeatedly ask for clarification, throw out the question or revise it. When conducting a situational interview, it's okay to repeat the question to ensure the applicant understands what is being asked. It's also okay to ask interviewees to state their assumptions about the meaning of a question so you know where they are coming from. But if you start rephrasing the question or giving additional information, you may inadvertently give this applicant an unfair advantage over others. Worse, the applicant may end up interviewing you, asking more and more questions until the desired answer becomes obvious.

Conducting the Interview

Most applicants have never experienced a situational interview, so after your usual welcome, start the interview with one or two sample questions. These shouldn't be scored. You are using them to get an applicant comfortable with this interview approach.

FURTHER EVIDENCE

Among the errors interviewers make repeatedly are *halo*, *similar-to-me, contrast, stereotype, first impressions*, and either *negative* or *positive* leniency.

Halo error occurs when an interviewer makes the mistake of judging a person as being excellent on one dimension (for example, working well within the team) because another dimension (for example, technical ability) seems so good.

Interviewers are often prone to hire people who are *similar to themselves* in attitudes, religion, education (for example, "we went to the same schools"), politics, and so on, even when the similarities are not job related.

Job candidates are typically evaluated in *contrast* to one another rather than against the job requirements. When "Pat Average" is interviewed following several "Sam Terribles," Pat is erroneously judged to be a winner.

Stereotyping is the mistaken conclusion that all people in a given category are the same (for example, "I would never hire anyone from Harvard; you know what those people are like").

In most unstructured interviews, the decision to hire a person is made within the first four minutes. The remainder of the interview is devoted to seeking confirmatory information. Hence the importance for a candidate to make a great *first impression*.

Nevertheless, some interviewers are prone to rating everyone too low (*negative leniency* error) or too high (*positive leniency* error).[8]

Once the interview begins, one person should ask the questions while everyone else on the interview panel records the answers. If only one person takes notes, important details of an answer may be missed. Interviewers should not score the answers on the fly. Wait until the interview is done; then have interviewers score their answers independently of one another.

Note that the situational interview is rigorously structured. This makes it possible to administer such an interview by computer or as a written questionnaire. Nevertheless, I do not recommend that you do so. Most managers want to talk to an applicant before making a selection decision so that they can see what it is like to interact with the person. Thus, the people who do well on a written situational questionnaire will undoubtedly *Interviewers are often prone to hiring people who are similar to themselves.* be called in for a follow-up, in-person unstructured interview ("So, tell me about yourself . . ."), at which point all the interviewer errors that the situational interview is designed to minimize will reappear. Instead, by making the situational interview the in-person interview, you will fulfill the hiring team's desire to meet candidates in person while relying on an evidence-based method to make a hiring decision.

The Patterned Behavioral Interview

The patterned behavioral interview is another evidence-based tool that will help you identify and hire high-performing employees. It enables you to collect data on how an applicant has behaved in the past (for example, on skill in building a high-performance team) so that you can predict future behavior on the job.[7] In this type of interview (unlike the situational interview), the interviewer explains to the applicant the aspect of the job that is being assessed (for example, team playing) to probe the past. So it should be used as a follow-up to the situational interview.

FURTHER EVIDENCE

John Bargh, a psychologist at Yale University, studies sub-conscious processes. He found that we are biased in favor of applicants who imitate our physical mannerisms such as leaning forward or backward, crossing our legs, and head movements during the selection interview.

The procedure for developing and administering the patterned behavioral interview parallels that of the situational interview:

1. Conduct a job analysis.

2. Design interview questions.

3. Develop a scoring guide.

To design the interview questions, return to the critical incident job analysis conducted for the situational interview. Use that information to develop a series of questions that assess what applicants have done in the past. For example, if the job analysis shows that teamwork is critical in a given job, you may want to state that you stress teamwork in your organization and then ask a question such as "Can you recall a time in your recent past when you demonstrated team-building skills?" This question is asked to assess the candidate's past behavior as a member of a team.

You could then ask the following questions to probe an applicant's team-building skills:

"What were the circumstances?"

"What exactly did you do?"

"What was the outcome?"

"How is that an example of team-building behavior?"

"Is there someone whom I may call to verify what you just told me?"

Note that focusing on "what" trumps emphasizing "why." Paul Green, a well-known organizational psychologist, has written extensively on this interview technique based on his professional practice. As he points out, people sometimes misuse this interview method by asking an applicant why an action was taken. The correct way to use this interview tool is to ask an applicant what was actually done. An emphasis on "why" invites applicants to speculate on reasons for their actions. This in turn invites self-promotion. An emphasis on "what," however, focuses on a description of actual behavior. Once you have a description of what was done, you are in a position to evaluate the applicant's answer to a question.

Focusing on "what" trumps emphasizing "why."

Keep in mind that your objective here is solely to predict someone's job performance before you decide whether to make a job offer. In a one-hour interview, you will never figure out everything there is to know about an applicant. Nevertheless, you can assess what people have done in the past and use that as a basis to predict what they are likely to do on the job in the future. As with the situational interview, you will want to develop a scoring guide for evaluating applicants' answers to the patterned behavioral interview. You develop this scoring guide in the same way you did for the situational interview. In fact, the two scoring guides are often identical.

FURTHER EVIDENCE

A meta-analysis, which is quantitative analysis of all the validation studies on comparisons of the SI and PBDI, shows that the criterion-related validity of the SI is higher than the PBDI. Nevertheless, both interview formats should be used rather than choosing one over the other. Using both selection techniques will increase your accuracy in identifying an applicant who will prove to be a winner on the job. (see *International Journal of Selection and Assessment*, 2013, vol 21, pp 264–76).

As is the case with the situational interview, the effectiveness of this selection tool is influenced by whether your interview questions are content valid—that is, are getting at all aspects important to doing well on the job. This technique may sound time-consuming, but Green recommends that two or more questions be asked with regard to each job competency that was identified in the job analysis you conducted. Green found he could cover six competencies in little more than an hour.

Job Simulations

The situational interview asks a job applicant to imagine the future: "What *would* you do in this situation?" The patterned behavior interview examines the applicant's past: "What *did* you do in that situation?" A simulation looks at the present: "Show how you can handle this situation." Simulations, when custom tailored for your organization, are an excellent (that is, in research terms, *reliable* and *valid*) way to assess a candidate's ability to handle job challenges based on present behavior in the simulation.[9] Rather than only listen to candidates' responses to interview questions, you get to see firsthand what the candidates can actually do. If you are part of a small or midsize organization, you can use an inexpensive simulation tool: a role play. A role play requires only that you and a candidate participate in a scripted job simulation. As is the case with the two structured interviews—situational and patterned behavior—develop a behavioral scoring guide that lets your assessors evaluate each applicant's behavior in a uniform and consistent manner.

Role plays are useful in selecting high-performing employees because, as noted earlier, rather than responding only to questions in an interview, applicants must in addition actually do something in front of you that will be required of them on the job.[10] Suppose the job for which you are hiring requires conflict resolution skills.

In this case, you would want to include a role play in your selection tool kit to see whether a candidate has what it takes to resolve conflicts. Here's an example:

Good morning, Sam, my name is Dr. Latham. I understand you are applying for the position of VP of customer relations. Have a seat, please. This is your office. The three people in front of you are upset customers. Please deal with them.

The people in your organization who had been trained for this role play would then begin to whine and complain to the job applicant, all speaking at once.

To develop a role play, create a script that reflects an actual scenario that typically occurs in your organization. In the customer service role play, the three customers (in reality three assessors) would be scripted to behave in approximately the same way with each job candidate. The same is true of the person playing the role of board chair in the grocery chain example on page 18. The grocery chain story illustrates how using a job simulation can help the best candidate for the job rise above the others.

Employing a combination of simulations—in-basket simulation, leaderless group discussion, business games—can ensure a candidate doesn't have just some of the qualities needed for success in a given position but possesses the whole package. The Rolls-Royce of simulations is the assessment center. It takes time, money, and usually consultants to develop—but it is worth it. Take a look at the cluttered in-basket on your desk (or the cluttered email in-box on your computer, or both). In an assessment center, you can create cluttered in-baskets just like those on your desk. The assessment center in-basket assesses a candidate's skills in task prioritization and delegation, as well as an applicant's written communication skills. Typical instructions for an in-basket simulation are as follows:

Hiring a Grocery Chain President

A role play helped the hiring committee for a grocery chain select a new president of the "House," the central location from which owners of the individual grocery franchises were required to buy their inventory. Among the four people on the short list to replace the president were three outsiders as well as one insider from the grocery chain, who was the odds-on favorite. The role play was used to gather data on ability to take into account divergent interests. The role play brought to light why the odds-on favorite was far from the best candidate for the job.

In the role play, an assessor playing the board chair insisted that the candidates take a strong position against the grocery store owners. To our surprise, the favored candidate responded, "Consider it done." This candidate was a great guy. He simply wasn't the right person for this particular politically demanding job. The person who ultimately received the job offer was an individual from the outside who made it clear that he would not favor one group—either the store owners or the House—and explained ways that he would seek solutions that were in the best interest of the organization overall.

Congratulations, you have just been promoted to the job of VP of marketing, a vacancy created by your predecessor's sudden death this past Friday. It is now Sunday morning. You are to attend a mandatory meeting Monday morning in a city 600 miles away. The only available plane takes off in four hours. Quickly go through your predecessor's in-basket to get yourself up to speed before you leave for that meeting and prioritize what needs to be done before you leave. There is an organization chart showing the people who are now reporting to you.

Another assessment center simulation is the leaderless group discussion. A group of applicants is given a topic to discuss while the assessors, typically two or three managers, watch to see who emerges as the group's leader. An example of such an exercise is a simulated school board meeting in which one applicant is given a script that advocates allocating money to buy new school buses. Another candidate is given a script that advocates upgrading the library, while still another is required to argue in favor of refurbishing the school's roof. The money must be allocated at the end of this meeting or the school board will take it back.

Still another assessment center exercise, the business game, assesses how well a person works with others under pressure. In one such game, candidates are told they are in the business of manufacturing and selling toys with the goal of making as much money as possible. Suddenly, an unanticipated wholesale price cut goes into effect, so that what was true at a previous time regarding the profits the candidates can make is no longer true right now. This simulation enables you to assess teamwork skills as well as who takes the role of specialist and who takes the role of generalist. It allows you to see who stays patient and who becomes irritated in interactions with others on the team in determining how to respond to this crisis.

The assessment center gets confirmation from several exercises on whether an applicant is truly a high performer.

Although assessment center simulations are excellent for identifying high-performing employees, their downside is that they are typically too complicated for you to develop on your own. And it can be costly to hire a consulting firm to develop them. Nevertheless, if you are part of a large organization, you cannot afford not to use this excellent tool due to its high reliability and validity in identifying winners. This is because the assessment center enables you to get confirmation from several sources on whether an applicant is truly a high performer. In addition, this selection tool is excellent for assessing a candidate's communication skills, energy, sensitivity, planning and organizing, and decision making.[11]

The Realistic Job Preview

Once you have made your selection, use a realistic job preview. To entice audiences, a movie preview shows only the best parts of the movie to come. As a result, audiences are sometimes disappointed by the movie itself. You don't want the applicant you hire to experience similar disappointment with the job. A realistic—and hence effective—job preview explains what is good about a job as well as what stinks about it.[12]

Why would you tell an applicant—someone you hope will accept your offer—about the downsides of the job? It's simple: Applicants always know things about themselves that no interview or simulation will reveal. Once you've made your choice, the final decision rests with the applicant. So think of the job preview as the final backstop to your hiring selection: If the candidate still wants the job after seeing the preview—the good, the bad, and the ugly it entails—you can be sure you've found not just the right person but the right person who will stay.

A realistic job preview should explain to applicants first what's great about working for your organization, division, and team; what's great about the job; what's great about your organization's location; what's great about upper management. Then it should explain what's not so great about each of those areas. Again, why expose your dirty laundry? Face it: The candidate will have this information within three months or less on the job, so it's better to present it up front rather than risk a disgusted resignation later.

The situational interview and patterned behavior description interview, backed by a simulation and a realistic job preview, give you a comprehensive tool kit for identifying and hiring high performers. Except for the assessment center, all of them can be developed by you.

THREE ADDITIONAL TOOLS: COGNITIVE ABILITY, PERSONALITY TESTS, AND EMOTIONAL INTELLIGENCE

Some evidence indicates that cognitive ability tests and personality tests may be useful predictors of who will do well on the job. However, only a psychologist can administer and score them. These tools have strong upsides balanced by strong downsides to their use.

Cognitive Ability Tests

Cognitive ability tests, commonly referred to as intelligence tests, assess verbal and quantitative skills. This doesn't necessarily mean an applicant has to have high scores on both. Lawyers and librarians, for example, must have excellent verbal skills. Quantitative skills are less pressing for those professions.

Although IQ tests accurately predict performance in most jobs, they are controversial because different racial groups typically perform differently on them. Hiring one racial group to the exclusion of all others is an invitation for a lawsuit. An article in the *American Psychologist* shows that these tests are excellent for predicting a wide range of short-term and long-term academic and job performance, and that these tests do not underpredict the performance of minority group members. The study described shows that the higher a person's test score, the higher the person's performance is likely to be on the job. But, as the researchers acknowledge, basing hiring on cognitive ability tests will affect your pursuit of diversity.[14]

And diversity in your workforce offers many strong advantages. Both the Conference Board and the Society for Human Resource Management have reported that workforce diversity is a business imperative for organizational effectiveness and sustained competitiveness. Diversity enables an organization to attract and retain the best talent and gain and keep new market share, which in turn increases sales and profits. In short, customers demand it. The flow of information among employees, work teams, customers, and suppliers depends on the quality of relationships and talent in your organization.[15]

Personality Tests

Personality tests may be useful to you because they assess an applicant's innate traits, dispositions that are relatively stable across time and across situations. However, although highly respected researchers have obtained evidence for the use of personality tests to select people, other highly respected researchers question this evidence. An article in *Personnel Psychology* argues that the

FURTHER EVIDENCE

In 1999, the American Educational Research Association, the American Psychological Association, and the National Council on Measurement in Education published "Standards for Educational Testing." They concluded, "Educational and psychological testing and measurement are among the most important contributions of behavioral sciences to our society ... There is extensive evidence documenting the effectiveness of well-constructed tests for uses supported by validity evidence."[17]

correlation between how people score on most personality tests and how they perform on the job is typically so low that it is not worth the time and money to administer them.[16]

The following traits are those known as the "Big Five":

- Conscientiousness

- Emotional stability

- Agreeableness

- Extroversion

- Openness to experience

They are referred to by this name because meaningful distinctions can be made among all five, and statistical analyses on the thousands of words used to describe aspects of personality have reduced the vocabulary to this five-factor taxonomy. Moreover, the statistical analyses that revealed these five factors have been replicated in non-English-speaking cultures using different measurement techniques.[18] Conscientious people strive for accomplishment. They are self-disciplined, organized, and efficient in carrying out tasks. They get things done. These are the people you want in jobs that include a lot of autonomy.[19]

Emotionally stable people are not easily rattled under pressure. They are not stress prone, temperamental, anxious, or worrisome. As is the case with conscientious individuals, emotionally stable individuals typically exhibit high job performance.[20]

If you are selecting people to work in unstructured jobs with a lot of autonomy, you want conscientious, emotionally stable people. In fact, conscientiousness and emotional stability correlate positively with job performance in virtually all jobs.[21]

Agreeable individuals are cooperative, trusting, and affable. Hence people who score high on this test typically work well in a team. Agreeableness predicts interpersonal skills. In settings that require helping, nurturing, and cooperating with others, agreeableness may be among the best predictors of job performance.[22]

Extroverted individuals tend to be sociable and dominant. They are ambitious and seek excitement. Extroversion is worth examining in settings where competition, dominance, and assertiveness are the norm. This is because extroverts usually do better than others in competitive settings.[23]

Open-mindedness characterizes individuals who score high on creativity and unconventionality. A high score on this test predicts proficiency in occupations such as management, the professions, law enforcement, sales, and semiskilled work.[24]

I also recommend that you use a test that measures narcissism. Narcissists constantly defend their ego against unfavorable evaluations, even when presented with factual and accurate data that support the evaluation. Any comments they perceive as threats to their ego make them angry. Consequently, they look for ways to denigrate the evaluator, the appraisal instrument, and innocent third parties. Their purpose is to punish the evaluator and reaffirm their dominance over that person. They are terrible team players. So do yourself and your team a favor and test for this trait; narcissists are not high performers.[25]

Using personality tests in the hiring process offers another advantage: They are safer than cognitive ability tests from a legal standpoint, as there is no evidence that the test scores of one racial group, one gender, or one age group are higher or lower than another.[26] A drawback to personality tests is that they don't work as well in identifying talented people for jobs that are highly structured, such as assembly line positions, or those where strong organizational controls ensure that everyone essentially behaves in the same way.

Emotional Intelligence

As a middle or upper manager, or as an MBA student, it is unlikely that you will ever lose your job because of low cognitive intelligence (IQ). Cognitive intelligence assesses verbal fluency and quantitative skill (think SAT, GRE, GMAT). You could not be where you are today in business or in a business school if you did not have adequate verbal and quantitative skills. However, emotional intelligence is a different story. The Center for Creative Leadership has found that among the top reasons for a derailed career is low emotional intelligence.

Emotional intelligence (EQ) is not only your ability to read others, it is your ability to read yourself. It consists of four sub-abilities: self-awareness, social perception, emotion understanding, and emotion regulation. Needless to say, cognitive ability or IQ does not necessarily correlate highly with EQ. An individual can be high on one and low on the other.

EQ is important in the workplace because it predicts performance in jobs requiring complex interactions with others. It is especially important in work settings where there are emotional demands. In fact, EQ has been found to be more important for effective performance on the job in these situations than scoring high on the Big Five.[27]

Core EQ Abilities

Self-awareness refers to your ability to read yourself, to assess your emotions. Do you realize when you are reacting to an issue strongly? Are you able to consciously regulate your anger? Can you usually cope with stressful job experiences?

Social perception refers to your ability to read the emotions of others, including your boss, your team's members, and your customers. This dimension of EQ is especially important for you as a manager. Do you sense when your team is reluctant to raise an issue with you? Can you read a peer's nonverbal reactions? Are you able to discern customers' expressions that are authentic versus fake? High acumen on this dimension of EQ is necessary for navigating your interactions with others effectively (e.g., when leading an organizational change initiative).

Emotion understanding is just that—skill in understanding your feelings as well as the feelings of others. Are you able to identify the reason(s) for an emotion you and/or others are experiencing? Are you able to correctly predict the impact of an event (e.g., a diversity initiative) on the reactions of your team's members, as well as on your emotions? High acumen in this dimension of EQ will be helpful to you on a personal level in determining whether you should accept a job offer, apply for a stressful position in your organization, or invest time and money in a start-up.

Emotion regulation refers to your skills in increasing, maintaining, or decreasing the magnitude or duration of your emotions and the emotions of others. Would you know which emotions to display before announcing a layoff to your team? Are you able to reduce your anxiety level? Do you know both when and when not to give a fiery speech?

Emotional Intelligence Can Be Learned

If you answer no to one or more of the above questions, there is good news. Unlike IQ, EQ can be learned. It is not fixed at birth. However, in mastering EQ, be aware that there is a low correlation between your self-report and an objective measure of your EQ. It is important for you to know if you are deficient on an EQ dimension so that you will be motivated to improve this capability.

A first step to improving your EQ on one or more of its dimensions is to recall, in vivid detail, examples where EQ was important to your task effectiveness. Second, seek feedback from those who have credibility in your eyes on ways you could have used your emotions effectively. Third, set behavioral goals based on this feedback.

Use the situational interview and the patterned behavior description interview to assess an applicant's EQ on each of the above four dimensions.

CONCLUSION

The people you want in your organization, not with your competition, are high-performing employees. When you rely on the evidence-based methods discussed in this chapter to screen and hire new employees, you can be sure you will select winners. And by addressing the psychological characteristics of today's high performers as explained in this chapter, you can be certain you'll select top-level talent to join your organization.

QUESTIONS

1. What is wrong with using an unstructured interview to hire people? What are two alternatives? What are their advantages?

2. What rating errors plague the interview?

3. What are the advantages of using a simulation to hire an applicant? Describe the "Rolls-Royce" of simulations.

4. How and when would you use a realistic job preview?

5. What are the upsides and downsides of using cognitive ability tests to hire people?

6. What are the arguments for a diverse workforce?

7. What are the upsides and downsides of using personality tests to hire people?

8. What is meant by the Big Five?

9. What is emotional intelligence? How would you assess it?

INSPIRE YOUR EMPLOYEES TO EXECUTE STRATEGY

No matter how brilliantly thought-out your organizational or departmental strategy is—no matter how sophisticated or clever—the strategy will fall flat without buy-in from your employees. You must turn your vision into their reality.

When I refer to buy-in, I'm talking about the necessity for employees to believe that their own departmental strategy, which supports the larger organizational strategy, is worth executing. If your employees don't believe the strategy is worth executing, they will never commit to putting it into action.

You must turn your vision into their reality.

As a result, your primary role as an evidence-based manager is to inspire people to execute the strategic plan for your department or group. From this execution, the results you want as a manager will follow.

In this chapter, I walk you through a four-step, evidence-based process you can use to inspire your team—a road map that will help your team get excited about rolling up their sleeves and doing the work they need to do to execute the organization's strategy to attain the desired results. You are undoubtedly aware of each of these four steps. The enabling power comes from combining them into one package. The steps are as follows:

1. Develop an affective vision statement.

2. Set SMART goals.

3. Align metrics and demonstrate integrity.

4. Stay engaged.

Your employees will feel inspired to execute your organization's strategy when they connect with the underlying vision and when they see you acting in sync with the vision. What's more, by working with your employees to set specific goals for attaining that vision and by holding them accountable to performance metrics that underpin the action steps for goal attainment, you will clarify the steps critical for producing desired results. In addition, by aligning your performance evaluation metrics with your vision and goals, you will send a loud and clear signal about the importance of completing these action steps. An axiom in business and in psychology is "that which gets measured gets done."[1] Measurement signals to your employees what is truly important, as opposed to what just gets lip service. Throughout this process, you must remain actively engaged, accessible, and involved in working with people in executing the strategy to attain the goals that define the vision.

WHAT WORKS, IN BRIEF

When people in strategic management talk about developing an effective vision, they are telling you to use your head. Where do you see your organization going in the next three to five years? When those leaders appeal to your heart instead of your head, they are developing an *affective* vision statement. How will you give the people who report to you a cause they can believe in? Goals move the vision from a slogan to a set of concrete action steps. Your personal involvement in formulating the vision, setting the goals, and establishing the metrics will ensure employee engagement (see chapter 5).

Develop an Affective Vision Statement

Affect refers to emotion, the heart, the soul—what people feel. An affective vision statement does not appeal to the intellect. Its aim is not to instruct but to awaken emotion. Its real greatness is the quality and force of this emotion. Hence an affective vision statement is the source of inspiration that will energize your employees to put in the effort needed to attain high goals.

By developing an affective vision statement, you appeal to the heart so that your employees are motivated to make the vision a reality. An affective vision appeals to emotion. It is expressed in a few memorable words that capture the imagination. An affective vision statement with these aspects inspires employees to set goals and execute *Appeal to the heart to make the vision a reality.* strategy that will lead to it. So your job as an evidence-based manager is to craft a vision statement with your employees that has an emotional appeal and conveys a sense of altruism in a way that is concise and memorable and one that is in their words.

Set SMART Goals

No matter how inspiring your team's vision, and no matter how well delivered your message, an inspiring vision alone won't energize your employees to execute strategy: You must also work with them to set SMART goals (those that are Specific, Measurable, Attainable, Relevant, and Time-bound). It's simply not good enough to urge your employees to "do their best." More than a thousand experiments have revealed that those who are given a SMART goal show superior performance compared with those who are simply urged to do their best. For example, the *Journal of Applied Psychology* reported a study where members of senior management of an R&D organization wanted their engineers to attain excellence. Step one involved an agreed-upon definition of excellence and the metrics for assessing it.

FURTHER EVIDENCE

A review of the literature on employee motivation for the *Handbook of Psychology* found more than 1,000 studies on goal-setting theory and concluded that it was the 800-pound gorilla among theories of motivation. Goal setting is among the most effective ways to motivate people on the job, and it may be at the top of the list.[2]

Step two involved setting specific, high goals that were attainable within six months. Those who had SMART goals were evaluated by management as performing significantly higher than those who didn't have SMART goals but instead received praise, public recognition, or a monetary incentive.[3] SMART goals provide a concrete plan to unite and focus the efforts of your team's employees to attain them. Goals make people think (what researchers refer to as *cognition*).

Align Metrics and Demonstrate Integrity

A well-designed and well-communicated vision (step one) will get people excited about setting SMART goals (step two) and about generating a strategy for goal attainment (step three). A leader who shows integrity will model for people the necessity of remaining committed to goal attainment (step four).

If you don't support the vision, why should your employees?

By displaying integrity—sending signals that are consistent with your team's vision and goals—you will keep employees engaged in pursuing goal attainment because they will see that you too value the vision and goals. If you only talk up the vision and goals but act in ways that devalue, contradict, or undermine them, your employees will undoubtedly recognize this reality and abandon them. If you as the manager don't support the vision, why should your employees?

One of the best ways for you to demonstrate integrity regarding the vision and goals is to ensure that the metrics are directly aligned with the SMART goals. Such measurement conveys loud and clear what you really believe is important, as opposed to what you merely say is important. As a result, you want to ensure that the measurement system is aligned with the vision and SMART goals for the department or team.

Stay Engaged

Once the plan is in place—once goals and metrics have been established—you need to remain engaged in the process of strategy execution. A strategy is nothing more than a business plan that specifies the time frame for attaining specific goals and the plan for attaining those goals that is different from or better than your competition's. Even if you've armed your employees with a fantastic vision and a foolproof plan of action for goal attainment, you must stay actively engaged to ensure that they see your

Actively encourage dissent to prevent groupthink.

personal commitment to strategy execution. In particular, you must ascertain whether your people have the knowledge, skill, and resources to bring about the desired change. Shower your employees with attention when they support the vision and execute the strategy for goal attainment. Actively encourage dissent so that you prevent *groupthink*, that is, employees agreeing with that which they know is wrong so as to be seen by you as team players.[4]

EFFECTIVE INSPIRATIONAL TOOLS IN PRACTICE

It's useful to look at these tools one by one, based on research evidence, breaking down their purpose and showing how to use each of them. Collectively, they can inspire your employees to execute strategy and to knock themselves out in terms of commitment to attaining specific high goals.

Develop an Affective Vision Statement

A strategic plan is only as good as the motivation of the people who have to implement it. If your people are not motivated to execute it with excellence, the plan is not worth the paper it is written on. Before the goals are set, before the strategic plan for attaining those goals is written, people must identify with their group, division, or organization. They must feel that what they are doing is somehow making their world a better place. The first step in bringing this about is to develop a vision that appeals to affect.

The purpose of the vision statement is to galvanize people to unite under a common cause, to set goals, and to develop and execute a strategy to bring about goal attainment. Above all, the vision statement must make an inspirational case for why the goals are worth pursuing.

What makes a vision statement affective? Research has shown that to be affective, a vision statement must be

- Memorable

- Tailored to employees, not the wider world

- Emotionally appealing

Make It Memorable

For a vision statement to appeal to affect it must be memorable, and for a vision statement to be memorable it must

- Be short enough for people to recite easily

- Have enough impact for people to become engaged

Martin Luther King Jr.'s "I Have a Dream" vision statement is a great example. These four simple words are easy to recall and they made an impact. People remember this vision statement because it is short, simple, and inspiring. Its impact lies in its direct appeal to the heart, to the imagination. The dream incited and excited people

Churchill's Vision

Winston Churchill, who led Great Britain as prime minister during World War II, was brilliant in his ability to deliver affective vision statements to the British people. Churchill had the knack for creating vision statements that would excite and incite people to rally to action.

When flying a plane for the Royal Air Force was tantamount to suicide because of the superiority of Germany's aircraft, Churchill intoned, "Never was so much owed by so many to so few." This vision statement included the key characteristics of an affective vision statement. It was memorable (eleven simple yet powerful words), conveyed the altruism of the British soldiers, and stirred emotion by implication ("so much" was owed because the soldiers flying war planes so often gave up their lives in the process). Additionally, the statement spoke directly to the English citizens themselves, referring to courage and perseverance without self-consciousness or apology.

Churchill's vision statements and one word from him—one hand signal, one V for victory—inspired the British to resist Nazi tyranny.

to set goals, to develop strategy, and to take action to make the dream a reality.

Memorable affective vision statements are effective when they stay with employees throughout the process of goal setting and strategy execution, working again and again to provide motivation and keep employees on course with the strategic plan to attain the SMART goals.

Speak to Your Employees

Affective vision statements are designed primarily, if not exclusively, for internal consumption—they speak to employees, not to the outside world. Thus, evidence-based managers know how to ask their employees questions that enable them to craft their vision, a vision that speaks directly to the people who will carry it out. They know to make a distinction between a marketing statement (for example, Nike's "Just Do It"), which is meant to inspire customers, and an affective vision statement, which is meant to inspire employees.

The vision statement for a bank in the U.S. Northwest is "We steal." This vision obviously leaves something to be desired if it was meant to be shared with the general public: "Bank with us; we are the best thieves in the business." Nevertheless, the bank's president is serious about this vision of becoming "the outstanding thieves." In a staff meeting, he explained the source of his discontent:

Vision statements speak to employees, not to the outside world.

Americans are among the most creative people on the planet, yet the Japanese are better at taking good ideas from others and implementing them with excellence. At that point, he slammed his fist on the table and exclaimed to his staff, "I do indeed want thieves. We will steal ideas, we will steal customers, we will steal market share."

He asked each member of his senior management team where they were going on vacation. "When you go there, I want you to visit three banks and open an account in each one. When you return from vacation, I want you to tell us three things each of these three banks does better than us. The rest of you will then have thirty days to figure out how we will do each of those things better than they do. I want you to become the most creative thieves in this business."

"We steal"—short, memorable, and not suitable for the bank's customers—was just the thing to inspire employees toward continuous improvement.

Appeal to Emotion

An affective vision statement causes people to feel the necessity to execute strategy, not just to know in an intellectual sense that it's the right thing to do. One of the reasons that King's "I Have a Dream" speech was so effective in inspiring people was that it appealed to the heart, not just the head. Microsoft's affective vision statement is "Create an environment where the very best people can do their very best work." This vision appeals to everyone's desire for personal effectiveness.

Make sure your vision statement has an emotional appeal and you'll win employee commitment to both goal pursuit and strategy execution.

Go Ahead and Build It: Your Vision Statement

How will you develop a vision statement that is emotionally appeal-ing, tailored to employees, and memorable if you lack the oratorical skills and charisma of Winston Churchill or Martin Luther King Jr.? Fortunately, a vision that appeals to employees' emotions and sense of altruism is usually generated from the bottom up rather than the top down, providing you with a clear path. An affective vision state-ment is expressed in the language of your employees, using words that are memorable and meaningful to them, not necessarily to your board of directors. And, most important, an affective vision state-ment describes the future that they, the employees, want to create.

Here is a straightforward way you can develop an affective vision statement with your employees. Ask them these three questions to stimulate thought as well as feeling:

- Why do we exist?

- Who would miss us if we were gone?

- What really ticks us off?

Why Do We Exist?

Walt Disney and his employees did a good job of answering the first question: *We exist to educate through entertainment.* They

Who Misses a Newspaper?

During a tension-filled day, management and staff at a local news-paper faced up to the second question, "Who would miss us if we were gone?" The newspaper was in a relatively small city about a thirty-minute drive from Seattle. The owners back East decided to close the paper because it had operated in the red year after year. So who would miss this paper if it ceased to exist? It seemed that no one would, because everyone in the community read the *Seattle Times*.

The local paper's publisher called a meeting of his staff. After a long day of discussion, the answer to "Who would miss us if we were gone?" suddenly became crystal clear: the roughly one million people living in the county who wanted the local news. Nearly all read the *Seattle Times* for global news—but the *Times* rarely informed them of the news in their county.

Hence, the vision: The paper was THE source of news about Sno-homish County, not merely a source of news for the county.

translated this vision into a specific high goal: to build the Epcot Center theme park. Their goal was to make their customers wiser at 6:00 p.m. upon leaving Epcot than they were at 8:55 a.m. waiting in line to enter the park—and to provide entertainment in the process.[5]

Who Would Miss Us if We Were Gone?

The dual reason for asking the second question is to pinpoint who the customer is and what behaviors are needed to retain and grow an organization's customer base.

The *Snohomish County Tribune*'s vision needed to inspire a change in employee behavior that would enable the paper to survive and grow. If you want to be THE source rather than a source of news for a million or so readers, what are you as a newspaper going to start doing? And what are you going to stop doing?

To answer the first question, you are going to start focusing on local news. Which high school in Snohomish County won the girls' basketball tournament? If the U.S. Navy moves into the county, will it drive property taxes up or down? Is the county picnic scheduled for the weekend before or after Labor Day? Very few readers of this book have any interest whatsoever in the answers to these questions. But there are a million people who do—and that's a solid customer base.

To answer the second question, you are going to stop focusing on national and global news. Who is doing what in the Middle East? Read the *Seattle Times*. What's happening on Wall Street? With all due respect to investment bankers, the reporters of the county newspaper are not going to cover them anymore—though what's happening to the local banks and businesses as a result of what's happening on Wall Street may get a lot of coverage.

So did THE source of local news for the county return to the black? You bet it did.

What Really Ticks Us Off?

This third question differs from the first two. All three tap employee emotion, but this third question gets at what employees are sick and tired of and, therefore, what issues motivate them to redefine who they are.

The new vision of the maintenance department changed the behavior of the maintenance employees *and* their colleagues in production: "We resource those who plan." Production units that worked with maintenance to set quarterly goals were given first priority. Those who set no goals fell into the "We'll get to you when we can" category. Production employees stopped being reactive. They became proactive in setting maintenance goals. Within eighteen months, production and maintenance were working together as one team.

Potential Vision Statement Pitfalls

A strict ground rule is that a bottom-up vision must be compatible with that of your organization as a whole. In the paper mill story,

The Maintenance Shuffle

Maintenance employees at a paper mill were at war with their counterparts in production. The first-line maintenance supervisor got his people in a room to pose this third question: "What really ticks us off?" They were furious at a phrase their production colleagues had coined: "the maintenance shuffle." It was particularly offensive because it was more than a tad accurate. If a machine required repair, two or three maintenance workers would be observed shuffling slowly toward it. Should they eventually reach the final destination, it was all but a sure thing that they would not have the needed part. A maintenance employee would then use a two-way radio to call two or three additional maintenance workers, who would eventually arrive for an informal chitchat that inevitably concluded with the discovery that the part had to be ordered. By that time, the production workers would be fuming.

There are, as you well know, two sides to every story. Maintenance employees didn't rush toward what production deemed momentarily to be a dire emergency—because, from maintenance's point of view, production people never knew what they truly wanted. "Maintenance, we need you here, right away!" Only to be followed by, "Forget that; we now need you over there." Or, "No, we need you over there instead."

An hour into this discussion, an employee got up and said that he had no use for this meeting. "We aren't going to get anywhere with those *** people in production until they start to plan." As he started to walk out the door, the maintenance supervisor yanked him back in. "What did you just say?"

What the worker said, minus the vulgarity, became the basis for the maintenance department's affective vision statement: "We resource those who plan."

the vision statement of maintenance worked because it was compatible with the goals of production; similarly, the vision of production could not be in conflict with that of marketing or other divisions.

And, of course, there are upsides and downsides to every bit of good advice. Here's the downside to all I've discussed thus far: Many vision statements are nothing more than hollow rhetoric. What's worse, an affective vision statement often raises employee expectations—only to have them dashed by management that doesn't follow through by setting goals and gaining commitment to them. Thus, a vision statement can become a tremendous source of cynicism within the workforce. To make sure the vision statement amounts to more than rhetoric, you need to set specific, high goals—SMART goals.

Set SMART Goals

Goals move the vision statement from galvanizing words to concrete action steps. As noted, Disney's goal was to build Epcot Center. Microsoft wanted to attract and retain the best people. By moving quickly beyond the vision to setting specific high goals, evidence-based managers are able to align employee actions with employee aspirations. But effective goals must be SMART. Much has been written and explained about SMART goals, and they are almost standard operating practice in business. So I am spending just a short time on what makes goals SMART before moving on to less well understood aspects of goal setting.

Do you recall John F. Kennedy proudly telling the American people on television, "We will become the high-quality, low-cost

---

SMART GOALS DEFINED

S = specific

M = measurable

A = attainable

R = relevant

T = time-bound

FURTHER EVIDENCE

In our reviews of the literature about goal setting, Ed Locke and I found that in 90 percent of the experiments, the quality and quantity of performance was higher in the cases where a specific high goal was set rather than a vague one such as "to do your best." Why? With all due respect to the Girl Scouts and Boy Scouts, a vague goal such as "do your best" allows too much leeway. Some people kick themselves in the pants undeservedly whereas others are undeservedly patting themselves on the back. A goal that is SMART allows you to evaluate your performance in relation to a specific goal, to make adjustments where necessary, to increase your effort, and to persist until the specific goal is attained. This is difficult, if not impossible, for you to do when you are only urged to do your best.[6]

space explorers in the world"? Of course you don't. He never said it. A statement such as this is nothing more than a marketing slogan. Instead, Kennedy set a SMART goal: "I believe that this nation should commit itself to achieving the goal, before this decade is out, of landing a man on the moon and returning him safely to the earth." When the television cameras went off, his aides raced up to him and said, "Mr. President, you never should have said that." Kennedy flashed his famous grin and replied, "Yes, I know."

Goals provide a road map to unite and focus the efforts of your team. Goals stimulate the creation and implementation of plans for where to go and how to get there. What criteria should be used to allocate the resources necessary for goal attainment? Which activities should be pursued? Which should be avoided? Goals are especially effective because they provide people with a challenge and give them a sense of accomplishment as progress is made. Goals remove any ambiguity regarding the criteria to which you hold yourself and your employees accountable.

In the forest products industry, harvesting trees hour after hour can be tiring, monotonous work. At the American Pulpwood Association, I asked loggers to set a specific high goal as to the number of trees each person should cut in a day and in a week. As a result of these goals, both their attendance and their performance soared within the very first week.[7] People immediately started bragging about their accomplishments the way some might brag about their score on the golf course. This is because goal setting and goal attainment increased their sense of personal effectiveness.

> *Goals provide a road map to unite and focus the efforts of your team.*

BENEFITS OF GOAL SETTING

- Creates focus.
- Sets up a challenge.
- Builds a sense of accomplishment.
- Reduces ambiguity.
- Often reduces stress.
- Improves performance.

In short, what we psychologists have learned about goal setting is that specific, high goals lead to higher performance than no goals or general and abstract goals. If a person is committed to the goal, then the higher the goal, the higher the performance. The nature of the goal, affects choice, effort, and persistence. Therefore, praise, feedback, participation in decision making, and monetary incentives increase performance only when they lead to the setting of and commitment to a specific, high goal.[8] The following sections present some additional keys to effective goals.

Set High but Attainable Goals

One of the interesting tensions in goal setting is that goals should be high, but they should also be attainable. If at 8:00 a.m. someone promises to respond to five emails before noon, it is a likely sign of low goal commitment. However, if the promise is to get five hundred answers out by noon, that too is likely a sign of low commitment. Chances are that the employee knows it's not attainable and is merely giving you a socially desirable response. In short, a goal that is too high is likely a warning sign that the person who set it is not truly committed to attaining it. If a goal is perceived as too high by employees, they will at best give it lip service in your presence, but they won't be committed to attaining it.

> A goal that is too high is a warning sign that the person who set it is not truly committed to attaining it.

Set Three to Seven Goals

For goals to increase performance, they need to be few in number: from three to seven. If the goals are too many—say, thirty-seven—they end up increasing stress because people try frantically to attain the impossible if they believe they have an outside chance of attaining all of them. What's worse, give your people too many goals, and they'll quickly lose the focus that goal setting normally provides. Setting too many goals invites employees to cherry-pick the easy ones—and procrastinate on the important ones.

Set the Right Kind of Goals

SMART goals fall into two types: performance or outcome goals and learning goals. A performance goal is one that focuses on the outcome or result (for example, increase production by 25 percent, cut costs by 10 percent). A learning goal, as the name implies, focuses attention on the discovery of effective strategies, processes, or procedures necessary for goal attainment.

When people have the necessary knowledge and skill to attain the goal, a SMART performance goal should be set. However, when people lack the knowledge or skill for goal attainment, a SMART learning goal is the right type.[9] For example, a good golfer with a low handicap should set a goal to reach a desired score (a *performance outcome goal*). A poor golfer might set a goal to acquire the skills necessary for using a 5 wood or mastering the use of the putter (both *learning goals*). Setting learning goals increases individuals' knowledge and skill to the point where they are then ready to set SMART performance goals.

Setting Goals for an Uncertain Future

Among the biggest impediments to the effectiveness of goal setting is the uncertainty of the future—that is, environmental uncertainty. A sales goal that looks attainable at the start of the year may look ridiculous six months later after changes in the marketplace. The more uncertain the environment, the more difficult it becomes to set a SMART goal. The

Set subgoals as stepping-stones toward the final goal.

solution is to set subgoals that act as stepping-stones toward the final goal. For example, a goal could be to increase sales 70 percent by year-end; the subgoal could be to make fifty sales calls and generate twenty-five solid leads within the first three months.

Take an industry that suffers dramatic price fluctuations. Setting a specific high-performance goal can result in profits that are significantly worse than a vague goal to "do your best." But when people set proximal or subgoals in addition to the performance goal, profits are significantly higher than with a single performance goal.[10]

Why is that? In a highly dynamic environment, it is important to actively search for feedback and react quickly to it. Subgoals improve error management. Besides the increase in information from setting proximal goals, attaining them increases your employees' overall goal commitment and reinforces their belief that the end goal is indeed attainable.

More generally, subgoals can ensure employee commitment to long-term projects. A distant goal can seem too far off to motivate people to attain it. Subgoals provide milestones to meet and in so doing increase the probability that people will meet their deadlines.

By pairing your vision statement with the right kind of goals—those SMART performance- and learning-based goals—you'll convey loud and clear the specific results you desire.

Align Metrics and Demonstrate Integrity

People are quick to see any lack of congruity between what you say and what you do. Thus, to motivate your employees to maintain their efforts for goal attainment, you must demonstrate your commitment to the vision and SMART goals. Through your actions, you demonstrate integrity. If your actions are out of sync with the vision statement or the SMART goals, employees will detect

A CEO's Example

Donald Carty, when he was chairman and CEO of AMR Corp., the parent of American Airlines, told union members that their cooperation was of utmost importance to keeping the airline out of bankruptcy. Consequently, the union offered AMR major concessions amounting to $1.62 billion in savings. Not long after, though, the union reconvened and voted to rescind the agreement—after they learned that Carty was due to receive a $1.6 million bonus if he stayed with the airline for another three years, and that his senior managers had awarded themselves lavish retention bonuses plus a generous supplemental pension plan. Carty had managed to convince the union to execute the company strategy—in this case, provide for significant cost savings—but his behavior demonstrated that he lacked the integrity to do the same. Carty's words didn't match his actions, and the union knew it. Only after Carty tendered his resignation did the union agree to renegotiate.[11]

this contradiction and abandon the goals. Why should they knock themselves out for something you seem to have little interest in?

Sending Signals

As a manager, you may often be unaware of the signals you send to your employees. For example, if you walk by an employee who is behaving inconsistently with your team's vision and goals, and— lost in thought—you ignore the behavior, you send an inadvertent signal that such behavior is acceptable. Do this repeatedly, and people will quickly discern what they perceive to be your real, as opposed to your claimed, level of commitment to your team's goals. Such signals can do much to damage your integrity as a manager and diminish your employees' belief in your commitment to what you and they are trying to accomplish.

Seeking Feedback

An effective way to assess whether your words and actions show integrity regarding the vision and goals is to invite your employ- ees to give you feedback. Periodically ask your people: "Are there things that I say or do that suggest that I am not committed to our vision and goals?" During this process, you must find ways to make people feel comfortable informing you about what they believe is behavior incongruent with the vision or SMART goals. You can often accomplish this better by informal means, such as a discussion over coffee, in the hallway, or at lunch. The following questions are good ones for soliciting feedback:

- Are the vision and goals still applicable? Do they still motivate you?

- Are we pursuing the right SMART goals? Are they too hard or too easy?

- Is there anything in our situation that is keeping us from reaching our goals?

A President's Lunch Program

Rob Pritchard, when he was president of the University of Toronto, knew that by virtue of his position he would frequently be among the last to know what was taking place on the university's three campuses. To solve this problem, each month he chose names at random to form a small group of faculty with whom he would meet once for lunch. (I know the names were truly chosen at random by the look of the folks around me in the month that my name popped up.)

Rob's opening remarks went something like this: "I hear what the deans *want* me to hear. What is it that I *need* to hear?" In this informal setting, we spilled our guts. Consequently, his knowledge of what was going on in the university was truly amazing. And if there was anything he was unintentionally doing that was undermining the appearance of his integrity—his commitment to the university's vision and goals—he quickly found out.

- Is there anything I am saying or doing as the leader of this team that is getting in the way of, or reducing, goal commitment? What would you like to see me start doing, stop doing, or continue doing in this regard?

If you don't ask, it is all but guaranteed that you will be among the last to know the answers to these questions. People are often reluctant to say something that may cause them difficulty with their boss.

Like Rob Pritchard, in the example above, you need to be aware that the members of your team will typically have access to essential information long before it reaches your office. They will almost certainly know how your customers and potential customers experience your department's products and services.

Further examples of integrity among leaders abound:

- Sir John Bond, when he was CEO of Hong Kong Shanghai Bank, demonstrated his commitment to the company's goal of minimizing costs with a number of seemingly small actions. He turned the lights off in his office when he left it. When he went to the airport, he often rode his own motorcycle instead of taking the company limo. His actions signaled to the bank's employees they should always be frugal with shareholders' money.

- At the Harvey Hotel in Dallas, members of the senior management team frequently drive the courtesy van incognito so that they can listen to customers' comments and complaints. By doing so, they send strong signals to employees that customers' opinions are truly important to the hotel's ongoing success.[12]

- Bill Marriott Jr. flew more than 200,000 miles a year so that he could interact with Marriott Hotel employees. He wandered into Marriott kitchens early in the morning to see whether the food was being cooked properly. He questioned employees about service, signaling his commitment to high-quality service.[13]

What stands out about these leaders is their knowledge that, over the long haul, seemingly small gestures will do more to signal their commitment to organization goals than any number of speeches or memos to employees. Following their example will help keep you from inadvertently undermining your vision and goals by sending the wrong signals. Informally seeking feedback from your employees ensures you find out if you are going off track.

When Metrics Don't Align

Among the best ways to show integrity is to align the metrics you use to measure the results of SMART goals with the vision statement.

Conversely, one of the best ways to demonstrate lack of integrity, and thus to undermine goal pursuit, is to measure employee performance using metrics that don't align with the goals and vision.

HR's Mismatching Goals

To help the human resources department better respond to line management, one company named a line manager as the new HR director. When I asked line managers a year later how the HR director was faring in the new role, they seemed mystified: "How could HR ruin a good person so quickly?" The mystery was removed by examining the goals against which the HR director and the HR department were measured. The metrics were not consistent with the goals of the line managers. HR had its own agenda, and its new manager was pursuing it.

How you measure performance conveys loudly and clearly what you believe is important, no matter what you say is important. Evidenced-based managers make sure that the measurement system is aligned with the vision and goals. If people are rewarded and promoted on metrics that do not support the vision and goals, only zealots will remain committed to the vision, while everyone else will focus on what they see getting measured.

For example, if promotion from assistant to associate to full professor at a university is based solely on research, don't be surprised when the faculty gives minimum attention to developing teaching skills. If a paper company rewards speed of production, don't be surprised if quality is constantly a problem.

Aligning Metrics to Support Vision and Goals

The right metrics will serve as a motivator for your employees to execute the strategy, because these metrics will measure progress toward and attainment of SMART goals and the company vision.

When dysfunctional behavior is observed in a team, the cause frequently lies in a faulty measurement system rather than in the person exhibiting the behavior. If you align the measurement

Carlson's Matching Metrics

At Carlson Companies, a variety of metrics consistently measure employees' awareness and understanding of the company's strategy. Carlson also relies on metrics that highlight when behavior changes are necessary. Armed with metrics such as "census and pulse," "event-specific evaluation," and "learning evaluation" surveys, Carlson's senior managers know that they must initiate and maintain ongoing communications through myriad channels tailored to their respective operating groups. They know they themselves will be assessed primarily on how well they engage their employees, create developmental opportunities, and coach people to embrace change and to attain goals. Carlson managers are even assessed on how well they measure and celebrate short-term as well as long-term successes with their employees.

system with goals that further your team's vision, the right employee behavior—strategy execution that leads to the attainment of desired goals—will follow. The following examples show how different organizations realigned their metrics to support their goals—with great results.

In a professional consulting firm, senior managers exhorted partners to help reduce voluntary staff turnover, which was creating a host of problems, including loss of bench strength as employees capable of being promoted to partner left the firm. This turnover also resulted in loss of money invested in developing staff who subsequently departed and in loss of competent people to work on accounts that the partners were bringing in.

No metrics were in place for assessing or rewarding efforts to decrease turnover. Instead, partners were evaluated on how well they attained revenue goals for new and existing clients. Partners' paychecks, year-end bonuses, and status within the firm were all

FURTHER EVIDENCE

A study in the journal *Applied Psychology: An International Review* showed that seeking feedback correlates with promotion to a higher-level job. It is hard to foul up when you're aware of what your boss, peers, and subordinates expect of you.[14]

based primarily on the client revenue they generated. Consequently, the partners devoted all their time to their clients and ignored their staff. Partners' sole focus on clients was detrimental to both staff development and to the overall good of the firm.

The answer was to shift goals and metrics. The firm implemented a balanced scorecard that set SMART goals for clients, employees, and the firm as a whole. The partners now have three equal priorities instead of one. The expected outcome from earning perfect 10s on client goals (for example, revenue generated) and firm goals (for example, serving on internal committees) and a 0 on staff development is that the partner will be asked to leave the organization. The formula is clear:

$$10 \times 10 \times 0 = 0.$$

Similarly, a large bank gave employees bonuses for getting customers to take one or more loans. However, the bank did not measure the quality of the loans the employees made to their customers. The number of loans increased dramatically; the bank lost money because so many of the loans went bad. The solution was straightforward: Assess employees on the number of loans and, in addition, the number of defaults on loans.

It may be an old saying, but the evidence shows it's true: That which gets measured against specific goals almost always gets done. So it's important for you as an evidence-based manager to examine your metrics when employee behavior seems dysfunctional. If your metrics are out of sync with your goals, it's time to realign your measurement system. When you do so, you'll quickly see a positive change in your employees' behavior.

Stay Engaged

To ensure both that your employees are capable of attaining the goals and that they remain committed to attaining them, you need to stay *engaged* throughout the process. It's difficult—if not impossible—to be an effective, evidence-based manager if you aren't actively engaged with your employees. The vision, the goals, and the metrics won't do much good if you aren't around to show your appreciation of your employees.

Here's what you need to do to show the folks on your team that you are engaged and want to help them be successful:

- Ascertain whether your people have the knowledge, skill, and resources to execute strategy for goal attainment.

- Shower your employees with praise for the little things they do to support the vision and pursue the goals.

- Actively encourage dissent with the vision and goals.

Making Sure Your People Have What They Need

Performance is the product of ability and motivation.[15] Few things are more unfair than expecting an employee or team to pursue goals when they lack the ability or the tools to do so. You need to ensure that your people have the know-how and are given the necessary resources (for example, training and up-to-date equipment) to do the job before you can motivate them to pursue your team's goals.

Showering Your Employees with Positive Attention

If you praise your employees when they execute strategy for goal attainment, you are likely to elicit more of the same behavior. They will know your expectations of them. This is a straightforward way to maintain goal commitment. In contrast, when managers don't provide praise and appreciation for desired behavior, employee apathy often sets in, and apathy is the enemy of goal attainment. But apathy has a relatively easy antidote: Praise your people for what they do—especially the little things. It's feeling like a nobody that breeds apathy. That feeling stems from lack of attention from significant others for who I am and what I do. In contrast, when you give an employee attention, that attention is a strong signal that you appreciate that individual as a member of the team.

Interestingly, attention can be effective even when it is negative. Shouting at an employee sends a strong signal that this person is a somebody; certainly you wouldn't waste your energy shouting at someone you believe can't be salvaged. It's when a person is ignored, when shouting is seen by you as a waste of time, that apathy occurs.

As a manager, you should praise your people for making progress toward the vision and goals. Providing praise is a critical step that, unlike setting a vision or goal, must be done on an ongoing basis to ensure that people do not conclude that they are being taken for granted. But when individual employees are not carrying their weight, let them know immediately or you risk sending a signal that slacking off is okay.

Science can teach the importance of giving people attention; the art is in how that attention is provided—in your case as a manager, how you praise your employees for executing strategy and how you show your employees your appreciation of them and their work. Staying engaged means finding different ways of letting people know you recognize and appreciate the work that they do to attain your team's goals. Here are some examples of how to provide praise:

- In my own days as department chair at the University of Washington, I took a two-week vacation and returned to find the in-basket on my desk overflowing. (This was before the internet!) Tucked in the middle of all that debris was a small handwritten card from my dean that said: "Gary, have I ever told you how great it is to have you as a department chair? Welcome back." I still have that note to this day. Through her thoughtful attention, my dean won my commitment—she didn't have to buy it with monetary bonuses.

- At a financial services company in Minneapolis, a senior manager left a high-level position to join a competitor in New York City. It was widely assumed by her colleagues that she left for a significantly better salary package. They were shocked to learn she would be making less—especially given the much higher cost of living in New York compared to Minneapolis. So why did she leave? "Because in New York," she said, "I will be heard; my opinion will be appreciated."

- Rick Frost, a former CEO at Louisiana Pacific, mailed a letter, without informing an employee, to the employee's partner. His handwritten note read along the following lines: "If Pat has been difficult for you to get along with during the past 2-3 months, allow me to give you a possible explanation. Because of Pat's long hours at the job, because of Pat's commitment to our organization, we were able to accomplish . . . " Through the HR department Rick found out what some of the partner's favorite activities are. Based on that knowledge, Rick ended the letter: "In appreciation for what you may have had to put up with, I am enclosing two tickets for the opera [or whatever the partner will enjoy]."

How many of your employees feel they aren't being heard? Nothing gives most people more joy than feeling that what they say and what they do are appreciated. This isn't just rhetoric; research shows this to be true. As William James, the father of psychology in the United States, once said, "The deepest craving of human nature is appreciation." It's your job as an evidence-based manager to ensure that your employees experience that joy. They, in turn, will reward you with goal attainment.

Encouraging Dissent

Another important way of staying engaged with your employees is to encourage their dissent—something far too few managers do. The absence of dissent in the workplace usually reflects the fact that employees do not believe it will be welcomed. They may even fear retaliation. Jack Welch, the former CEO of General Electric, is fond of saying: "To get candor you reward it, you praise it, and you talk about the value of it. Most of all, you demonstrate it." By candor, Welch is referring to encouraging disagreement with you as the manager, and with the vision and the goals.[17] The absence of dissent reflects a decline in trust and the deterioration of your relationship with your people.

Apathy has an easy antidote: Praise your people for what they do.

An absence of complaints is often an indicator of an absence of hope. By embracing and welcoming criticism, you send your people a strong signal that you care about their concerns. They may have discovered that the vision and goals that were bang-on in the fall are no longer on target this winter. Dissent is an antidote to groupthink, which occurs when people agree with what they know to be wrong. A tragic example of groupthink occurred when engineers agreed that the space shuttle *Challenger* should be launched

The absence of complaints is one of the surest signs of a failing relationship.

the next day, January 27, 1986. They agreed to the launch as a team, yet as individuals they knew that the shuttle's O-rings might not seal when the temperature fell below 55° F. They agreed as a team, even though they knew the weather was supposed to be in the 50s the next day. The *Challenger* exploded within minutes after takeoff, taking the lives of everyone onboard.

A solution to groupthink is to ask for dissent: What are the downsides in what we are proposing to do? Another solution is to appoint and then rotate naysayers: "Pat, Samantha, Billy: Find the flaw in our proposal to reduce our asking price by 25 percent. Shoot us down." "Next week I want Ruth, Tom, and Coreen to find the flaw in our logic to sell our division in Kansas."

When listening to your employees' concerns, don't promise to act on everything they suggest. It's the listening—and acting when you believe it is necessary—that counts. Encourage dissent, and your employees' candor may alert you to problems in your team you couldn't see from your vantage point as manager. That kind of encouragement will ultimately strengthen the relationship between you and your people.

It's the listening that counts.

Be aware that a downside of encouraging constructive dissent is that you may find a queue at your door because you are the one person who gives people a chance to vent their concerns. While you want to provide a forum for dissent, you don't want people to become dependent on you. You can empower your people by asking questions that will help them realize solutions on their own, while refraining from providing them with immediate answers.

For example, in a personnel conflict, you might say: "You believe Sam is impossible to deal with. Okay, how might you approach Sam differently? What positive outcomes (if any) does Sam expect from cooperating with you? What negative outcomes (if any) does Sam expect from cooperating with you? Is there anything you can shift or change so that Sam can clearly see the benefits of working with (rather than against) you in attaining your goal?"

CONCLUSION

The four steps discussed in this chapter—developing a vision, setting goals, aligning metrics, and staying engaged—offer a complete package for evidence-based managers to inspire their employees to success. Together, they form a road map that will guide you and your employees to solid strategy execution for goal attainment. These steps are shown by research to be effective; as a result, evidence-based managers use these steps to bring about desired results in their own organizations.

QUESTIONS

1. What four-step process can you use to inspire your team?

2. What is the rationale for encouraging dissent within your team? How can you do so constructively?

3. How can you develop a vision that appeals to affect?

4. What is meant by SMART?

5. Why does an attitudinal goal to "do your best" have little or no effect on behavior?

6. What are the benefits of setting a specific, challenging goal?

7. What signals can you send that you are supportive of those on your team?

8. What happens when metrics are not aligned with the vision, goals, and strategy?

9. How can you let the people on your team know that you notice and appreciate them?

10. Are there downsides to setting high performance goals?

DEVELOP AND TRAIN TO CREATE A HIGH-PERFORMING TEAM

It may come as a surprise, but the truth is you don't need a big training-and-development budget to help your people become high performers. Using the six inexpensive evidence-based techniques in this chapter, you can develop and train your team to accomplish their goals. These methods are straightforward, powerful, and proven to work.

Chris Argyris, who was a revered professor at Harvard University, found that most people strive to be effective. He believed that people have an innate need or desire for personal effectiveness.[1] This chapter provides developmental techniques that will foster a high-performing mind-set in your employees. By using these techniques, you will help your people become creative risk takers and independent problem solvers who confront challenges head-on and take action that is in the best interests of your department—without having to constantly check with you for permission. High performers aren't born; anyone can become a high performer when armed with research-proven psychological techniques that empower the attainment of your team's goals.

> **SIX TOOLS FOR TRAINING AND DEVELOPMENT**
>
> **As an employee use:**
> - Functional self-talk
> - Mental practice
> - Self-management
>
> **As a manager:**
> - Show the flag
> - Maintain the organization's culture
> - Encourage mistakes

WHAT WORKS, IN BRIEF

The mind is a powerful asset. To help your people harness the power of a can-do mind-set and perform at a high level, teach them three cognitive techniques: functional self-talk, mental practice, and self-management.

Training and Development Techniques

Internal dialogue (self-talk) holds the key to performance. That is, when we actively influence our thoughts so that we think posi-tively, we can expect positive outcomes—and the opposite is also true. When we think negatively, we can all but ensure a negative outcome. You can teach your employees a four-step process for *functional self-talk* that will enable them to turn *dysfunctional* thinking into *functional* self-talk that engenders high performance.

Mental practice (also known as *visualization*) is a technique that teaches your people the power of rehearsing specific steps in their mind's eye to increase performance. While the old saying "Practice makes perfect" certainly holds true, there is ample evidence showing that mental practice, a type of scripted mental visualization, can do as much as physical practice to boost performance by reinforcing material learned in a training session.

Training in *self-management*, the third technique, teaches people skills in self-observation, especially the ability to compare their behavior to their goals and to self-administer rewards and punishment. It's an effective way to guide your employees to manage their own behavior—so you won't have to do so.

Your Actions as a Manager

No matter what your training content entails, you, as a manager, must still do three things to ensure that your training and development programs work. You need to show the flag, focus on your organization's culture, and actually encourage your people to make errors when mastering a complex task. Together, these techniques will demonstrate to your team that you believe in your organization's training programs, that you believe in your organization's values, and that—perhaps most important—you value an employee's ability to take creative risks to execute your team's strategy for goal attainment.

You don't want your people to, at best, tolerate a training program or a new initiative—you want them to believe in it, support it, and execute it in the workplace energetically. This requires you to "show the flag"—to visibly demonstrate your support for the training. You can do this by explaining its logic and by showing how what is being taught will increase participants' ability to attain goals both as individuals and as teams. You can also participate in the training program. You can drop by to praise the trainer and the trainees for devoting the time necessary to ensure the training content is mastered. When you drop by to show your belief in the importance of the training content, initiate a dialogue around

Show the flag by visibly demonstrating your support.

your department's goals and strategy and how the training content is related to them.

Your organization's rule book can only cover so much, and this is where your organization's culture and its values come into play. Teach employees your organization's values by talking about its everyday heroes, demonstrating these values, and taking a personal role in maintaining this culture by discussing and living those values. You'll give your team members the confidence they need to execute strategy when unfamiliar situations arise.

The third technique may seem counterintuitive: You need to encourage your people to make mistakes. You do this by orienting them toward learning goals rather than performance goals. Although encouraging mistakes may initially seem absurd, think about it: Truly high goals are rarely reached without making errors along the way. Encouraging your people to make errors—and to learn from their mistakes—will ensure that they won't be afraid to take risks by trying something different to attain breakthroughs.

EFFECTIVE TRAINING AND DEVELOPMENT TOOLS IN PRACTICE

Besides any job-specific content that needs to be covered in your organization's training programs, you will want to include the following essential developmental techniques to help your employees achieve top performance.

Functional Self-Talk

Self-talk refers to a person's internal dialogue. It's what we tell ourselves about ourselves—what we need to do, what we might say, what may go right, and what may go wrong. This internal dialogue is a collection of thoughts, both positive and negative, that research shows to have an important effect on performance.[2] As such, self-talk can be functional or dysfunctional. That is, a positive internal

FURTHER EVIDENCE

It is not ability per se that holds us back or propels us forward as much as it is our beliefs about our ability.[3] This belief is known as *self-efficacy*. Self-efficacy is task-specific confidence. I have high self-efficacy that I can write a book on evidence-based management that will be useful for you. I have no self-efficacy whatsoever that I can fix a leaky toilet. Self-efficacy explains why some people are overachievers and others are underachievers. One person with loads of ability as a singer may not perform nearly as well as her sister who has much less ability yet much higher confidence that she can "wow" an audience—and she does.

dialogue can help you succeed, while a negative internal dialogue can undermine your confidence and reduce your ability to perform effectively. As a manager, you can teach your employees to engage in functional self-talk—and thus guide them toward high-performance—using four steps:

1. Develop awareness.

2. Recognize alternatives.

3. Replace negative thoughts with positive ones.

4. Prevent relapse.

Here's a look at an example of functional self-talk in action, based on my own research with my former doctoral student Zeeva Millman.[4] This developmental technique was taught to managers who had been out of work for a year—a period when negative self-talk can truly get out of hand, damaging the displaced managers' belief in their ability

A positive internal dialogue can help you succeed.

to find a new job. We coached them to discard their negative self-talk using these four steps, which are the same ones your employees can use.

Develop Awareness

In the first step, you want to increase employees' awareness of their negative thoughts—the sum of their personal fears and insecurities—and, more important, how these thoughts affect their behavior in attaining their goals. You can do this by simply asking them to list them. "What are the reasons why this goal may not be attainable?"

We asked the unemployed managers to think about how their negative statements influenced their ability to obtain another job. In particular, we provided them with a diary to record every negative self-statement they made (for example, "I am too old to get an offer") regarding any job search activity they considered.

In the second session, the trainees reviewed their negative self-statements in a group discussion, and they began to realize that their negative self-talk consisted of generalizations rather than specifics. For example, they discovered that statements such as "I'm too senior, too expensive" and "Headhunters know when they are on to a loser" were generalizations. While possibly true in some instances, no one could point to any evidence that indicated that such a statement was true for themselves in all instances. Realizing that their negative talk was only true for some situations laid the groundwork for a can-do mind-set.

Recognize Alternatives

In the second step, you teach your people to look for positive alternatives that will counteract their negative thoughts. These positive alternatives are also called "transition statements." Specifically, you ask participants to look at the diary of negative self-statements they created in step one and to generate positive statements in response. This increases self-efficacy, a belief that "Yes, I can."

With the unemployed managers, we asked them to create a transition statement to counter this negative thought about their employment: "Why am I looking? There are never any jobs for me."

Second, we asked them to verbalize a transition statement that would connect their actions to their thoughts, which turned out to be: "Wait a minute, let me look at my job search behavior. The truth is, I haven't sent out any resumés in the past few weeks."

Replace Negative Thoughts

After recognizing a transition statement, the third step is to cement functional self-talk by formulating self-statements that focus on positives.

The unemployed managers generated such statements as "I have valuable skills that can enable me to contribute positively to an organization," "There are a lot of organizations that need my particular skill set," or, "I will bring priceless experience to my next employer."

Once these positive self-statements were on the table, we asked the trainees to do a job search activity while telling themselves out loud why their search would prove successful.

When training your own employees, you too will ask them to explain out loud to themselves what they will do to attain their goals. Verbalizing the positive action they will take will prevent them from entertaining negative thoughts. In addition, you will be aware of anyone who is not talking aloud because they are having difficulty generating positive action steps. After this training, your employees will not have to speak their actions out loud back on the job. They can do so covertly. But during training, overt self-talk is a method of self-persuasion. Self-persuasion is extremely effective because it is far easier to argue with the opinions of others than it is with oneself.

Generate positive statements in response to negative self-statements.

Prevent a Relapse

The fourth and final step is about preventing a relapse into old habits of negative, dysfunctional self-talk. To accomplish this, you will

FURTHER EVIDENCE

Training in shifting dysfunctional self-talk ("I can't") to functional self-talk ("I can") has also proven to be effective in turning highly competitive MBA students into team players in their study groups, as well as in enabling Native American high school students to find jobs. Although many managers and researchers fear that findings in the behavioral sciences may be applicable to Western countries only, this is not the case. This developmental technique also enabled Muslim women in Turkey, all over the age of forty, to find meaningful employment.[5]

want to ask your employees to generate ways they may fail and then to come up with coping responses. Relapse prevention is essential; without it, your efforts to reduce negative self-talk are in danger of being altogether erased.[6]

We asked the unemployed managers to discuss possible obstacles to conducting an effective job search as well as obstacles to using positive self-talk. Then we asked them to generate a list of ways in which they could overcome these obstacles. Obstacles included feeling silly about consciously speaking out loud when alone, needing a conscious effort to speak silently to oneself when in a public setting, facing fear of failure, and feeling like a loser in front of family and friends when finding a job takes longer than a week or a month.

The results of this training experiment make a powerful case for using functional self-talk to develop your employees to become high performers: Of the managers in the training group, 45 percent found a new job within six months and a total of 95 percent found a new job within nine months.[7] Meanwhile, only 12 percent of the managers in the control group—the managers we didn't train—found work.

In sum, self-talk is an inexpensive, straightforward training procedure for instilling a can-do mind-set. It has limitless applicability for developing resilience in any employee who has suffered one severe setback or multiple small ones. Setbacks lead to doubt, and left to itself that doubt can be more damaging than whatever caused the setback itself.

Mental Practice

Another training technique, closely related to self-talk, is called mental practice—also known as *visualization.* Mental practice involves thinking about a task before taking action, and it works on virtually any task—from sinking a putt on the golf course to making a successful presentation to prospective clients.

Using mental practice can help master both physical and mental activities.

It may seem like common sense that the only way to learn to parallel park a car is to get behind the wheel and try it. But experiments show that using mental practice—in addition to taking action—can help you master both physical and mental activities.[8] This technique is beneficial for both motor activities (such as parking or playing basketball) and mental activities (such as solving puzzles). The greater the task's mental or "cognitive" component, the greater the benefit of mental practice.

You can teach mental practice to your employees using a guided script that includes three elements:

- Step-by-step procedures for acquiring a specific skill

- Instructions for people to visualize themselves putting those steps into action

- Ways for people to use one or more of their five senses as they imagine themselves performing the task

For example, in teaching people how to successfully deliver a sales presentation, you might begin by breaking down the skills

Supervisors Practice Communication with the Union

A forest products company in Quebec conducted a one-day training program with supervisors and process engineers focused on improving skills of communicating with union shop stewards. But at the workshop's end, people expressed grave doubts that they could apply what they had been taught.

My former doctoral student Lucy Morin randomly selected a group of supervisors to mentally practice the communication skills they learned in the course.[9] Using the content of the training program as a script, they visualized themselves using specific, effective communication behaviors with a union official. Lucy read the following script: "Close your eyes and imagine that you are sitting comfortably in your chair, and you feel relaxed and calm. See a union leader coming toward you. Imagine yourself slowly standing up and welcoming that person with a smile. Feel the person shaking your hand. Now hear yourself say the following words that you learned in your training program . . . "

Several months later, here is what the supervisors who took the additional training in mental practice had to say:

- Visualizing the different scenarios prior to a disciplinary meeting helped me to anticipate problems with the union and to stay on track.

- Visualization was helpful to me in preparing for negotiations with the union.

Those who took the visualization training scored higher on a measure of confidence (that is, self-efficacy) in interacting with union officials than those in the control group who had not been trained in mental practice. And according to their peers, who were surveyed anonymously, the people who were trained were more effective in their interactions with the union leaders than those who had not been trained.

that your employees need to develop to attain a high level of performance when delivering the presentation to a large audience. Next, discuss the step-by-step procedure for acquiring or sharpening each of these skills. For example, to develop the skill of closing a sale, you will remind your employees that they need to do a, b, and c. Then guide employees through the mental practice of each of these steps by talking them through a visualized situation. "Begin to imagine that you are with a specific client whom you visited within the past month . . . " During this process, you will encourage people to use all five senses to make the experience real (for example, hear the people shifting in their seats, smell the flowers that are typically in that room). In essence, mental practice teaches people to visualize themselves taking concrete steps to attain their goal. Using this technique, you as an evidence-based manager can guide your people to mentally rehearse how they will attain each goal.

Perhaps the greatest benefit of mental practice is that it doesn't just teach people to better handle a negotiation or make a presentation to a large group; rather, mental practice increases self-efficacy, the belief they can improve their own job performance. By teaching mental practice, you put the tools to achieve high performance in the hands of your employees, tools they can use on their own, time and again.

Self-Management

A third development technique that instills a "can-do" mind-set is called *self-management*. This technique teaches people to discover the root of their problem, to set goals to resolve it, to reward success and punish failure, and to monitor their own behavior against the goal that they set.[10] You can teach this technique through a six-step self-management program:

1. List the reasons for this problem.

2. Set a specific goal.

3. Monitor personal success.

4. Provide a personal reward or punishment, depending on progress toward the goal.

5. Create a personal contract.

6. Prevent relapse.

The importance of setting a specific, high goal was described in chapter 2, as was the principle underlying step three: What gets measured (or in this case, self-monitored) gets done. The rewards and punishments should also be specific. They are contingent upon progress toward the goal (or lack thereof). In the fifth step, the employee summarizes planning for the first four steps by putting in writing the goal to be attained and the time frame for attaining it, along with the self-administered rewards for attaining the goal and the punishment that awaits failure. The self-written contract should also specify the behaviors that will enable an employee to attain the goal. Step six is about warding off a return to former behavior.

Collette Frayne, another of my former doctoral students, delivered self-management training to a group of unionized, hourly government workers to increase their job attendance.[11] Table 1 shows the steps of self-management training that were applied with the unionized employees.

The unionized hourly workers showed a dramatic increase in job attendance within three months of taking this training program. Self-management techniques enable employees to coach themselves to become high performers with a strong can-do mind-set.

THE MANAGER'S ROLE DURING TRAINING AND DEVELOPMENT

For your employee training and development programs to be most effective, you need to show your support for the programs and to help foster a high-performing mind-set.

To start, you as manager must visibly demonstrate your support for the program—or risk losing your people's support and commitment to training and development. Second, you must maintain your company's culture by teaching and communicating your

TABLE 1. STEPS IN SELF-MANAGEMENT FOR HOURLY EMPLOYEES

STEP	EXAMPLE
1. List the reasons for the problem.	Workers listed everything from legitimate illness to family problems to dislike of their boss as the reason for their low job attendance.
2. Set specific goals.	The workers each set a high goal for the number of days they would go to work each month.
3. Monitor behavior.	The workers (1) graphed their own attendance and posted the graph in a high-visibility area at home, such as on the refrigerator, (2) listed the reason for any absence, and (3) identified the steps they took to return to work.
4. Self-administer rewards and punishments.	Rewards included stopping for a beer with friends after work, while punishments included cleaning out the attic.
5. Create a personal contract.	Steps two through four were put in writing by the employee for the employee.
6. Prevent relapse.	Workers identified what might tempt them not to come to work and planned ahead for ways to cope with these situations should they occur.

organization's core values. These values will ultimately help guide your people to making the best possible decisions for your organization. Lastly—paradoxical as it may seem—you must encourage your people to make errors, because in pursuing high goals, mistakes are all but inevitable. These three steps provide an evidence-based foundation on which to train your employees to become high performers.

Showing the Flag

If you don't believe in a training program, why should your people? You need to "show the flag" if you expect people to buy in. This means communicating to your employees and modeling support for the organization's training programs, especially for the underlying vision and goals that the training is designed to support.[12] Companies such as IBM have found that manager support for a training initiative is critical, because managers set the example—when they model the desired behavior, their employees internalize that example and follow the managers' lead.[13] When you show the flag, you also help protect your employees from the inevitable pressure to revert to "the way things are done here." Why? Because you signal loudly and clearly what defines a high performer in your eyes.

Of course, you only want to show the flag if your organization's training is truly tied to its vision, goals, and strategy. If there is no relationship—or the relationship is tenuous at best—kill the program.

Maintaining Company Culture

Your organization's culture is made up of the values and behaviors that are reinforced and that differentiate it from other organizations (for example, picture Apple, IBM, Microsoft, or Salesforce). Creating and maintaining your organization's culture within your team is among the most important aspects of your job. You need to sell your organization's values to your people as aggressively and as steadfastly as you sell a product or service to your customers. Your employees need to know and understand your organization's values so they can execute strategy and make appropriate decisions when unfamiliar problems arise. They also need to hear about your organization's heroes—the regular folks who go to extraordinary lengths for the organization and clients—so they will have the confidence that if they take the risk in making a decision in unfamiliar terrain, they too may become a hero. Remember, modeling works.

Here's a look at what a few top-notch companies do to communicate and maintain their organization's culture:

- **They actively teach company values.** Disney stresses to its employees the importance of four company values: safety, courtesy, show, and efficiency. All Disney employees hear this in their orientation training. It is the first thing the trainers present. When employees encounter an unfamiliar situation, these four values help them decide what to do.[14]

  > *You need to sell your organization's values to your people.*

- **They share stories of their organization's heroes.** Leaders at American Express tell stories about "Great Performers." Among them, two customer service representatives in Florida got money to a woman in a foreign war zone and then helped her get a boat out of the country. Travel agents in Columbus, Georgia, paid a French tourist's bail so he could get out of jail. Another employee drove through a blizzard to take food and blankets to stranded travelers at New York's John F. Kennedy Airport. Still another employee got up in the middle of the night to take an Amex card to a customer stranded at Boston's Logan Airport. American Express distributes its "Great Performers" booklets to all its people worldwide.[15]

- **They take a personal role in maintaining their organization's culture.** Dominic D'Alessandro, when he was CEO of Manulife Financial Company, attended every weeklong executive education session, usually on either the first or last day, regardless of whether the session was scheduled

FURTHER EVIDENCE

Research shows that values, the hallmark of culture, serve as guiding principles in the life of a person. They influence behavior because they are normative standards used to judge and choose among alternative courses of action. The same is true for an organization's culture. It affects the guiding principles for what an employee should do.[16]

for Toronto, Boston, Hong Kong, Tokyo, or Shanghai. To do what? He simply sat on a bar stool for 90 minutes describing the values underlying the organization's strategy—and he emphasized how specific values, particularly integrity, affected his decisions as the CEO of this large financial institution. While doing so, he stressed how the content of the weeklong training program was tied to the goals he wanted the attendees to attain.

In short, developing and maintaining your organization's culture requires actively teaching and modeling the desired values and behaviors, as well as sharing stories about your organization's heroes. Your organization's culture is the foundation on which your employees can rely as they make decisions about how to handle sundry issues with clients, products, or services and ultimately how effectively they are able to execute your team's overall strategy.

Encouraging Errors

Henry Ford once said, "The beauty of failure is that it allows you to start over more intelligently." And Thomas Edison once noted, "Of all the lightbulbs that didn't work, every failure to me was something that I was able to incorporate into the next attempt." What were these great inventors and businessmen really talking about? They were talking about the value of mistakes. If you want the people on your team to take creative risks—to pursue challenges and to become high performers—you must encourage and celebrate errors. This is the cornerstone of a "learning organization." The critical step is for you to frame an error on the part of your employees as positive (for example, "The more errors you make, the more you learn"). This enables your people to keep their negative emotions in check, especially when working on tasks where solutions are not known. Explicit instruction from you regarding their self-talk is also critical. Encourage and model statements such as: "I have made an error. Great! I have just learned something." This helps people to keep their attention on the task at hand and away from themselves (for example, "I am so stupid").

Some of your people may have the ability to see errors as part of the natural course of learning, while others may inherently try to steer clear of tasks in which they risk mistakes or failure. That's because the ability to take creative risks is in part a product of heredity and in part a product of environment. Heredity includes personality traits, among them goal orientation.

Both goals and goal orientations come in two types: performance and learning.[17] People with a *performance* goal orientation paradoxically lack a high-performing mind-set, because they focus too much on their performance. Their goal is to look good in the eyes of others. As a result, they actively avoid situations in which they run the risk of seeming incompetent. Instead, they seek assignments in which they can perform effectively. On the other hand, people with a *learning* goal orientation seek to master new skills and knowledge. Consequently, they enjoy challenging, difficult projects. They even seek constructive criticism. This in itself is an effective

> *People with a learning goal orientation seek to master new skills and knowledge.*

strategy because pursuing high goals makes errors all but inevitable. As Paul Arbor, former executive creative director of global advertising agency Saatchi & Saatchi, has said: "The person who does not make mistakes is unlikely to make anything."[18] Constructive criticism enables people to learn from the errors they make.

> **FURTHER EVIDENCE**
>
> Research shows that the combination of providing train-ees with ample opportunity to make errors and explicitly encouraging them to learn from an error improves their performance on complex tasks. If you minimize opportunities for your employees to make errors, they may not learn to be resilient. They are likely to give up when they make one error after another. The research shows that people can be easily taught to frame errors as beneficial and consequently bounce back from foul-ups through encouragement for systematic exploration of alternatives.[19]

As an evidence-based manager interested in coaching employees to high performance, you will want to follow the research that recommends guiding your team members to have a learning goal orientation. The good news is that in this case environment trumps heredity. By using the training techniques discussed earlier in this chapter—functional self-talk, mental practice, and self-management—you can instill in your people a learning goal orientation, even if they have a natural preference for a performance goal orientation.

> *Emphasize that errors lead to learning successes, not performance failures.*

The research giant on goal orientation is Carol Dweck, an educational psychologist at Stanford University. She has worked primarily with children. Peter Heslin, another of my former doctoral students, now at the Australian Graduate School of Management, has shown that managers with a performance goal orientation can be taught a learning goal orientation. It is important to do so because some managers view an employee's ability as fixed, and this makes them reluctant to take the time to coach their employees. Their emphasis is on selecting the best, rather than training people to become the best. Managers with a learning goal orientation believe that employees are capable of continuous improvement. Hence, they believe that coaching is worthwhile.[20]

CONCLUSION

When it comes to training and development, research reveals the value of taking the approaches discussed in this chapter. First, train your employees in techniques that will help them become confident as high performers. Functional self-talk, mental practice, and self-management are three techniques that your employees can use on an ongoing basis to guide themselves to high performance again and again. Second, foster a climate for your employees that is conducive to learning and ultimately achieving high performance.

By showing the flag for training and development programs that are tied directly to the implementation of your organization's strategy, you will signal the value of these programs and reinforce employee engagement in the learning process. In addition, by actively ensuring the training is tied to the culture you are trying to create and maintain, you will help the employees on your team place the learning process in the larger context of your organization's vision, goals, and strategy. Lastly, your encouragement of employees' making mistakes during the learning process will communicate the value of taking risks and working to overcome challenges, which will consequently lead to the highest levels of performance.

QUESTIONS

1. What are six tools you can use for training and development?

2. In the context of training and development, what is meant by "show the flag"?

3. How can you use functional self-talk to improve your performance?

4. What is the benefit of mental practice? How can you apply it?

5. Where in your organization would employees benefit from acquiring skills in self-management?

6. Why is it important for you to "sell" your organization's culture to your employees? How can you do so?

7. What is the logic or rationale for you to encourage your subordinates to make errors?

8. What is meant by a learning versus a performance goal orientation?

9. How do you view the training and development programs in your organization?

10. Based on what you have learned in this chapter, how would you improve the training and development programs in your organization?

MOTIVATE YOUR EMPLOYEES TO BE HIGH PERFORMERS

4

At Tokyo's Imperial Hotel, a waiter overheard two guests discussing their college reunion, an annual event with a typically large turnout. The waiter thought that such reunions could be an untapped niche for the hotel, so he mentioned it at the weekly team meeting with his manager. The hotel pursued the waiter's idea. The result was an extra $600,000 of revenue in just two months.[1] How many of your frontline employees are sufficiently motivated to watch for such revenue-generating ideas?

The Imperial Hotel story is impressive. Yet the real challenge in motivating staff is not in the occasional "big win" but in smaller daily successes. Effective managers need to be able to motivate their people every day. If you are not taking steps to ensure your people are motivated, you aren't doing your job. In this chapter, I present five keys to unlocking your employees' inner motivation. I also share with you some surprising facts on what the research has to say about the "money factor" (for example, a simple pay raise may not have the motivating effect you expect) and discuss simple things you can do to avoid inadvertently demotivating your people. Every evidence-based manager should keep in mind five keys that will motivate employees to become high performers:

1. Attend to employees' physiological and security needs.

2. Make sure your employees have high, specific goals.

> **FURTHER EVIDENCE**
>
> Training increases a person's ability. Research shows that people with high ability show a proportionately greater improvement in their performance from an increase in motivation than do those individuals with lower ability. To train the people on your team, to truly increase their ability, and then to fail to take steps to motivate them is an inexcusable waste of your organization's money. You can't focus on one and overlook the other if you want the people who report to you to be high performers.[2]

3. Focus on job performance.

4. Understand and change the work environment if necessary.

5. Avoid demotivation.

WHAT DOESN'T WORK, IN BRIEF

Money is not the end-all motivator many managers believe it to be. The relationship between money and worker motivation is quite complex. Just handing out a raise or an occasional bonus typically does not get you much improvement in performance.

Money is a funny thing: If you think that just giving your employees a raise or doling out an occasional bonus will do the trick to motivate them, think again. Walt Disney once said, "You don't work for a dollar; you work to create and have fun." Research shows there may be something to that way of thinking.

Studies show that receiving a monetary reward for doing what one would have done anyway because of its intrinsic appeal reduces motivation as well as satisfaction, because the money is seen by the recipient as "controlling."[3] These findings are likely applicable to people working in volunteer organizations. I have knocked myself out in volunteer leadership roles and never received a dime for doing so. But I would have walked away disgusted if I had been given $100 in recognition for my efforts. Nevertheless, it is nonsense to believe most of us would perform our day jobs in the absence of our salary. Pay is important to the extent that it enables employees to satisfy their needs for security and autonomy. Pay is not motivating if it is not tied closely to performance. If high performers are paid the same as low performers, both job performance and job satisfaction will be low. Money is motivating to the extent it leads to the setting of and commitment to high goals.[4]

WHAT WORKS, IN BRIEF

The first motivational element—a prerequisite, in fact—is fulfillment of employees' *physiological and security needs*. Until those needs are met, the motivation to perform at a high level will not exist and no motivational techniques, however ingenious, will energize employees to deliver high performance on their own.

Focusing on job performance boosts motivation far more than focusing on job satisfaction.

The second element—*setting high, specific goals*—is based directly on goal-setting theory, discussed throughout this book. Some managers fear that setting high goals will overwhelm employees and discourage them from performing well. But as long as the goals are specific and attainable, challenging goals will serve as key motivators of performance improvement in the workplace.

Many managers believe that among the best ways to motivate employees is to focus on increasing job satisfaction. Yet the third element for motivating employees, *focusing on job performance*, actually boosts motivation far more than focusing directly on improving satisfaction. Incidentally, job satisfaction increases as a by-product of improving performance because most people enjoy doing what they can perform well.

The fourth element for motivating employees is *understanding and changing the work environment*. This includes taking into account characteristics of the job, the schedule for administering rewards, employee perceptions of organizational justice, and societal values.

The final element is to *avoid demotivation*. Just as you, the manager, have the ability to motivate your employees, your actions can also demotivate them. Organizational justice has to do with perceptions of fairness in the workplace. The unspoken agreements between you and your employees constitute psychological contracts, and ignoring the principles of organizational justice—especially failing to honor those psychological contracts—will rapidly deflate your employees' motivation.

MOTIVATIONAL TOOLS IN PRACTICE

Motivating your team to high performance requires understanding how your employees' needs, goals, performance, and work environment interact and influence the desire to execute your team's strategy. Once you understand this interrelationship, as explained in detail in this chapter, you'll have the tools to create the conditions necessary to build your employees' desire to become high performers.

Addressing Employees' Needs

In the aftermath of Hurricane Harvey in 2017, it would have been lunacy for managers in Houston or Puerto Rico to expect employees to focus on their jobs when so many homes were destroyed and communities broken apart. Smart employers took steps to make sure that employees' basic needs were met as soon as possible. That may seem like common sense, but common sense is often lacking among those who are not evidence-based managers. Research provides a theoretical framework—which I've given here as a five-point checklist—of the needs that must be met before an employee can be motivated to become a high performer:[5]

- **Physiological needs**. These are the absolute basics required for life—food, water, and shelter. They affect a person's survival and well-being, making them the starting point of motivation.

- **Security**. In the work setting, the need for safety goes beyond physical safety to include job protection (for example, tenure, a union contract) as well as the desire for a savings account and for insurance (for example, health, unemployment, disability).

- **Affiliation**. This is a desire to get along with the people on the team and know you have your team's support.

- **Self-esteem**. People need to have a high opinion of themselves based on achievement that leads to respect from others.

- **Self-actualization**. This is a desire to feel fulfilled, to maximize one's potential, "to be all that one can be."

These five points make up the taxonomy of needs first introduced by Abraham Maslow. His theoretical framework is a useful diagnostic tool in the workplace because it provides you with a checklist you can use to identify what's wrong when an employee is not pursuing agreed-upon goals.*

Once the basic physiological and safety needs—needs for food, water, shelter, and security—are met, that's it. Those needs are satisfied. For example, once I'm full, I'm not motivated to order another pizza. The same is true for affiliation—working well with

---

* Behavioral scientists have dismissed justifiably the scientific premise of this theory, namely, that a lower need must be satisfied before attention is given to finding ways to satisfying a higher need. This is not always the case. Nevertheless, I find this taxonomy to be a useful checklist when dealing with clients and students.

TABLE 2. MEETING EMPLOYEES' FIVE NEEDS IN THE WORKPLACE

NEED	EXAMPLES OF WAYS TO ADDRESS
Physiological	Ensure that employees have access to healthy food.
Security	Make clear what people have to do to keep their jobs.
Affiliation	Hold team-building sessions; teach conflict resolution skills.
Self-Esteem	Let people know that what they are accomplishing is noticed and appreciated. Celebrate their successes.
Self-Actualization	Explore ways an employee can grow in the organization—ways they will be wiser and more proficient in three to five years.

people on the team. This is not the case, however, for a person's needs for self-esteem and self-actualization. When goals for these two needs are met, a person will set even higher ones. For example, if someone's goal is to be promoted to supervisor, you can be pretty sure that once the promotion comes through, the new supervisor will soon set another goal to reach the next rung on that management ladder. These two higher-level needs—self-esteem and self-actualization—are inexhaustible.

That means they are always available for you to use as tools of motivation. Table 2 provides practical guidance on how you can address employees' needs to increase motivation to perform and a checklist for diagnosing problems. As the area doctoral coordinator in the business school, if I see a new PhD student having difficulty performing well in seminars and conducting research, I immediately want to know whether the person is having difficulty finding a suitable place to live, lacks adequate funds to cover living expenses,

A Manager's "Three Cheers"

One manager sends out "Three Cheers" notices to the organization every time he sees a member of his team excel. He provides public recognition for what a specific employee has done. In addition, he has one or more discussions a year with each of his employees on where they want to go in the organization and how the two of them can make it happen. If an employee likes the way things are and does not want a promotion, he encourages discussion on what that person might like to start doing, stop doing, or be doing differently in the present job so there is continuous learning and boredom does not creep in from doing the same old things.

or is experiencing trouble making friends with fellow doctoral students. I use the five-point framework to problem-solve issues with that individual.

Although the importance of addressing employees' basic needs may be most evident in times of crisis—such as in a natural disaster like Hurricane Harvey—the evidence shows that you must ensure that your employees' needs are met if you want to be able to motivate your employees to become and remain high performers.

Setting Employee Goals for High Performance

Goal setting is a fundamental theme of this book, and I bring it up again here because as an evidence-based manager, you can use goals as a tool of motivation. But to serve as effective motivators, the goals you set must be challenging to attain and specific in nature. There is a direct relationship between the *difficulty* of a goal and a person's job performance. High goals inspire people to put in more effort and persistence than moderately difficult or easy goals. What's more, goals that are *specific*—rather than something vague such as "do your best"—also lead to higher performance. Goals that are both difficult and specific provide an unambiguous basis for employees as well as you to judge their effectiveness. That is ultimately what makes it possible for them to feel successful at their job.[6]

Interestingly, experiencing success does not depend on the absolute level of employees' performance; it depends on their per-formance in relation to established goals. The relationship of goals to employees' sense of well-being is straightforward: The greater their success in attaining high goals, the more employees experience job satisfaction and happiness. When employees attain a high goal, they not only feel satisfied with their performance, they like the task more than they did previously—and this satisfaction can serve as an effective motivating tool. This is because attaining goals validates the person's effectiveness. Moreover, feelings of competency increase, as does job satisfaction.[7]

> *Experiencing success depends on performance in relation to established goals.*

A study published in the *Journal of Organizational and Occupational Psychology* on a broad range of managerial and professional jobs found that feelings of exhaustion did not go up among those with high goals. Their sense of well-being increased only when high rather than easy goals were attained. In hindsight, these findings seem rather obvious, but they do reaffirm the value of setting high goals with the people on your team. What is astonishing is the additional findings that lack of goal attainment in one's personal life was related to a higher sense of well-being when a person experienced goal attainment on the job. Compensatory switching occurred when people shifted their focus from home life to their work setting.[8]

Here's a look at how setting difficult, specific goals affected job performance in both blue- and white-collar workers. The American Pulpwood Association wanted to increase the productivity of independent pulpwood crews in the South. Many of the people on the crews had little or no formal education, and when we asked them how they knew whether they had a "good" day or week,

FURTHER EVIDENCE

Job satisfaction increases organizational commitment. Commitment is a powerful source of motivation in that it leads to persistence in a course of action, even in the face of obstacles. People who are committed to their organization continue to set and commit to high goals.[9]

they merely shrugged and said they had no idea. So we set up an experiment.[10]

Different crews were organized into comparable situations (for example, same type of terrain, same type of equipment, similar experience levels). But the crews were given different goals. Some crews were told to "do your best to cut as many trees as possible." Other crews had a specific (and high) number of trees to cut down. All the crews were paid on a piece-rate basis—that is, the more trees they cut down, the more money they made.

Can you guess the results? Within the first week, productivity— as well as job attendance—soared for the crews that were given a specific, high goal. Why? Goal setting instilled a sense of purpose in what they had previously seen as a tedious and physically exhausting job. Attaining the set goal didn't just earn these pulpwood workers more money, it met their need for self-esteem, giving them job satisfaction and the chance to earn the respect of their peers.

What about work that is mentally rather than physically challenging? The senior vice president of the Weyerhaeuser R&D department wanted the engineers and scientists to attain a level of performance excellence so high that line managers would stop trying to cut back their budget.[11] We couldn't set a simple productivity goal as with the pulpwood workers, so we conducted a job analysis to define "excellence" in behavioral terms (for example, finds practical solutions to seemingly impossible problems plaguing

FURTHER EVIDENCE

The research explaining the benefits of appraising employees on job behavior is described in chapter 10. A bottom-
line measure such as revenue generated or costs reduced
is often not available for evaluating an individual employee. And even when
it is available, it is often affected by factors beyond the person's control.[12]

line managers). We set up four comparable groups. We provided
two groups with specific, high behavioral goals: One group's goals
were set by managers; the other group had goals set with the input
and suggestions of employees. We told a third group to "do your
best." All three of these groups were promised praise, recognition,
or monetary bonuses depending on whether they were scored as
excellent by their supervisors six months later. We also had a fourth
group with which we did nothing; they didn't even know they were
part of the study.

The results? The performance of the employees in the third
group (the ones who were told to "do your best") was no better at
the study's end than the fourth group for whom we did nothing—
even though the "do your best" group was promised the opportunity to receive praise, recognition, or money.

So "carrots" such as praise, public recognition, and even money
do not motivate people to improve their behavior unless they are
backed by the setting of and commitment to a specific, high goal.
This study also revealed the importance of involving employees in
the setting of goals.[13] Goals that were set following a discussion by
an employee with a supervisor (referred to as *participatively set
goals*) led to higher performance than goals that were assigned by a
manager. That's because the participatively set goals were significantly higher than the goals assigned unilaterally by a supervisor.

The commitment to reaching the goals was the same for both groups.

Focusing on Performance

The widespread belief that improving employee motivation requires improving job satisfaction is not borne out by the research. Instead, research points to the ability to be productive in one's job as the real heart of motivation. The evidence shows that job satisfaction, in turn, typically results from being productive. Thus, if you want motivated employees, you should focus on ways your employees can be high perform-

> *The ability to be productive is the real heart of motivation.*

ers, rather than focusing on ways to increase their job satisfaction per se.[14]

Your employees may love their jobs because they enjoy a great salary and supportive colleagues. Yet that doesn't mean they're as productive as they could be—or as motivated as they should be—to achieve the highest performance possible. But there's good news here for your employees' productivity level and your team's bottom line: Focusing on ways to increase someone's productivity (for example, training, changing characteristics of the job) will simultaneously motivate that person to improve performance. A productive employee is often happier and more dedicated to improving performance than the employee who likes being on the job but doesn't do much during the day. By focusing on ways to increase the performance of your team members, you'll also help them develop the motivation to attain higher and higher goals.

Most people get such a thrill from attaining their goals that they will set even higher ones next time, rather than lapsing into a state of contentment (or worse, laziness). So focus on ways to help your people become more productive—and watch job satisfaction increase while absenteeism and turnover decline. Help them boost their productivity, and your people will continually look for ways to improve themselves and their job performance—on their own.

Understanding and Changing the Work Environment

The workplace environment affects your employees' motivation in a variety of ways. *Environment* in this case constitutes more than the physical space in which your employees work. It goes beyond four walls, assembly lines, or cubicles. In fact, the environment is among the most complex aspects of motivation. It includes elements such as these:

- Job characteristics
- Rewards for performance
- Influence of societal culture on the workplace

Job Characteristics

What makes a job a *great* job? A great job is one that consists of task variety, feedback, recognition, responsibility, opportunities for acquiring new skills, advancement, and most of all, autonomy.[15] In psychology, such jobs are called *enriched.* "Jobs that are too simple can lead to depression. They can even stunt someone's personality."[16] Overall, regardless of where in the world your employees are, most want job opportunities that permit growth and autonomy so that they can exert control over their environment.[17] They want jobs that are enriched.

> *Give people the training and resources they need and then turn them loose.*

Keep in mind, however, that a prerequisite for performing well in an enriched job is task knowledge. Giving people a lot of autonomy without the knowledge to complete a task or execute strategy can be overwhelming for them and hurt motivation.[18] That's where the training and development techniques discussed in chapter 3 come into play.

FURTHER EVIDENCE

A survey of 121 jobs in five plants found that jobs that score high in job enrichment have incumbents who have higher performance, higher satisfaction, and less absenteeism than those that are unenriched. Similarly, another study showed that enriched jobs increase an employee's personal initiative.[19]

Hence evidence-based managers give people the training and resources they need to do the job, and then turn them loose (give them what the researchers call *autonomy*). They make sure the employees know they have the responsibility to get things done without having to constantly check back with the boss. They take steps to make sure the people on their team are not doing the same things day in and day out (allowing *task variety*). Instead, they are on the lookout for opportunities for their team members to grow by developing new skills. They also make sure that each employee gets feedback on what to continue doing or start doing differently and recognition for what is done well.

Rewards for Performance

Simple rewards can make otherwise tedious work more interesting. Rewards are, of course, a classic tool of motivation. But what you may not know is that the schedule you choose for administering rewards to your employees can increase their motivation or dilute it—depending on the frequency with which the rewards are given.

Hundreds of laboratory experiments with rats and pigeons have shown that a variable schedule, in which an animal gets rewarded on a seemingly random basis, is more motivating than a fixed reward schedule that enables an animal to learn exactly when rewards will be distributed.[20] The same holds true for people in the workplace.

What do these results mean for you? Reward your inexperienced, just-learning staff continuously and consistently every time they do

A Trappers' "Lottery"

Rodents may be highly prized in laboratory settings, but the opposite is true in forest products companies, which often battle against a rat-like creature called a mountain beaver. These rodents devour newly planted seedlings. Consequently, forest product companies employ trappers whose sole job is to bait and trap the rodents. In one company, an executive became so frustrated with the rodents—and the unionized trappers' performance—that he angrily declared he could step on more rodents than his employees could catch. Moreover, the trappers had a bad reputation for complaining about everything from the seats in the bus that took them to the forest to the frequent bad weather and long work hours—grievances that were too often the result of boredom. The union executive commit-tee and company managers were exasperated.

The solution to the dual problems of the rodent overrun and the trapper complaints? Bring Las Vegas to the woods.

The trappers were randomly assigned to different groups.[21] The trappers were initially paid on a continuous schedule of reinforce-ment, which paid each trapper a $1 bonus over and above his hourly rate for each rodent trapped. At the end of four weeks, one group of trappers was switched to a variable schedule, during which they received $4 per rodent if they *also* correctly guessed the color of one of four marbles the supervisor picked out of a bag (a one-in-four chance).

Not only did the trappers' productivity soar, their grievances stopped. The excitement of possibly winning money replaced boredom. The experienced trappers were more productive on the variable schedule, while their inexperienced counterparts had higher productivity on the continuous schedule—but both the inexperienced and the experienced employees loved the variable schedule.

Believe it or not, employee excitement with the marbles con-tinued for years.[22] Not a single grievance was ever filed. In examin-ing employee reactions to the two schedules, the variable schedule contributed to feelings of task accomplishment, recognition, and meaningfulness of the work. In addition, the trappers began to set higher goals on their own for how many rodents they would catch.

something good. And give recognition and other forms of rewards on a predetermined variable schedule (for example, on average once every five times a person does something well) for your experienced people who have mastered the task. But don't tell your team about this schedule. And don't confuse a variable schedule with one that is haphazard or "catch as catch can." If you do, you are likely to forget to give people the credit they deserve. Do that, and apathy will creep into your team. Set a predetermined variable schedule for giving rewards and watch performance soar.

If your organization has a high absenteeism problem, create a variable-interval reward schedule. Have a "lucky bonus day" with a predetermined variable schedule. Approximately every 22 days give people a bonus for coming to work. Sometimes two bonus days will happen back-to-back. Other times 35 days may go by before the bonus day comes up. Only you, the evidence-based manager, know when the bonus will be given—just as is true for the person who programs a

A variable reward schedule will do more to motivate experienced employees than a fixed schedule.

slot machine in Las Vegas. Watch people race to work in fear that they won't be there at 8:00 a.m. when the alarm goes off signaling that today is Bonus Day. (Note that I picked the number 22 arbitrarily. The interval should be relatively low at first. As job attendance improves, you should increase the number of days between payouts, such as approximately every 75 days.)

One note of caution: Recall the axiom "that which gets measured gets done." So be sure that the behavior you reward is the behavior you want to see from your employees. A hotel I know tells its employees that they should make every effort to satisfy the customer. And yet this hotel simply evaluates its employees on budget-mindedness. So what do you think the hotelier's employees do? They focus on ways to cut costs rather than on ways to increase customer satisfaction. Similarly, if you strongly advocate team performance but you only reward individual performance, you can say goodbye to team playing. The key to high performance is to reward both.

Societal Influences at Work

This last aspect of a job environment has gained importance as the world has become more globally interconnected. Many organizations have their operations spread around the world: sales in one country, manufacturing in another, and research and development in yet another. What managers worldwide must remember is that the societal culture in which employees work affects their values, and these values influence the nature of the workplace environment.

What kind of values are important in the workplace? Different cultures often have very different concepts of what constitutes inequality. For example, one country may value the individual (as in the United States or Germany), while another values the collective (China or Mexico). Yet another difference is evident in how one culture places importance on personality traits such as assertiveness, ambitiousness, and competitiveness, especially in regard to material success, while another puts greater emphasis on quality of life and interpersonal relationships.[23] Other differences are the acceptability of differential versus flat salaries and top-down versus two-way communication styles.

You can do three things to be culturally attuned in ways to motivate your workforce, wherever in the world you may be:

- Identify the cultural values of the country.

- Know your own cultural values.

- Keep in mind the meaning of various managerial practices in cultural terms in the countries where you do business.

Projecting your values onto employees from other cultures can damage employee motivation, interpersonal communication, and the overall performance of your workforce.[24] In *high-context*

Cultural Deafness

Even with 20/20 hindsight, one wonders what role communication style may have played in the September 11, 2001, terrorist attacks on the World Trade Center in New York City and the Pentagon in Washington, DC. In the three years before the terrorist attack, United States and Taliban leaders met to discuss bringing the terrorist Osama bin Laden to justice. According to former CIA station chief Milton Bearden, "We never heard what they were trying to say . . . We had no common language. Ours was, 'Give up bin Laden.' They were saying, 'Do something to help us give him up.'" When the Taliban publicly stated that they no longer knew where bin Laden was, the low-context United States interpreted it as an effort to evade responsibility for turning him over. However, a more high-context interpretation of the statements suggests that the Taliban more than once set up bin Laden for capture by the United States. Bearden noted, "Every time the Afghans said, 'He's lost again' they are saying something. They are saying, 'He's no longer under our protection.' . . . They thought they were signaling us subtly, and we don't do signals." High-context cultures communicate using signals, yet low-context cultures apparently don't "do" signals, potentially with disastrous results.

cultures, meaning relies heavily on "reading between the lines," that is, understanding what is said through the context of the situation. In contrast, in *low-context* cultures, meaning is explicitly delineated—what you say is what you mean. And tragic mistakes can occur when people fail to take into account differences between cultures.[25]

Avoiding Demotivation

Evidence-based managers know they bear responsibility for not *demotivating* their employees—and they know how to watch for warning signs so that they can avoid undoing all they've done to

FURTHER EVIDENCE

Research on job enrichment showed that salary is often a source of dissatisfaction. This is likely because people could not see the relationship between what they accomplished and the salary increase they received.[26]

motivate the people on their team. The risk of demotivation lies in employee perceptions of unfairness in the workplace.

The Unfair Workplace

Nothing deflates employee motivation faster than a loss of trust in you, your employees' boss. And loss of trust in you has much to do with their perceptions of fairness and justice. Failure on your part to put principles of justice front and center will kill worker motivation as feelings sweep through your team that some people are getting a better deal than others.

> *Few things kill an employee's motivation faster than perceptions of injustice.*

The principles of organizational justice are listed here as a check-list of five questions that you must keep in mind to ensure that you're seen as fair:[27]

- How will resources—salary, bonuses, office space—be distributed?

- Do you have agreed-upon processes or systems for determining who gets what (for example, a salary increase, a bigger office) and why?

- Have you explained to your people the logic of your decisions as to who gets what?

- Are the agreed-upon processes for making decisions applied consistently?

- Have you taken your employees' viewpoints into account before you make your decisions?

The concept of "having a voice" at work is fascinating; it can be a powerful source of motivation or disillusion. Here is one scenario:

Pat argues for relocating your division to Chicago. Sam argues why the division should stay here. You and your team decide to remain here rather than move to Chicago. Pat supports the decision; within days Sam's résumé is on the street. Does this make sense? It will.

Before the decision was made, you gave Pat his day in court by calling on him repeatedly. Hence he knows he is a "somebody" on this team because his opinion is always solicited. He knows that he can't win them all, but he feels his voice has been heard. Now that the final decision has been made, he supports it even though it is counter to the position he originally advocated.

Following the meeting, Sam phones her partner. "I am leaving the firm," she says. "Why," her partner asks, "when every decision you have hoped for in the past year has been made by the firm?" "Because those decisions were made in spite of me rather than because of me." She is right. Rarely have you sought her opinions. Modeling their behavior after yours, her colleagues likewise usually ignore her input. Consequently, she is seldom if ever heard. I personally applaud her decision to leave your team. Why should Sam stay with people who ignore her?

A perceived lack of justice is a primary source of stress in the workplace. Not surprisingly, perceptions of injustice can lead to aggressive retaliation against you, the boss.[28]

Using the five-point organizational justice checklist regularly, particularly when key decisions are at hand, will help ensure that your employees perceive your actions as fair. Have a process in place to allocate resources, seek feedback from your team, be sincere, and communicate the logic behind your decision to your people. By

FURTHER EVIDENCE

Back to the issue of money. There is evidence that people who feel they are compensated fairly for their effort are more committed to their organization than those who believe their compensation is unfair.[29]

doing so, you'll avoid falling into the trap of unintentionally demotivating the people on your team.

Breaching the Unspoken Agreement on Expectations

Whether or not your employees work for you under a written contract, there is an implicit agreement between you that you may not even be aware of: the *psychological contract*.[30] Psychological contracts so thoroughly pervade human social behavior that they are like the air we breathe; they attract no special notice—until they go bad.

A psychological contract is the set of unwritten expectations between an employee and an employer. Your employees' expectations typically include a sense of dignity, worth, and an expectation that you will provide opportunities for them to learn and grow on the job. Your expectations as manager include loyalty, commitment, and productivity from your employees. Thus, a psychological contract is the very essence of an employee's link to you; it's an implied promise of reciprocity in exchange for action. It allows for cooperation and trust under conditions of uncertainty.

> *Violating an unspoken contract can engender distrust, resentment, and indignation.*

Violating such an unspoken contract—which happens when promises are perceived to be broken—can engender feelings of distrust, resentment, and indignation on the part of your employees.

A Promise from the Past

Wharton School of Business Management attempted to recruit an assistant professor away from us at the University of Toronto. Panic-stricken over the prospect of losing a stellar researcher, the dean and I put a retention package together that included a large office—an office that unbeknownst to us had been promised by the previous dean to a senior professor as soon as it became vacant. To this day that senior professor won't speak to me. He feels his unwritten contract with the earlier dean, who had left long before for another university, had not been honored and hence his expectations had been unfairly violated.

The root of the problem is that the senior professor failed to see the necessity for renegotiation of his psychological contract when the new dean arrived, and the new dean—unaware of the standing promise—could not propose to renegotiate the contract. The only good news here is that the assistant professor chose to remain at the University of Toronto. The lesson is to remember the necessity for renegotiating a psychological contract whenever conditions change with the employer or employee.

This, in turn, can damage the employees' organizational commitment and job performance. In short, violating a psychological contract can kill motivation because it is seen as unjust. Ultimately, such a violation will result in your employees' wanting to leave the company.[31] See the example above.

How do you honor a psychological contract with your people? When you are appointed manager of an existing team, ask the members the following questions:

- What do you consider to be your "sacred cows"—things you hope I don't change?

- What don't I know about you and this team that you believe I should know?

- What can I, in my new role with this team do to be, and to be seen as fair?

The importance of psychological contracts for motivation in the workplace cannot be overemphasized. Employees' feelings that this kind of contract is respected will foster commitment to and support for organizational policies and procedures. However, feelings that a contract has been violated will often result in a host of counter-productive behaviors, such as a decrease in performance and an increase in employee turnover. And take note: Negative feelings over a perceived act of injustice can last for decades.[32]

CONCLUSION

There is a saying that managers cannot motivate their employees; they can only create the conditions that enable people to motivate themselves. This is a half-truth. It is based on the fact that an enriched job environment is more motivating than one character-ized by routine—an environment where people lack autonomy, responsibility, task variety, and opportunities to acquire new knowledge and skills. Most employees are highly energized in an enriched environment. It has a positive impact on their job satisfaction.

The evidence also shows that managers do directly impact employee motivation. Motivation increases when managers take into account an employee's needs, set specific and high goals, focus on ways to increase job performance rather than job satisfaction, and administer rewards on a continuous schedule for inexperi-enced employees and on an intermittent schedule for those who are experienced. Motivation decreases when managers fail to take into account factors that affect perceptions of organizational justice. Motivation also decreases when the societal values where the orga-nization is located are ignored.

QUESTIONS

1. Can you explain how you would use a five-point checklist to ensure the needs of your direct reports are being met?

2. How would you apply goal setting as a motivational technique?

3. How can money be used as a motivator?

4. What societal influences affect motivation? How can you avoid cultural deafness?

5. What is meant by job enrichment?

6. How would you use the principles of organizational justice to minimize demotivating your team?

7. Why is "voice" so important?

8. What is a psychological contract?

9. When it comes to motivation, where should you as the team's manager put your emphasis?

10. After reading this chapter and chapter 2, how can you keep apathy from creeping into your team?

ENGAGE YOUR EMPLOYEES

Some behavioral scientists argue that employee engagement is nothing more than "old wine in a new bottle." By that they mean that focusing on ways to engage your employees in their work is no different from focusing on ways to increase their job satisfaction or organizational commitment. They are wrong. These three concepts overlap one another, yet they are different. And all three require focus if you want to build a high-performing organization.

JOB SATISFACTION

Job satisfaction is discussed in chapter 4, "Motivate Your Employees to Be High Performers." Recall that taking steps to increase the job performance of your employees will increase their satisfaction with their job. As stated in that chapter, research shows people like that which they do well. But, people also can be satisfied with their job for reasons having nothing to do with the work they perform. These reasons include satisfaction with their supervisor, coworkers, office, business location, pay, benefits, etc. Hence, you may find that a focus on only these job characteristics results in low performers happily remaining in your workforce.

To ensure that your employees are satisfied with their job for the right reasons, you want to be certain that your employees have the ability and resources to do their job. Provide them autonomy, task variety, job responsibility, performance feedback, and the opportunity for their further growth and development on the job, then get out of their way.[1] High-performing employees are prone to asking, "Will I be smarter or wiser if I remain on this job for the next three years?" If they can't answer the question positively, they are prone to looking for work in another organization. To keep high performers from leaving your team, or worse, your organization, you must focus on ways of ensuring their job satisfaction. It is just as important as keeping your eye on organizational commitment and employee engagement.

ORGANIZATIONAL COMMITMENT

Your employees can be highly satisfied with their job for the above reasons. The question remains: "Are they committed to doing their job in your organization?" Commitment is a desire by your employees for an enduring relationship with your organization. You want the commitment of your employees to your organization, lest you waste time and money in their training and development only to see them leave you shortly thereafter. By focusing on both job satisfaction and organizational commitment, you will greatly reduce the likelihood that your high performers will leave you to work elsewhere.

Two leading researchers on organizational commitment are John Meyer and Natalie Allen, behavioral scientists at Western University in Canada.[2] They identified three types of mind-sets regarding commitment.

- **Emotional:** The first and most important mind-set of the three is emotional commitment. The reason for its importance to you is that employees who are committed emotionally to your organization are the same people who stay with your firm, demonstrate low absenteeism, have high job performance, and are good organizational citizens. Good organizational citizens are constantly on the lookout for ways to advance the well-being of their organization and fellow employees.

- **Cost**: A second mind-set toward commitment is cost-based. These employees stay with their organization to avoid the undesirable costs of leaving (e.g., moving to another city when a child is a senior in high school, disrupting a partner who has a high-paying job, loss of pension). People who remain in their organization to avoid the costs of leaving it typically do what is required of them on the job and little more.

- **Obligation**: A third form of commitment is a sense of obligation. These people stay with their employer, but they do not buy in to their organization's goals the way those with emotional commitment do. They remain out of a sense of duty (e.g., my company paid for my education; therefore, I feel obligated not to seek employment elsewhere).

There are four steps that you can take to increase your employees' emotional commitment to your organization. First, select people whose personal values are reflected in the values of the organization with regard to the nature of the business, the products and

FURTHER EVIDENCE

Both empirical research and case studies have shown that employees who are engaged in, as opposed to merely satisfied with, their job embrace an organization's core values, including respect, entrepreneurship, passion, and customer orientation.

services provided, and the ways they are marketed. Employees have a strong desire to advance the interests of their organization when their values are aligned with their employer's. Therefore, include a realistic job preview in the selection process. Recall the discussion in chapter 1 on the importance of telling job applicants the downsides as well as the upsides of accepting an offer to join the organization. Note too that the honesty shown by the organization for giving potential employees a complete picture of the job predisposes them to see your organization as supportive of them should they accept a job offer.

The second step involves daily work experiences. Make sure that your employees' roles are clear rather than ambiguous. Foster good interpersonal relationships among team members. And, as is the case for increasing job satisfaction, give employees challenges and important responsibilities.

Third, ask yourself whether your organization shows visible support for your employees. Employees emotionally commit to their organization to the extent that they can see that the organization is concerned with their well-being and that it values their contributions. Providing job security is an excellent way for an organization to show this concern.

In addition, provide training opportunities to your employees. Doing so enables them to feel confident in their ability to better perform their job. This is a proven way of increasing emotional commitment to an organization. Family-friendly practices such as flextime and daycare facilities also are straightforward ways to increase emotional commitment to an organization.

Fourth, adhere to the principles of organizational justice. As emphasized in chapter 4, few things demotivate employees faster than unfair treatment. Even decisions to lay off members of the workforce will have a minimal detrimental effect on commitment if these justice principles are followed (i.e., principles of distributive, procedural, and interactional justice). Employees must understand the rationale for decisions that will impact them negatively. In addition, they must see that decisions are implemented in a

FURTHER EVIDENCE

In a review of the research on employee engagement, Dr. Michiel Kompier and his colleagues at Radboud University in the Netherlands found that improvements in job resources, decision authority, communication, and social support led to increased employee engagement in Denmark, Germany, the Netherlands, and Sweden.

uniform and consistent manner regardless of whether an employee is affected negatively or positively.

EMPLOYEE ENGAGEMENT

Now let's ratchet things up a notch. Employees who are engaged in their work show vigor in and dedication to their job. They are fully absorbed in it. They experience meaningfulness and enthusiasm in what they do. They derive inspiration from their work. For them, time passes quickly because they are so engrossed in their job. Hence, employee engagement is a key predictor of creativity and innovation, customer service, high job performance, and strong financial results.

Among the leading researchers of employee engagement (alternatively called work engagement) is Arnold Bakker, a behavioral scientist at Erasmus University in the Netherlands.[3] His research shows that engagement peaks when employees perceive their job as meaningful and they have the necessary resources to perform it. As is the case with job satisfaction, they also must be given autonomy when doing their job as well as task variety and social support. There are two strategies for increasing employee engagement: top down and bottom up.

Top-Down Strategies for Increasing Employee Engagement

Four management practices will improve your employees' engagement in their work. The first, as is the case for emotional organizational commitment, involves your selection procedures. Through the use of structured interviews, particularly the situational interview and the patterned behavior description interview discussed in chapter 1, you must ensure that the values of the applicants you hire are in sync with the values of your organization. In addition, administer one or more personality tests. People who score relatively high on conscientiousness, proactivity, emotional stability, and extroversion are predisposed to becoming engaged in their work.

A second step you can take to foster engagement is to provide socialization initiatives for people who are newly hired. Pair them up, as in a "buddy system," with people who are also relatively new to the job (e.g., 12 to 18 months). These people can give the most recent newcomers a heads-up, or what is called tacit knowledge of the informal "do's and don'ts."

Third, set monthly performance and development goals for newcomers. Through the use of technology (tablets, smart phones), provide them relatively instant performance feedback and recognition for goal pursuit.

Fourth, and arguably most important, is the day-to-day leadership you provide to your people. Here are seven questions to ask yourself:

1. Do you find ways to inspire your employees?

2. Do they trust you?

3. Do you provide them daily support?

4. Do you give them autonomy?

5. What about recognition for a job well done?

6. Are you perceived as fair, as having high integrity?

7. Have you ensured that they have the resources needed to perform their job?

If you don't know the answer to one or more of these questions, find out through informal discussions and 360-degree surveys (see chapter 10). If one or more of the answers is no, fix it. Start by becoming an excellent listener, and then act on what you hear.

Bottom-Up Strategies for Increasing Employee Engagement

There are at least four ways that employees themselves can take the initiative to increase engagement in their work: self-management, job crafting, taking advantage of their character strengths, and mobilizing ego resources. Self-management techniques include setting long-term and sub-goals, developing a plan to attain them, self-monitoring goal progress, and self-administering rewards and punishments (e.g., clean out attic). A study conducted by Bakker and his colleagues revealed that when there was a relatively low workload, work engagement was particularly high when employees were given the freedom to self-manage. However, when work involved new, complex issues, transformational leadership had a positive effect on employee engagement and performance.

Training employees in ways to craft their respective jobs begins with increasing their awareness of their work situations and the freedom they have to change them. These changes include seeking ways to increase their networks for social support, initiating one or more challenging projects, expanding their range of tasks, and actively seeking feedback on their performance. What makes crafting your own job so effective for increasing work engagement is that it improves the fit between your goals and those of the organization.

A fourth method to increase engagement in work is to mobilize an individual's cognitive and affective resources. That is, engage one's thoughts and feelings. This can be done both on and off the job. For example, on the job an employee can interact with enthusiastic coworkers or work on mastering a new task. Off the job, an employee can take a walk, read a book, or engage in a favorite pastime (e.g., skiing) to restore mental energy while not thinking about work.

Taking the time to detach from the job is an excellent way to engage thoughts and feelings. Minibreaks at work are helpful, as is exercise. People also need to take the time to get away from the workplace and just relax. Energy accumulated off the job can spill into the workplace.

Work-Family Balance

Traditionally, behavioral scientists have believed in the resource drain theory. This theory states that we have finite amounts of psychological resources to expend in terms of energy. These finite, expendable resources can and usually are depleted on a daily basis. Hence, the demands of work versus family compete for psychological energy. As a result, we often have to make difficult compromises between these two spheres of influence. Doing so often exhausts us.[4]

Good news: emerging evidence supports an "expansionary" perspective. This research suggests that our work and family lives can enrich one another. That is, our positive experiences in one role can increase our energy and positive emotions in the other role. The good news is that our positive emotions and attitudes spill into the other domain because new energy is generated from our behaviors in the other role.

Family-friendly policies, as I noted earlier with regard to emotional commitment to the organization, have a spillover effect to the job. Those policies include:

- Flexible work scheduling

- On-site childcare facilities

- Child or elder care financial assistance

- Telework arrangements
- The opportunity to switch from permanent to temporary work
- Parental leave
- Family-related medical leave

For example, employees who have access to elderly care support and childcare assistance experience less stress and hence are more engaged in their work than employees who do not have these benefits. Employees who are given autonomy have control over ways to cope with the boundary between their work and family. This is because they have relative freedom to choose when to perform sundry work activities versus family tasks.

Positive, stress-free family experiences generate energy that can be subsequently used on the job. The converse is also true: the ability to fulfill one's potential in the workplace generates energy that can be expended at home. The passion and positive feedback that one receives in work and family domains provide reciprocal energy in these two spheres.

The mere existence of family-friendly policies does not mean that your high performers will take advantage of them. They may perceive that using them will signal to others their lack of commitment to the organization. Hence, family-friendly policies must be embedded in an organization's culture if they are to have a positive effect on your workforce. An excellent way to ensure this is for your organization's leaders to be seen taking advantage of them. Doing so will minimize the likelihood that employees will burn out from overengagement in their job. Burned-out employees typically have high absenteeism, occupational accidents, and poor job performance. Wilmar Schaufeli, a research professor at KU Leuven University in Belgium and Utrecht University in the Netherlands, has developed a reliable and valid questionnaire, the Energy Compass, which you can use to assess the likelihood of work engagement/job burnout in one or more areas of your organization.[5]

Volunteers

Fostering volunteer engagement in nonprofit organizations is arguably more challenging than fostering employee engagement in the private sector. How do you get people to feel a high level of enthusiasm, inspiration, and pride in their volunteer work (e.g., serving food in a soup kitchen)? The answer is worth exploring because the evidence shows that engaged volunteers work longer, perform better, and remain longer in their respective nonprofit organizations than those who are not engaged in their work.[6]

Key drivers of a volunteer's work engagement include:

- Identifying with the organization's goals

- Commitment to the organization's goals

- Flexibility in carrying out duties

- Autonomy in carrying out duties

These final two drivers have been shown to increase the meaning of work. The methods for bringing all of this about can be found in two contradictory leadership styles.

Participatory and Directive Leadership

A participative leadership style has multiple benefits for bringing about an engaged workforce. The same is true for engaging volunteers in their work. Involving volunteers in work-related decisions intrinsically motivates them. It increases their personal identification with their work as well as feelings of control over what they have volunteered to do. But a directive style of leadership is necessary too.

A hands-off leadership style, that is, a style that is too participatory, can lead to poorly defined roles and uncertainty among volunteers as to efficient and effective procedures for performing their tasks. This can lead to task, process, and interpersonal conflicts

FURTHER EVIDENCE

Research shows that employees need time to psychologically disengage from their work. Recovery in the evening through leisure time is related to work engagement the next day and, hence, job performance.* Another study showed that high-duty off-the-job activities such as housework reduce engagement the following day.

among volunteers. The overall result is the perception among volunteers that they lack the support of their leaders. Consequently, volunteer leaders must set clear goals and ensure that the work procedures to attain them are aligned among the volunteers. Clear communication and detailed instructions regarding the attainment of specific goals enable volunteers to understand what to do and why to do it. In short, a volunteer leader's participative and directive leadership styles complement one another.

In practice, participative and directive leadership styles can be combined as follows. Volunteer leaders can set specific, challenging goals for the volunteers during the orientation process. They can explain to each volunteer how fulfilling his or her role will have a positive impact on the nonprofit organization's goals. They can explicitly detail the tasks that a volunteer must complete (e.g., making phone calls, selling goods at a fundraising event, teaching English to refugees). As a volunteer leader, you can then involve your volunteers in discussions on the ways they believe these tasks should be performed.

A second tension volunteer leaders often must resolve is that between monitoring versus trusting volunteers to do their jobs effectively. Monitoring is almost always needed when the

---

* See special issue on this topic in the journal, *Organizational Dynamics*

volunteers do not have the knowledge and experience to perform the tasks assigned to them. By offering guidance, a volunteer leader can minimize confusion and work disengagement. The danger to avoid is the perception of not trusting the volunteers.

High-quality interpersonal trust between volunteer leaders and their direct reports is crucial for volunteers' engagement. Trust is a type of job resource in that it gives volunteers a sense of psychological safety to make and act on decisions without fear of subsequently being belittled. A way to resolve the push-pull between trusting and monitoring volunteers is for you to stay close by and check in regularly with new inexperienced volunteers without micromanaging them. As soon as you see they understand and can perform their tasks, monitor them at most at the end of the day or only once/twice a week.

A third tension for volunteer leaders to resolve is that between flexibility versus giving instructions. Allowing volunteers flexibility in what to do and how to do it enhances their engagement, because it gives them the opportunity to craft their roles. A perception of autonomy among your volunteers helps them feel responsible for their work. Consequently, they put in the needed effort, and they show a high level of engagement. However, teaching new volunteers "the ropes" about how things are done is a pivotal leadership task.

When a skill set is required that volunteers do not possess, or when the workload is high, volunteers need and appreciate instructions on efficient and effective ways to perform their job. Failure to do this on the part of a volunteer leader can result in volunteers feeling overwhelmed.

To increase perceptions of autonomy on the part of new or inexperienced volunteers, a volunteer leader can pair them with experienced volunteers, enabling the latter to share experiences with the newcomers. Doing so will reduce the newcomers' dependence on you, the volunteer leader.

Similarities between Job Satisfaction, Organizational Commitment, and Work Engagement

Research on employee engagement emphasizes the importance of ensuring that employees have resources to meet the demands of their job. If the demands exceed an employee's resources, the probability of that individual becoming engaged with the work is greatly diminished. Job demands include organizational features of a job that get in the way of attaining job goals. Among the detrimental demands of a job are work and role overload, job insecurity, role ambiguity, role conflict, administrative hassles, and organizational politics.

Job resources include granting employees job autonomy, participation in decision making, task variety and significance, performance feedback, recognition, social support, role clarity, and opportunities for growth and advancement. These drivers of engagement with one's work will also drive increases in satisfaction with one's job and emotional commitment to one's organization. And as is the case with emotional organizational commitment, process variables are important, especially the principles of procedural and interactional justice (see chapter 4).

Human resource managers should integrate these variables in employee surveys as well as their selection, performance management, and training and development systems. Senior management should include employee engagement, job satisfaction, and organizational commitment in the organization's goals and strategy.

CONCLUSION

Globally, it has been reported that only 21 percent of employees are fully and completely engaged. One report suggests that employee engagement is on the decline worldwide, and that across North America as of 2017 it had hit a four-year low.[7] When employees are consistently asked to do more with fewer resources, burnout is likely lurking around the corner. When employees experience a chronic state of work-related stress, they burn out. They feel emotionally drained. All jobs include demands as well as resources. Job demands are the aspects of a job that require an ongoing mental or physical effort. Job resources are aspects of the job that (a) facilitate the attainment of an employee's job-related goals, (b) minimize job demands, and (c) stimulate an employee's personal growth. Among the list of job resources are supervisory and coworker support in goal pursuit, performance feedback, and autonomy regarding the ways to attain job-related goals.

When job demands exceed job resources, burnout occurs. The converse occurs when job resources exceed demands—work engagement, including organizational commitment, job satisfaction, and superior performance, are among the positive outcomes. Job resources spark an employee's energy. Whereas high job demands and few job resources result in employee burnout, only a high amount of job resources results in employee engagement. Thus, by increasing job resources, such as providing social support, autonomy, specific and challenging goals, and performance feedback, two birds are hit with one stone: feelings of burnout are minimized and engagement in work increases.

QUESTIONS

1. How can you increase the job satisfaction of your employees?

2. What can you do to increase their commitment to your organization? What mind-set regarding commitment most requires your attention?

3. What differentiates employee engagement from job satisfaction and organizational commitment?

4. What are the top-down strategies you can use to increase work engagement?

5. What are the bottom-up strategies employees use to increase work engagement?

6. How would your organization benefit by implementing family-friendly initiatives?

7. How can you foster work engagement in volunteer organizations?

8. What similarities between job satisfaction, organizational commitment, and work engagement can you take advantage of?

9. What is meant by job demands versus job resources?

10. When is job burnout likely to occur?

ENSURE YOUR CAREER SUCCESS

Career success is as much about the quality of your journey as it is about the destination.[1] What steps can you take to up the odds that you will have a successful career, that when you retire you will be pleased with what you have accomplished? A first step is to ask yourself what it is you truly enjoy doing, and then find a way you can get paid for doing it. By doing so, you will become fully engaged in your work (see chapter 5 on employee engagement).

To bring this about, first ask yourself, "What can I do well?" Answer this question in terms of your education, experiences, knowledge, skills, and abilities as well as your work accomplishments.

A second question to ask is, "What do employees, customers, and/or clients want?" Secondary questions include:

- What will be required of me to excel in their eyes?

- What major challenges am I likely to face?

- How are the present job/role requirements likely to evolve over the next three to five years?

You are likely to find answers to these questions through company reports, business analysts, blogs, and networks.

A third question for you to answer is, "What do I want?" Secondary questions include:

- What skills do I enjoy using?

- Similarly, what types of roles, situations, and people do I enjoy/not enjoy?

- When I retire, what accomplishments do I hope to be proud of?

- What do I want my legacy to be?

In answering these questions, examine what is called a career anchor.[2] A career anchor is the one thing you would be most reluctant to go without. It is something your job must provide for you to experience job satisfaction. There are eight career anchors:

1. **General managerial competence**, whereby you would not want to sacrifice opportunities to show your competence as a manager because you have a strong desire to advance up the managerial hierarchy.

2. **Technical functional competence**, whereby you would not want to forego the opportunity to further develop and apply your skills in a particular specialization.

3. **Entrepreneurial creativity**, whereby you do not want to pass up opportunities to create your own business.

4. **Autonomy**, whereby you would not want a job where you would lack the freedom to make the decisions on ways to perform your work.

5. **Security**, whereby you would not want to give up the opportunity for long-term employment.

6. **Service**, whereby you would not want to jeopardize the opportunity to engage in work that contributes to the betterment of society.

7. **Pure challenge**, whereby you would not want to give up the opportunity to work on seemingly impossible problems and overcome tough obstacles.

8. **Lifestyle**, whereby you would not want to give up a work-life balance.

Each anchor reflects how you prefer to be managed, rewarded, and developed. Understanding each anchor will minimize the likelihood of you moving into a situation where your values are incompatible with the setting.

Edgar Schein, a professor emeritus at MIT, has developed a 40-item self-scored survey, the Career Orientations Inventory, to help you manage your career. An example of a service-oriented question is, "I dream of being in a career that makes a real contribution to humanity and society." A typical general management question is, "I will feel successful only if I become a high-level manager in some organization." And a typical technical functional question is, "I want to be so good at what I do that others will seek my expert advice." Your answers to such questions will help you to discern the career path you want to take.

As an aside, you can also use these anchors to analyze the jobs in your organization. Doing so will enable you, as a manager, to provide career advice to your employees, particularly in regard to succession planning. You can also use these anchors when hiring applicants and mentoring employees to increase the probability that the person you hire or promote is a good fit with the job.

Lifestyle as an anchor is steadily rising in importance with today's workforce, and it is likely to become a dominant anchor in the near future for many people.

Still another key factor to take into account in managing your career is an organization's culture.[3] Your "fit" with your employer is heavily influenced by the extent to which your career interests and personality align with the organization's values and goals.

There are four types of career cultures:

An **apprenticeship culture** has strong intrinsic values. Hence, the focus is on assimilation and strong identification with the organization (e.g., West Point, Bain & Company). Mentorships and apprenticeships are the lifeblood of this culture.

A **prestige culture** is typically found in professional service firms, such as Deloitte and PricewaterhouseCoopers, where the firm's reputation is critical to its success. Recruiting is often restricted to elite universities. Employee work attire must convey power and prestige. Companies such as Goldman Sachs pride themselves as serving as a springboard for employees to develop their professional reputation. Entry into a prestige culture is more difficult than entry into the other three cultures because of their high level of selectivity.

Protean cultures are characterized by an emphasis on each employee being clear about his or her passion and hence wanting to take the initiative to pursue that passion. In this culture, individuality, creativity, and being a team player are highly valued characteristics. The organization structure is typically flat (e.g., Google, Zappos). Employees enjoy a great deal of autonomy. This can be unsettling if you desire a hierarchical, structured approach to your career.

In a **meritocracy culture**, (e.g., GE) you are required to continually prove your worth through your job performance. This culture attracts people with a high need for achievement. Opportunities are earned, not granted. Thus, you will advance in the organization contingent on your successes. However, loads of opportunities will be provided for you to increase your abilities through training and development programs. This is because merit cultures make it a priority to help employees succeed and advance in the pursuit of career goals.

It is advantageous to your organization to be clear about its cultural values when recruiting. Doing so will increase the probability of attracting and retaining individuals who will thrive in the firm.

Before accepting a job offer, you should seek answers to the following questions: In which one of the four cultures are you most likely to be comfortable? What are the messages you have heard about how people develop their career in this organization? Are your career priorities similar to what the organization expects of you to be successful?

Author and business management pioneer Peter Drucker, in an article entitled "Managing Oneself," observed that "knowing where one belongs makes ordinary people . . . outstanding performers." Be sure your career values and goals are aligned with the organization's culture before you accept a job offer.

Definitions of Career Success around the Globe

In 2004, a research team was formed to conduct a global study on how people define career success. A survey was administered to 15,000 people in 30 countries. Seven major meanings of success were identified:

1. Financial security

2. Financial achievement

3. Learning and development

4. Work-life balance

5. Positive relationships

6. Positive impact

7. Entrepreneurship

Financial security involves the ability for you to provide the basic necessities for living on an ongoing basis. It is an especially strong indicator of success in economically less-developed countries.

Financial achievement is viewed as a measure of success across countries. It is typically viewed in terms of the rate of financial increases you receive during your career, such as job promotions and gaining higher social status. It is commonly used as an indicator of success in achievement-oriented countries, such as Canada, the United Kingdom, and the United States. The amount of money you make is viewed as a visible signal to others of your career success.

Learning and development are viewed as ongoing, sustainable, and renewable forms of career success. They can occur informally through continuous learning on the job or formally through training and education initiatives. This view of career success is usually held only by those individuals who already have financial stability.

Work-life balance is judged in terms of the time an employee has for nonwork interests and activities. This definition of success is especially important in collectivistic and individualistic societies, where employees are in dual-working marriages, distant relationships, and/or have children in daycare.

For many people, career success is viewed in terms of positive relationships with colleagues in the workplace. They want to work with people they like and respect, as well as with people who give them appropriate recognition for a job well done. They especially appreciate coworkers who give them constructive feedback. People in all countries want appreciation for the work they perform.

Having a positive impact on others and performing work that has a beneficial effect on society is viewed as a career success by those of us who are advanced in our careers. As Albert Einstein argued: "It is high time the ideal of success should be replaced with the ideal of service." In organizational life, service often takes the form of mentoring, a subject dealt with shortly in this chapter.

Entrepreneurship includes starting your own enterprise and/or pursuing your own projects. It reflects the importance to you of being able to invent and develop your own projects in the workplace.

Knowing these seven definitions of career success will help you in a wide variety of scenarios, such as when launching an initiative internationally with a virtual team consisting of members from markedly different countries (e.g., China, South Africa, United States). One-on-one conversations with each individual on your team can help you understand how each person views success.[4]

Being Proactive and Wise in Advancing Your Career

Being proactive means taking action rather than remaining passive when you believe it is important for you to do so in order to attain an outcome you desire. Proactive behaviors include those having to do with your workplace (e.g., improving the way to perform tasks, improving a system, speaking up on needed changes). Proactive behavior will contribute to your career success when your behavior is viewed by others as positive.

Proactive strategic behavior involves identifying issues and raising awareness of future opportunities and threats to your organization. This is an effective way for you to get the attention and appreciation of senior management.

Another proactive behavior is taking steps to improve your fit. If you just joined your organization, schedule a meeting with your boss to request feedback. Within the first year of your employment, seek a senior person to become your mentor. In short, take charge of your own development. By doing so, you will be promoted more often, receive more salary increases, and become highly satisfied with your career.

Now, there are downsides to everything in life (e.g., too much exercise, too little exercise. Too much Vitamin D, too little Vitamin D). This is true for being proactive in the absence of wisdom, as in, not using your head. Being proactive often means challenging the status quo and, hence, the people who are staunch defenders of it. In short, being proactive can be risky. To minimize the risks of derailing your career because you are proactive, you must take into account the context or situation, the people affected by the ideas you are championing, and you yourself.

With regard to the context, setting, or situation, you must do your homework before you propose your initiative to others. Does your initiative address an important problem? Have you talked to key stakeholders who will be affected by your proposal to get their reaction? Have you built a coalition of advocates for your ideas? Insensitivity to the reactions of others has been shown consistently to be a prime cause of career derailment. A wise person becomes aware of how others will perceive a proposed change before advocating it in a public forum. Are you able to make clear how your initiatives will prove helpful to others? As for yourself, ask this question: Are you able to lead this initiative?

The way to advance your career lies not in passivity, nor does it occur through egocentric proactivity. The path forward for your career is wise proactivity.[5]

Career Resilience

Very few of us live a charmed existence. Almost all of us experience setbacks. For example, we may get passed over for a job we thought was all but ours. Our mentor may bolt to another organization. We may be laid off. Our personal life may become unhinged. The key question is simply this: How are you able to get back on your feet after being "knocked down"?

Psychological Strategies

Failing to acknowledge your negative emotions after being knocked down hurts resilience rather than enabling it. Attempts to deny your anger, frustration, and resentment often result in excessive alcohol or illicit drug consumption, overeating, mindlessly watching television, or playing endless computer games. Dwelling on your negative emotions is also dysfunctional. Instead, try one or more of the following strategies:

1. Focus on your development. Look for ways to improve your underdeveloped skills necessary for attaining your career goals.

2. Surround yourself with people who inspire you to grow.

3. Practice, practice, practice your newly acquired skills.

4. Celebrate your errors: "Great, now I know what not to do." "How am I smarter/wiser?" "What will I do differently next time?"

5. When you experience setbacks, know that they signal the necessity for better strategies and an increase in effort rather than your lack of ability.[6]

Minimize the Likelihood of Setbacks

There are at least four strategies you can use to minimize the likelihood of setbacks in your career: (1) develop a solid working relationship with your boss, (2) enroll in training and development programs relevant to your career interests, (3) seek job challenges, and (4) develop a career network.

Perceived similarity in goals and values between you and your boss can pay big dividends. Start by being sensitive to the environment in which your boss works as well as his strengths, weaknesses, and preferred work style. The latter has to do with your boss' preferred level of formality, expected frequency of you "checking in," and the preferred mode of communication (e.g., face-to-face, phone calls, emails). A good relationship with your boss can lead to developmental opportunities, autonomy in your job, and opportunities to take on increasingly challenging jobs.

Looking for training and development opportunities will further embed you in your organization. Doing so may also connect you with important people who will increase your political acumen within the workplace. Furthermore, it will send a signal to higher management that you have a continuous-learning mind-set.

FURTHER EVIDENCE

The Center for Creative Leadership reports that seeking out challenging assignments and performing them well is an excellent way of earning a promotion.

Among the most effective ways to be resilient when confronted with a significant setback is to maintain a large professional network so that you can make use of those contacts when necessary. Open your network to people inside and outside your organization. Such a network will provide you with the psychological and the social support that will enable you to be resilient in the event of setbacks.

Negotiating Idiosyncratic Deals (I-deals)

Idiosyncratic deals, or i-deals, refer to special arrangements that you negotiate with your boss that are relatively unique for you. They are typically negotiated when you are presented with the opportunity for a promotion or transfer, but only if you have a good relationship with your boss. Typical i-deals involve negotiations around your development, tasks, flexibility, workload, and financial arrangements.

Development-related i-deals include opportunities for high-quality training and advancement and assignments to important committees. Securing these opportunities will give you a leg up on your coworkers for a promotion.

Task-related i-deals involve adding, modifying, reducing or eliminating job duties. A successful negotiation of this type enables you to focus on aspects of your job that you find meaningful. Hence, you will become increasingly engaged in your work.

Flexibility i-deals will likely prove a boon to your ability to balance your work and family life, but coordination issues may arise between you, your clients, and your coworkers. If you are successful in gaining this i-deal, be sure to make your subsequent accomplishments visible to others. Keep your boss and coworkers informed of the milestones you have met, contributions you have made, and the assistance you have provided to others.

A variation of this option involves negotiating a reduced workload. This i-deal may be an excellent way of dealing with health issues or transitioning to your retirement. Again, if you are successful in this negotiation, keep people informed of your accomplishments, lest colleagues eventually see you as "deadwood."

Financial i-deals can be a two-edged sword. The increase in money and perks you negotiate will be great from your standpoint. But, this i-deal can lead to perceptions of unfairness on the part of your coworkers and, hence, their reluctance to cooperate with you on future assignments (see chapter 4 on perceptions of organizational justice). The i-deal you negotiate must not reek of favoritism in the eyes of others. Where possible, be able to explain how your i-deal will benefit your boss and your team's members. Continually look for opportunities to help your coworkers. In short, manage your workplace relationships effectively. [7]

Mentoring Relationships

Having an excellent mentor is a highly effective way to advance your career. Typical outcomes you can expect include job and career satisfaction and increases in opportunities for promotion. In addition, you are likely to experience increases in self-confidence and optimism in your workplace.

For these outcomes to occur, you must have a close relationship with your mentor, a relationship characterized by trust and commitment. Having a mentor will enable you to quickly learn the norms and expected behaviors in your organization as well as the "landmines" to avoid. A distinguishing feature of a mentoring relationship is the focus on your growth and development in the organization, as well as your visibility. A mentor will help you understand confusing experiences and give you support when you experience stress.

A mentor may not be your boss. Your mentor may not even work for the same company. Some mentors are assigned to you by your organization. Others may develop informally, and others may agree to serve in this role at your request. The key is for you to have a mentor who is in an influential position and can give you sage advice, "open doors," help you learn about other areas in the organization, and offer you protection should you need it.

The dynamics of a mentor-protégé relationship should be a two-way street. As an expert on mentoring, Belle Ragins, a behavioral scientist at the University of Wisconsin, noted that the dynamics between you and your mentor should reflect a needs-based approach. Instead of thinking in terms of, "My role is to teach you," a better approach is, "What do you need and how can I help?" This dynamic will move you from being a passive recipient of your mentor's knowledge to a relationship of mutuality: "Let's figure this out together." In addition, this change in dynamics will likely prove empowering for you: "Wow, maybe I can do this!"

The key skills you want to acquire in a mentoring relationship are those that can be used across jobs, roles, and organizations. These include listening, perspective taking, giving constructive feedback, managing conflict, communicating, and networking.

Although having a high-quality mentor-protégé relationship is beneficial for all of us, it is particularly valuable for those of you who are subject to exclusion and discrimination because of your sex, race, age, religion, color, national origin, disability, or sexual preference. Such exclusion or discrimination shouldn't happen, and in most cases it is illegal. But the unfortunate reality is that it still occurs in many workplaces, sometimes in overt ways and sometimes more subtly.

A high-quality mentoring relationship can help you develop strategies to overcome such exclusion. A high-quality mentoring relationship may also prove to be a comfortable way for you to explore and reflect on your own beliefs and attitudes. A positive mentoring relationship offers a "safe space" to discuss diversity in the workplace and to come to the realization that diversity is not only a legal and a moral issue, it is a business necessity demanded by customers in a heterogeneous society.[8]

CONCLUSIONS

The message in this chapter is straightforward. You must actively take charge of the advancement of your career. To do this, you must become aware of your career anchor and the career culture where you are likely to flourish. But to do so, you must be wise in the ways you become proactive. If you offend people in your attempts to grow and develop in your organization, you may become derailed. Hence, you must develop ways to be resilient if this should happen, or better still, become adept at ways to minimize the likelihood of a career setback. Given that you develop a strong working relationship with your boss, you may be in a position to make idiosyncratic deals. But again, be aware of the potential landmines when doing so. Among the most important steps to take to advance your career is to find a mentor who will provide a role model for you, giving you sage advice on effective ways for you to advance in your organization.

QUESTIONS

1. What is your career anchor? How do you prefer to be managed, rewarded, and developed?

2. In what type of career culture are you most likely to thrive?

3. What is your definition of career success?

4. How can you be both proactive and wise in advancing your career?

5. What psychological strategies can you use to be resilient if you are confronted by a setback in your career?

6. How can you minimize a career setback?

7. What are the different types of idiosyncratic deals you might make?

8. What are the "landmines" of making one or more of these deals?

9. What are the benefits of having a mentor?

10. How would you describe the dynamics of the ideal mentor-protégé relationship?

CREATE A PSYCHOLOGICALLY HEALTHY WORKPLACE

Tinline and Cooper, two organizational psychologists in the United Kingdom, believe that the most straightforward way to minimize job-related stress is to change the working environment. The two most important environmental factors to focus on for you as a manager are job security and work relationships (recall the emphasis, discussed in chapter 4, on the importance of satisfying an employee's concerns for security and affiliation).

JOB SECURITY

Organizational restructuring and head-count reduction have become the new norms. Not surprisingly, this can cause your employees to fear for their job security. If they remain employed, many of them fear that they will not have the ability to do what will soon be required of them. As a manager, you need the skills to increase your self-efficacy and the efficacy of your team (hence, the importance of reading chapter 8). Building your self-efficacy and the efficacy of your team will transform perceptions of what's known as "hindrance stress" to "challenging stress." Hindrance stress occurs when your employees perceive job demands as having little or no purpose. Thus, sources of hindrance stress are viewed

FURTHER EVIDENCE

The American Institute of Stress reported that 80 percent
of us experience job-related stress, and more than half of
the 550 million working days lost annually in the United
States from absenteeism are stress-related. Other environmental factors
that are turning job stress into a virtual epidemic are workload, work pace,
work scheduling, job content, and poor interpersonal relationships.

as major barriers to success. "Challenge" sources of stress, on the
other hand, are opportunities to master new skills. Hence, challenge sources of stress typically increase job satisfaction, organizational commitment, and job performance.

To transform hindrance stress as challenge stress, you must
provide your team with opportunities for growth and development.
The workplace should be viewed by them as a domain that provides
a sense of purpose and mastery. With regard to mastery, you must
lobby senior management for the resources (e.g., training, equipment) your team needs to perform their jobs effectively. In addition,
you must guard against excessive or unreasonable job demands by
your boss. It is you who serves as the voice of your team to senior
management.

In short, it is you, as your team's manager, who plays an integral
role in forming a psychologically healthy workplace. This is because
you provide training opportunities for your direct reports and recognition to them for work they perform well. It is you who can
involve them in decisions that will affect them in the workplace. So
now let's turn to work relationships.

WORK RELATIONSHIPS

In a global study of 20,000 people, Christine Porath, a behavioral
scientist, found that people rated respect as more important to

them than any other interpersonal factor in the workplace. In 2013, Canada introduced a National Standard for Psychological Health and Safety in the Workplace. This standard, although not a legal requirement, identified 13 critical workplace psychological health and safety factors. Yet, many managers express bewilderment as to how to implement them. The steps are straightforward.

You can increase your team's well-being through your own working relationships with them. You can start by modeling respectful, civil, fair, and ethical behavior. In addition, you can:

- Dedicate time for one-on-one meetings with each person on your team

- Encourage them to exercise their voice on ways to improve their performance, the team's performance, and your performance

- Encourage them to use the organization's programs and initiatives for developing a healthy workplace (e.g., employee assistance programs, leaves of absence, flextime, telecommuting)

Research in the behavioral sciences suggests a number of additional practices you can apply to promote your team's mental health. Give your team members autonomy by giving them the freedom to decide how to pursue their individual and team goals. Hold team meetings to explain upper management's decisions, and solicit their ideas on how to implement them.

TAKE CARE OF YOU

In addition to being supportive of your direct reports, you must take care of yourself. Seek opportunities to develop both your technical and psychological skills (e.g., communication, negotiation, conflict resolution).

Along with informal chats with your boss, peers, and direct

FURTHER EVIDENCE

Jack Welch, the former CEO of General Electric, said, "Before you are a leader, success is all about growing yourself. When you become a leader, success is all about growing others."

reports, administer 360-degree feedback surveys (see chapter 10) to learn what you are doing well and what you should consider doing differently. Arla Day, a leading expert on building psychologically healthy workplaces, has concluded that self-care is among the most underrated leadership skills. Find time for you to disengage from your job, or you will risk burning out (see chapter 5, "Engage Your Employees"). You are the key to creating and monitoring a psychologically healthy workplace for your team. You can't do so if you are the one who is experiencing excessive hindrance stress.[1]

YOUR MENTAL HEALTH

Your mental health is the *sine qua non* for inculcating a psychologically healthy workplace. In fact, St-Hilaire and Gilbert go so far as to argue that a focus on your mental health as the manager of your team is the first step in fostering a "virtuous circle."[3] That is, the better the mental health of you, the manager, the higher the likelihood that you will adopt and model healthy management practices that in turn will promote the mental and physical health of your employees.

Sadly, being a manager today is not always a healthy choice. Among the consequences of organizational restructuring and headcount reductions are an increase in the number of employees you will be supervising, an increase in your workload, and more responsibility with fewer resources. All of these factors can increase your job-related stress. Yet, many managers are uncomfortable talking about their stress, fearing that it signals weakness. Their fear of being judged negatively, and perhaps being demoted, keeps them tight-lipped.

Ongoing exposure to a toxic work environment, where the job demands greatly exceed the resources, has consequences for your health. These consequences can include:

- Mental health problems such as depression

- Psychosomatic disorders

- Behavioral reactions, such as absenteeism

- Excessive use of alcohol

- Heart problems, abdominal discomfort, and sleep disorders

This situation often leads to the overuse of prescription drugs for reducing anxiety, insomnia, and depression. One or more of these reactions to stress will have an adverse effect on your ability to make wise decisions. Worse, these reactions are conducive to you shifting to an abusive supervisory style with your team. In short, your relationships with your employees can influence your mental health. The stresses you endure—particularly as a result of toxic employees—eventually will prove harmful to you.[2]

Promoting Your Mental Health through Subordinates

In today's work environment, where nearly everyone is experiencing stress, it can be highly beneficial to bring mental health experts into the workplace. Such professionals can teach you and your team

FURTHER EVIDENCE

According to the World Health Organization, at least one in four people will experience a mental illness at some point in their lives.

FURTHER EVIDENCE

In Canada, over $20 billion is lost each year because of disability-related costs. The total cost to the economy is more than $150 billion. In the European Union, just under 5 percent of the gross domestic product is lost each year due to people experiencing depression.

how to identify sources of stress and who among your team is experiencing stress-related problems. Most importantly, these experts can explain why it is as important for your employees to reduce your stress as it is for you to reduce their stress. Subordinates can offer social support for you by listening to your concerns and asking how they can help when you are overwhelmed and feeling out of control. Discuss tasks with your subordinates that they can take on in order to lessen your workload. Becoming aware of organizational hindrance stressors and who is experiencing them can bring about a healthy work environment for you and them.[3]

Mental Health Problems Are Managers' Problems

Dimoff and Kelloway, organizational psychologists in the United States and Canada, respectively, report that in the United States alone, between $150 billion and $300 billion is lost annually as a result of mental illness. Hence, the necessity for management to create and maintain a psychologically healthy workplace. Management solutions include: (1) Increasing mental health literacy, that is, an understanding of mental health issues and treatments so that there is no stigma or discrimination surrounding employees who have a mental illness; and (2) providing employee-assistance programs (EAP) where employees are free to discuss and resolve issues related to psychological and physical health, child-parent issues, domestic abuse, and interpersonal problems in the workplace. With one in three people reporting that they experience an extreme amount of stress at work, an EAP is a necessity. Hence, it is critical for you as a manager to promote the use of an EAP to your employees by raising awareness of the benefits of using it as a resource. As stated earlier, you need to model the use of an EAP so that your staff is not afraid of using it. At a minimum, use EAP staff to teach you and your team how to recognize and thus support colleagues who struggle with stress. This is necessary because two in three people who have a mental illness strive to hide the fact, fearing that it will negatively affect their career (e.g., fear that colleagues will avoid them or pro-motion opportunities will suddenly disappear).

Early recognition improves the prognosis for a mental health issue. Moreover, employees report that if you as their manager are supportive, they experience considerably less stress. Those employ-ees who do not receive your support early on typically experience further deterioration in their mental health. In addition, repeated sick leave frequently increases, as does a decrease in their job per-formance. This in turn is likely to negatively impact your work and the work of your team, which results in a decrease in customer service. In short, the mental health problems of employees are management's problems and must be dealt with in a timely, pro-fessional fashion. See table 1, where Dimoff and Kelloway give the warning signs that an employee may be experiencing a mental health problem.[4]

MENTAL HEALTH AWARENESS

Mental Health Awareness Training (MHAT) is a three-hour workshop that teaches managers how to recognize and respond to mental health issues as well as the skills for supporting and refer-ring an employee to workplace resources such as an employee assistance program. This workshop has led to significant savings in disability costs up to one year following its implementation (e.g., an average reduction of 19 days per claim). Three aspects of the

TABLE 1.

WARNING SIGNS THAT AN EMPLOYEE MAY BE STRUGGLING WITH A MENTAL HEALTH PROBLEM INCLUDE:	
Emotional Changes	Expressing dissatisfaction or being unhappy at work Expressing that he/she wants to quit Mentioning how stressed he/she is Crying at work
Withdrawal	Withdrawing from coworkers Withdrawing from social activities (i.e., weekly coffee with coworkers) Engaging in fewer helping behaviors with colleagues
Extreme Behavior	Expressing thoughts about harming oneself or others Expressing thoughts about suicide or the intent to commit suicide Behaving in inappropriate or counterproductive ways (e.g., theft) Neglecting personal hygiene or appearance Bringing or consuming drugs or alcohol at work or before work
Attendance Problems	Being absent from work Staying home or coming to work sick Arriving late to work
Performance Concerns	Failing to perform to his/her usual standards Missing deadlines Being forgetful (e.g., misplacing documents, failing to return emails)

workshop explain its effectiveness. First, the workshop provides managers factual information about the prevalence of mental health issues and the steps that you as a manager can take. Second, the workshop includes video clips and case studies that help reduce the stigma around mental illness. Third, this training increases your

FURTHER EVIDENCE

The Mental Health Commission of Canada defines stigma as a form of prejudice that manifests as a collection of negative attitudes and behaviors that are perpetuated by misinformation and fear. Stigma is a primary barrier to seeking help for mental illnesses.

self-efficacy so that you can assist and support an employee who is experiencing an excessive amount of hindrance stress, burnout, depression, anxiety, or substance addiction, five of the most common mental health problems that affect employees.

In summary, Dimoff and Kelloway, experts on dealing with mental health issues in the workplace, have emphasized the following points. By providing managers with techniques to recognize and respond to warning signs of mental health issues, an organization can increase a manager's self-efficacy for supporting employees. Doing so can increase the organization's ROI. Remove the stigma that often surrounds mental health issues, and these issues become correctable.

WORK CLIMATE

All of the above becomes much, much easier if the work climate facilitates and maximizes the benefits to employees of disclosing early on their mental health problems in the workplace. Legislation in Canada, the United Kingdom, and the United States specifies that disclosure is a first step for an employee to seek formal accommodation for a mental health problem. There is evidence that an employee is more likely to explain a mental health issue to you, the manager, than to coworkers or HR managers. This disclosure in itself has been shown to reduce an employee's anxiety. Many employees, however,

FURTHER EVIDENCE

In 2015, the *Journal of Clinical Psychiatry* published a study showing that mood and depression disorders alone result in an estimated economic burden of $210.5 billion per year in the United States alone. A large portion of these costs was due to missing days of work or being at work but providing low productivity.

perceive the costs of disclosure to be much greater than the benefits. For example, they often see disclosure as framing their identity and hence how they will be seen by others. This will result in negative emotions by others toward them and discriminating behaviors against them by their colleagues. In short, they believe they will be devalued. This, in turn, can reduce self-esteem and induce feelings of demoralization and shame. As a result, an employee is likely to feel embarrassed and withdraw from work.[5]

ORGANIZATIONAL BENEFITS OF DISCLOSURE

It is to your organization's advantage to create a climate where employees feel comfortable disclosing mental health difficulties. This is because it is you, the manager, who will have relevant information on ways to support the employees. Moreover, disclosure will prevent you from attributing an employee's increasingly poor performance to bad character, which could make the situation worse by engaging in inappropriate sanctions toward the employee.

To create a climate that supports disclosure, organizational psychologists Bonaccio, Lapierre, and O'Reilly support the following steps:

1. Present good mental health as a goal for every team member to attain and sustain. Share your own experiences with a mental health problem—how you coped with it, and how the support from others helped you cope with it. Disclosing your

personal struggle with stress will exemplify your courage and conviction that mental health should be discussed openly. It will certainly gain you the admiration of many people on your team.

2. Involve your staff in generating ideas to ensure the mental health and a low amount of hindrance stress for everyone on your team. For example, involve them in a brainstorming exercise on ways to accommodate flextime while still attaining the team's performance goals. Giving your people a voice in such issues as flextime will ensure that they consider them fair.

3. Take the time to support each member of your team. Working with an employee to come up with an appropriate accommodation can be viewed as an idiosyncratic deal (see chapter 6), that is, a special arrangement between the employee and you that meets that employee's needs without having an adverse effect on the team's performance.

In short, go the extra mile to increase the emotional connection between you and your team's members.

FURTHER EVIDENCE

A mistaken belief is that accommodating employees with mental health problems is expensive. A survey conducted by the Job Accommodation Network, a service within the US Department of Labor, showed that for 59 percent of the companies surveyed, such accommodations cost $0. The majority of the remaining companies reported one-time costs of less than $500. Of the companies surveyed, 73 percent reported that accommodations increased employee productivity, 90 percent said that the accommodations helped to retain valued employees, 56 percent reported increased employee attendance, and 38 percent indicated an observable saving in worker compensation and other insurance costs.

QUESTIONS

1. Why are you, as a manager, a key player in building a psycho-logically healthy workplace?

2. What can you do to facilitate good working relationships among the workers of your team?

3. How can you take good care of yourself? Why is it important for you to do so?

4. In what ways can your subordinates promote your mental health?

5. What are the warning signs of a mental health issue?

6. What are the benefits of Mental Health Awareness Training (MHAT)?

7. What are the benefits to your organization of an employee's early disclosure of a mental health issue?

8. How can you create a climate that supports early disclosure?

9. Explain the difference between hindrance stress and chal-lenge stress.

INSTILL
RESILIENCE
IN THE FACE
OF SETBACKS

Every individual and every team faces setbacks. It's how your direct reports and team handle setbacks that will set them apart. Losing a key client or engaging in a number of production mishaps can create feelings of doubt and uncertainty, which can build into stress and paralyze performance. It's what psychologists call "learned helplessness." An evidence-based manager can instill resilience even when disappointments cloud a team's vision and failures make goals appear unattainable.

It's all about resilience: How are you going to bounce back from disappointments and inspire the people around you to do the same? The answer is in two extensively researched methods: linking actions and outcomes (what researchers call *outcome expectancy*) and building a can-do mind-set (or *self-efficacy*). These two steps will help develop resilience:

1. Link actions and outcomes.

2. Build a can-do attitude.

WHAT WORKS, IN BRIEF

Feeling helpless—that frustrating "I just can't do it" sensation—is a mind-set that we learn over time. A display of such helplessness in the face of setbacks may emerge automatically for some employees, but that feeling of helplessness is not innate, nor is it unchangeable. Instead, helplessness is learned from experiencing one severe setback or many lesser ones. That's good news for managers because it means that employees can *unlearn* helplessness and replace it with the positive, can-do mind-set needed to bounce back and overcome challenges. Once you understand the outcomes your people expect, you will understand why they do what they do.

Linking Actions and Outcomes

People choose their behavior based on their expectation of the results of their actions: If they expect a behavior to yield a desired result, they are more likely to engage in it; if they do not, they are less likely to take that action. Expectations for the outcome of a given behavior are what psychologists call "outcome expectancies." People will not do what is needed to succeed unless they see and believe that there is a link between those actions and a desired outcome. As a result, expectations are an important area to target when trying to foster high performance. By teaching your people the link between actions and outcomes—by helping them develop accurate outcome expectancies—you can arm them with resilience to recover quickly from setbacks.

Believing in Achieving—a Can-Do Mind-set

A second key to instilling resilience in the members of your team is teaching them to believe that they can succeed—fostering self-efficacy. People have high self-efficacy when they believe strongly in their ability to successfully perform a task, to successfully attain a goal. When your people have high self-efficacy, they won't crumble in the face of obstacles; instead they are apt to be excited because they see the obstacles as challenges they can and will overcome. But remember that self-efficacy is domain-specific rather than general. You as an evidence-based manager must be ready to increase your

> **FURTHER EVIDENCE**
>
> Countless studies show the importance of taking into account a person's outcome expectancies and self-efficacy to predict, explain, and influence that person's behavior.[1]

employees' self-efficacy whenever they encounter a situation where they have doubts that they will be successful.

You can build self-efficacy in at least four ways: by enactive mastery, by use of appropriate models, through persuasion by a "significant other," and through functional self-talk. These methods are as effective with a team as they are with an individual, and they are as effective with an 8-year-old as they are with an 80-year-old. I discussed *Teach your team to believe they can succeed.* functional self-talk in chapter 3; this chapter covers the other three methods.

RESILIENCE TOOLS IN PRACTICE

Setbacks are inevitable; failure is not. A key differentiator of an effective manager from an ineffective manager is resilience—your ability to bounce back and your ability to simultaneously get the people on your team back on their feet.

One severe setback—or multiple small ones—often creates feelings of doubt: "I can no longer do this." Doubt, in turn, can result in *learned helplessness*. Let me give you two examples.

My son called from his first year in college to inform me that he was going to drop his chemistry class. "I got a D on the exam," he said. I replied, "Why don't you do something never done before in the history of your university?" "What's that?" he asked. "Try going to class," I said. He did.

What did he get for his effort? Another D. "Try reading the book in addition to going to class," I suggested thoughtfully. He did. The result? Another D. He learned that effort and persistence were useless. He learned helplessness.

Learned helplessness is not a genetic infliction, nor is it the result of a poor attitude. Rather, learned helplessness is based on observable data. My son's chemistry grades were real, not imagined.

Here is a second story:

I work with a professional consulting firm in which the partners are evaluated on revenue generated from both existing and new clients. A newly elected partner came to me in considerable distress. Although he had exceeded the firm's goals for revenue generated from existing clients, he had generated nothing from other sources. "I can't make cold calls," the partner concluded emphatically. The zero dollars he had generated so far supported this conclusion. He had learned helplessness from lack of revenue from cold calls.

> **Your job is to help people break the "I can't do it" cycle.**

Your job as an evidence-based manager is to help your people break the "I can't do it" cycle. The paralyzing stress and lack of confidence that people experience from setbacks can be overcome by taking the two steps described here: strengthen outcome expectancies and increase a person's self-efficacy.

Strengthening Outcome Expectancies

When people say they "don't get it," what they mean is that they don't see the relationship between what they are doing and the outcome they would love to expect. Here's another look at my son's poor chemistry grades and the consulting partner's lack of revenue generation from new clients.

Needless to say, as a university professor, I was chagrined that my initial advice to my son on ways to improve his grades had not worked. Then, in a flash of the obvious, I suggested that he see the TA. "What's a TA?" he asked. Eureka! I knew I was on the path to a solution. At large universities, there is often little or no relationship between what the professor emphasizes in class (to the 1,500 students crowding the lecture hall) and the questions that appear on the exam. That's because the chores of writing exam questions and grading answers are left to a graduate student known as the teaching assistant, or TA. A visit to a TA increases the likelihood a student will discover what the TA will put on an exam. So, I said, "See the TA, my son. See the TA." My job as a parent was to help him see the relationship between visiting the TA and getting a high grade. And he did.

Now, about the partner in the consulting firm: I asked him to explain the steps he had recently taken to far exceed his revenue goal with a long-standing client, a bank. I asked how he achieved such success, given the many changes among the bank's key personnel that year. The point was to make the partner see how his present client, as a result of all the personnel changes, had in reality become a new client. My job was to get him to understand that what he did so well with that bank, with minor adjustments, he could also do with another bank, one new to him. He did. The revenue from new clients began to flow because the partner could now see the relationship between what he was doing and the outcome he desired—new business.

The *empathy box* that follows in figure 1, reported in *Personnel Psychology*, is a tool to understand and change your employees' outcome expectancies.[2] This box allows you to see issues from the viewpoint of your employees. It is based on two principles:

FIGURE 1. THE EMPATHY BOX

The Goal:

	POSITIVE OUTCOMES EXPECTED +	NEGATIVE OUTCOMES EXPECTED −
DESIRED BEHAVIOR: honesty	CELL 1	CELL 2
UNDESIRED BEHAVIOR: steal	CELL 3	CELL 4

- If you understand the outcomes people expect, you will understand their behavior.

- If you change the outcomes people expect, you will change their behavior.

Here's how the empathy box works in action: A company wanted to slash employee theft from more than $1 million a year to $1,000 a year or less. Together, company and union managers randomly selected employees to interview. Interviewees were guaranteed anonymity regarding their answers to these four questions:

1. **What positive outcomes do you expect for being honest?** (cell 1) The most common answer turned out to be "none."

2. **What negative outcomes do you expect for being honest?** (cell 2) The answers included harassment by and isolation from peers, which fostered a "hear no evil, see no evil" culture.

3. **What positive outcomes do you expect from stealing?** (cell 3) Employees confessed they stole for the "challenge" and the "thrill"; no one was selling the stolen goods or even using them. One said, "We're so good, we could steal a head rig from a sawmill." (A head rig weighs more than a ton.) The thieves said, "Tell us what you want, Doc, and we will get it out within 45 days."

4. **What negative outcomes do you expect from stealing?** (cell 4) No one feared dismissal because the employees knew the company had to meet its major supply contract—or face financial penalties. Employees also knew the company feared a union strike. In fact, the thieves were only concerned about losing arguments among themselves as to whose turn it was to house the stolen goods. "The stuff is clogging up our garages, basements, and attics," they said.

Suffice it to say, things aren't always as they seem, and to the managers, some of the employees' answers were more than a bit surprising. The value of the empathy box is that it provides a systematic way to understand employee behavior. To find a solution to the employees' lack of positive goal commitment, I posed a fifth question: "What has to change to get people to commit to the company's goal for honest behavior, to get people into cell 1?" Clues to potentially correct answers can usually be found in the answers to questions in cells 2 and 3, as seen in figure 2.

Here is the resolution: To eliminate the thieves' expected thrill from stealing—an undesirable goal—the company adopted a policy from the public library. The employees were informed that they could now borrow whatever equipment they wanted. The organization's legal department produced reams of paper that required the borrower's signature indicating that, should the borrower get hurt while using the equipment, the company was not responsible. With that, the excitement of stealing was removed.

Copying another policy from the public library, the company announced an amnesty day during which people could return stolen material under the assumption that they "were returning it for a friend." So much was returned from clogged garages and basements that the company extended the amnesty from a Friday to Saturday and then from Saturday to Sunday. These changes are reflected in figure 3.

By creating policies that reduced the negative outcomes of goal commitment (cell 2) and positive outcomes of goal rejection (cell 3)—as described by the employees themselves—the organization was able to gain employee commitment to the goal of honesty (cell 1). There is a caveat to the empathy box, however: When deciding

FIGURE 2. THE EMPATHY BOX BEFORE MANAGERIAL ACTION

The **Goal:** Honest Behavior

	POSITIVE OUTCOMES EXPECTED	NEGATIVE OUTCOMES EXPECTED
DESIRED BEHAVIOR: honesty	None	Peer disaproval
UNDESIRED BEHAVIOR: steal	A thrill	Storage problem

FIGURE 3. THE EMPATHY BOX AFTER MANAGERIAL ACTION

The Goal: Honest behavior

	POSITIVE OUTCOMES EXPECTED	NEGATIVE OUTCOMES EXPECTED
GOAL COMMITMENT	No more storage problem	No thrill
GOAL REJECTION	None	Storage problem

on a solution, putting emphasis on punishment in cell 4 should always be viewed as a last resort. A focus on punishment in cell 4 can create a punishment culture in your organization that may lead to a "don't get mad, get even" mind-set among employees.

The benefit of the empathy box is that it helps you get to the root of why employees aren't committed to your goals or why they are resisting change. It offers clues as to how to gain their commitment. Understand the outcomes your employees expect, both positive and negative, and you'll understand their behavior. Take action to change the outcomes your people expect, and you'll be able to change their behavior too.

Self-Efficacy: Believing in Achieving

The second method for preventing or overcoming learned helplessness is to increase a person's *self-efficacy*. This concept differs from self-esteem. Self-esteem is based on your feelings toward yourself, which you take with you no matter the situation or place. How much you like yourself at home is pretty much how you like yourself in Paris, London, or Rome. Self-efficacy, on the other hand, is the belief that you are capable of attaining a specific goal.

Self-efficacy and self-esteem are not necessarily correlated. Someone can have high self-esteem and low self-efficacy, or the converse. This is because self-efficacy is domain- or task-specific confidence. For example, I could have very high self-esteem, but if you ask me to help you start your car—because it won't—I'd probably just shrug my shoulders and say, "Sorry," because I don't believe I have the ability to do anything mechanical.

You want the members of your team to have high self-efficacy for goal attainment for at least three reasons:

- Even if you get the outcome expectancies correct, and your people connect the dots between a given action and the outcome, people with low self-efficacy still may not take action. "*I see now what has to be done, but I lack the confidence to try.*"

- People with low self-efficacy look for tangible reasons to abandon high goals. Setbacks and failures prove to them that they are wasting their time, so they quit. "*I am out of here. It can't be done.*"

- People with high self-efficacy commit to high goals—the stepping-stones toward high performance. Setbacks and obstacles generate excitement, not helplessness. "*We can do this. We will do this! All we have to do is . . .* "

My advice is to leave self-esteem to the clinical psychologists; there is little you yourself can do as a manager to deal with people who have severe self-esteem issues.* Self-efficacy, however, does fall within your domain. The three methods outlined in the

---

* Reread chapter 7 on ways you can create a psychologically healthy workplace.

following sections can help you improve your employees' self-efficacy and, in doing so, foster in them the resilience they'll need to
bounce back from setbacks.[3]

Guaranteeing Success through Small Wins

To overcome low self-efficacy, assign tasks and sequence them in
such a way that all but guarantees that the person will attain the
goal. That's what "enactive mastery" is all about. It's the straightforward principle that small wins build confidence.[4] You can use
enactive mastery to build confidence in
novices, as well as in senior team members
who once had the confidence to make things
happen but lost it as a result of one or more
setbacks. Although ability is certainly vital

*You can set your
people up for failure or
success.*

to performance effectiveness, lack of ability is usually not what
prevents people from mastering a task, executing strategy, or
attaining high goals. It's the belief people have about their ability
that will ultimately propel them forward or hold them back.

You can set your people up for failure, or you can set them up
for success. Essentially, enactive mastery is the science of setting
people up to succeed. Doing so is relatively simple. Give them an
assignment that they are likely to master. On a task that is complex
for them, help them break the task down into subtasks. Sequence
the tasks so that success is likely. These steps can guide your team
toward attaining any number of goals, whether on the production
line or in the sales field.

Learning from Role Models

Yet another way to help improve an employee's self-efficacy is by
identifying an appropriate role model. The first role model who
comes to mind may be the best person on your team. But, surprising as it may be, this individual is often not the best choice to model
a task for someone who has low self-efficacy. Instead, you want to

find a model with whom your employee can identify, someone who has either just mastered the task or is in the process of doing so. Here's an example:

> A company in Maine benchmarked its performance against a great company in the same industry in Connecticut. Visits to a benchmark company are often smart because they can provide a picture of what is possible and keep you from having to reinvent the wheel. So the Maine company's senior management team, the union executive committee, and I got on a bus together and drove to Connecticut.
>
> The trip exceeded everyone's expectations. As we boarded the bus for home, all remarked how worthwhile and inspiring the trip had been. But just a few hours later, everyone was depressed. What had happened? We had seen the promised land and concluded that we would never get there. The union executive committee members said, "Did you see their management team compared to our Neander-thals?" The senior management team said, "Did you see their labor contract? We would never be able to negotiate something like that." As a result of benchmarking against an outstanding model, the group's efficacy was lower than it was before the trip. The team did not see themselves in the same league as the benchmark organization.
>
> Does this imply that benchmarking is a bad idea? No. My client's people simply had to take an additional, critical step. They needed to find a model that would leave them thinking, "If they can do it, so can we."

A model has to be an individual with whom the person can identify.

So the person on your team who delivers a flawless performance nearly all the time is usually not the person to pair with someone who has low self-efficacy. As with the Maine company, it's too easy for someone with low self-efficacy to write off such high performance as the result of innate talent or other factors that are beyond control. To be effective in increasing self-efficacy, a model has to be an individual with whom the person you are coaching can identify.

Having Significant Others Who Energize

This third method for boosting an employee's self-efficacy focuses on the influence of "significant others." A significant other doesn't have to be a spouse or romantic partner; it can be anyone you allow to "whisper in your ear" and who energizes (or de-energizes) you as a result of doing so. Here's a look at the power of significant others in action:

A psychology professor in a white lab coat welcomed two groups of Fortune 100 executives to the university's four-week advanced management program. As an icebreaker, he told one group of executives the following:

"Welcome to our university. This afternoon we are going to put you through a simulation. A simulation, as the name implies, simulates the kinds of things that you as senior executives confront on an ongoing basis. As you may be aware, a person's intelligence is not fixed. We used to believe that in the 1950s. But today we know that this is not true. Intelligence is based on your ability to learn from the people around you and to apply that knowledge. We know you are going to have fun and get a lot out of this simulation. It's 1:05 p.m. See you at 6:00 p.m. Have fun with the simulation."

To the second group, the same university professor in the same white lab coat gave a slightly different speech:

"Welcome to our university. This afternoon we are going to put you through a simulation. A simulation, as the name implies, simulates the kinds of things that you as senior executives confront on an ongoing basis. As you may be

aware, a person's intelligence is fixed: You either have it or you don't. We have voluminous data on this fact going back to the 1950s. We know you are going to become frustrated; we know you are going to get upset. It's 1:10 p.m. Hang in there and I will see you at 6:00 p.m. Please keep in mind that intelligence is fixed; you either have it or you don't."

At 6:00 p.m. the professor slowly pushed back a sliding wall that had been separating the two groups. How do you think the first group was feeling as the simulation ended? They were upbeat. Everyone complimented the university in developing a simulation that was so realistic. One former cynic admitted that he had told the pilot of the corporate jet to stick around in case the course turned out to be a waste of time. Now he was convinced it would be a highly meaningful experience. Another executive said that the cost of the course had already paid off for her in terms of the knowledge she had gained that afternoon from those around her.

In stark contrast, the second group of executives reported that they didn't get anything out of the simulation; they said it was a waste of their time. The issues they worked on, several executives argued, had no answers. Then they demanded that they be given the opportunity to go through the same simulation as the first group. But of course, they had already gone through the same simulation as the other group.

The people we listen to closely can influence the way we see the world.

The critical question is this: Who allowed the university professor to play with the minds of these talented executives? Who allowed him to do this in less than one minute? The answer to both questions: The executives did. Those in one group allowed him to make the afternoon productive and enjoyable; those in the other group allowed him to make the afternoon terrible for them. Both groups had let him "whisper in their ears"—to a very positive end in one case and a very negative one in the other.

The point is that significant others—people we listen to closely— can wield tremendous influence over the way we see the world. As an evidence-based manager, you must

- Recognize your effect as a significant other on the people on your team.

- Teach your people the positive and negative influences significant others can have on their ability to do their job well.

- Be conscious of who you allow to whisper in your ear and what you are whispering into the ears of your employees.

To the extent you are respected by your employees, your position as manager typically confers on you the status of significant other. As such, you need to be highly conscious of what you say to whom, because your words can carry special weight to foster either positive or negative results. In addition, you should also always be on the lookout for people who either energize or de-energize people on your team, and you can make suggestions as to whom to see or avoid according to those observations.

Developing Learned Optimism

Pessimism is an attribute of helplessness when it is felt on a long-term basis with regard to everything an employee has done and has remaining to do. But pessimism can be challenged—and optimism learned. Martin Seligman, a clinical psychologist at the University of Pennsylvania, developed a series of questions to pose to pessimists, people with a can't-do mind-set resulting from one or more setbacks.[5] The purpose of these questions is to enable a pessimist to discover evidence for optimism. The following questions, based on Seligman's research, are designed to enable you to get an employee to snap out of this kind of funk and become optimistic about goal attainment.

- Does the failure or setback you have experienced apply to everything you have done, or just this one thing?

- Is this failure or setback an enduring one that will affect you forever, or are its effects only temporary?

- Is this failure or setback due solely to what you did or did not do, or were there additional factors involved?

In asking these three questions you are forcing an employee to examine the evidence that shows the basis for pessimism is not justified. Your discussion should result in an employee seeing that the sky is not falling and that one setback or failure does not mean the end of the employee's world.

There are specific, productive ways to manage this type of discussion. The goal is to have employees acknowledge that they are doing some things well, and that this one setback is just that—one setback, not 100 setbacks, and not a promise of an endless string of setbacks to come. An employee may be justified for feeling bad about this one mishap, but the evidence does not warrant the conclusion that everything this person has done has been ineffective. During such discussions, help employees generate the evidence that this is true by getting them to list those things that they have done and are now doing well. Be specific; be concrete.

In discussing the answer to the second question, acknowledge (that is, validate) the person's feelings of pessimism: "Yes, there is (was) an issue. Yes, you are right. I understand why you feel bad." Now, shift the discussion to brainstorming ways the issue will be corrected, and to ways to minimize its occurrence in the future. Recall chapter 3 on training: the benefit of encouraging errors when an employee is attempting to master complex subject matter. ("Great, you made an error. How are you wiser now?") What you are doing here is restoring this person's feeling of being back in control (self-efficacy; "I can do this").

Answers to the third question flow from the second. The purpose here is for you to help an employee see all the factors that contributed to the setback. ("Aha, so it was not all my fault.") Ask, "Were the necessary resources such as time, money, equipment, and people available for attaining the goal? If not, how will you get them?" "Did others who were accountable for goal attainment coordinate their efforts? If not, how will you get them to do so?" These are illustrative questions, but you get the idea—engage the employee in a discussion that leads to positive action steps, steps that will put the person back into the driver's seat so that feelings of pessimism shift to feelings of optimism. This methodology fits nicely with the discussion of shifting from dysfunctional to functional self-talk that I explained in chapter 3.

CONCLUSION

Setbacks in mastering a task or pursuing a goal often inflict doubt—a "can't-do" mind-set. Helping your employees see the relationship between what they do and the outcome they can expect (called *outcome expectancy*) plus increasing their confidence (their *self-efficacy*) that a task will be accomplished—that the goal will indeed be attained—instills a "can-do" mind-set. Applying these two concepts, outcome expectancy and self-efficacy, will enable you to instill resilience when one or more people on your team suffer setbacks.

The empathy box enables you to gather evidence on the outcomes employees expect. To the extent that you understand what these expected outcomes are, you will understand why employees say what they say, why they do what they do. Change the outcomes a person expects and you will change that person's behavior. The empathy box is a great tool for you to use in gaining goal commitment, in getting people to embrace rather than resist change.

If feelings of pessimism have infected one or more people on your team, ask the kinds of questions that force an examination of the evidence showing why these feelings are inappropriate:

- Global versus specific (for example, everything is wrong versus one thing is wrong)

- Enduring versus temporary (for example, the effects of this mess will last forever versus the effects will last at most a week, month, or quarter)

- Situational factors (for example, this is all my fault versus all we need are the following resources)

Feelings of helplessness and pessimism are learned. Fortunately for you and your team, so is resilience.

QUESTIONS

1. How do you define resilience?

2. What is meant by the term outcome expectancy?

3. How would you apply the empathy box to real-world issues?

4. What is meant by the term self-efficacy?

5. How are self-efficacy and self-esteem different?

6. What are the different ways to increase an individual's self-efficacy?

7. What three questions can you ask an employee to develop learned optimism?

MAKE GOOD
DECISIONS

As human beings, many of us are prone to procrastination. We avoid making decisions in fear that we will make bad ones. This fear is often justified. We place blame for ineffective performance on an individual without taking into account the situation. Our decisions are often contaminated by biases. We are stymied by issues that bewilder us. Hence our preference to avoid making a decision. When we do summon the courage to make a decision, we frequently let our emotions cloud our judgment. The purpose of this chapter is to provide evidence from the behavioral sciences on ways to cope with these issues so as to improve the quality of your decisions.

FOCUS ON THE SITUATION FIRST

When we observe an employee, we are likely to attribute the reasons for that person's behavior to personal characteristics (e.g., conscientious, careless, agreeable, toxic) rather than to situational factors. When we learn that our organization is on the verge of bankruptcy, most of us attribute it to incompetent senior managers (e.g., flawed judgments). In short, most human beings attribute undesirable behavior to the failings of an individual or team. In doing so, we may be misdiagnosing the issue. This misdiagnosis, because it is made by so many of us, has a name: "the fundamental attribution error." That is, we overattribute the cause of someone's behavior to their traits and characteristics without considering the power of the environment to shape behavior. The solution to this error is to examine the context, that is, situational factors, for an explanation of your employee's behavior before attributing causes to that individual.

Consider, for a moment, the fact that your star employees as well as your CEO frequently are not as successful in another organization as they were in your organization. This is because the situational factors, such as market dynamics, interpersonal relationships, and the deep knowledge that they had in your organization often no longer exist in their new organization. With regard to your CEO, people are predisposed to point to leadership or the lack thereof to explain the organization's successes and failures. They overlook situational factors. Yet there are almost always situational factors that explain many of the "whys," that is, the root causes for the decisions CEOs make and their subsequent behavior. This is ironic in that we as human beings are also predisposed to the "self-serving bias," namely, explaining away our own ineffective decisions and behavior due to situational factors.

In summary to this point, when looking for causes of poor decisions made by an employee, first do an analysis of the situation; second, look at the individual or team for what they did or did not do.

I had a client who was frustrated continuously with the HR director they promoted from within the organization. They then hired a HR star from one company followed by a HR star from another company. Finally, they put in a line manager to head HR. Ten months later I asked how the line manager was doing. "How HR could ruin such a good man in so short a time we will never understand." The problem here was not the person; the problem was the situation, specifically, the mission and reward structure for

FURTHER EVIDENCE

Charles Duhigg reported in the *New York Times* that Google found that "the who [was on the team] part of the equation didn't seem to matter." Instead they found that building group norms was the key.

the HR department in general, and the HR director's role in particular (see chapter 2 on metrics). So, what I am asking you to do as an evidence-based manager is to look at the situational factors that influence the decisions that are at issue before looking at individuals. In the above example of the HR director, the same mistake was repeated and repeated: replacing one HR star with another HR star to solve the problem of an HR department that was not seen as responsive to the line managers. The solution was to change the environment, the mission, and the measurement system for assessing the HR department's effectiveness.

The research evidence is clear. If you want better decision outcomes, design different job environments. In changing the environment, you will change your employees' behavior. To build a high-performing team, you must build a work environment where your employees have clear goals, can speak without fear of reprisal, and can trust the people around them to be dependable and supportive.

The above evidence suggests the following three action steps for improving your decisions regarding employee performance.

1. Before assigning fault to one or more individuals, examine the situation.

2. Create contextual "containers" that encourage appropriate behavior.

3. Tell stories to your team that signal what is valued, where to start in diagnosing human resource problems, and the

behavior on your team that is appreciated. Employees are prone to internalizing a memorable story.[1]

Nearly half of all organizational decisions fail to lead to goal attainment.[2] This is due to managers rushing to judgment, imposing their preferred solutions, ignoring uncertainty, downplaying risks, and discouraging a search for alternatives. Fortunately, there are six additional evidence-based practices that minimize bias when making decisions.[3]

1. To avoid the pitfall of solving the wrong problem, such as focusing first on the individual rather than the environment or context, start with a search to find the correct decision frame. Ask lots of questions until you thoroughly understand the issue.

2. Address the politics, including those that are subtle. Is there a "decision sponsor"? If yes, what are the individual's biases and interests? Appeals to broader interests and superordinate goals can often help frame an issue in a legitimate way. This in turn can broaden the problem you and your team are tackling, and ultimately generate additional options and choices.

3. Generate several distinct alternatives. When only one alternative is considered, it is almost certain that important information is being ignored. Give systematic attention to the upsides and downsides of each alternative, including the odds of the success of each one.

4. Use multiple criteria for defining success. As Albert Einstein stated, not everything that can be counted counts, and not everything that counts can be counted. Having several criteria for defining success deepens the evaluation of each alternative. Consequently, you and your team are likely to deliberate the upsides and downsides of each alternative rather than be tempted to go with intuition.

5. Take into account all the stakeholders rather than a select few. Doing so will improve decision making due to an increase in your understanding of the issues, including those with regard to implementation. Moreover, this step will help you address such questions as who will benefit, who will be the losers, what other actions might be possible, and what are the implementation challenges.

6. Use more than one type of information from multiple sources, and then appraise how good each source is. This action step will minimize the likelihood of you being swayed by tradition, such as past practices, and the opinions of powerful people. Gather information from multiple sources, including scientific evidence, company records, shared experiences of team members, and expert judgment. In gathering this information, the key question is: What would you like to know? The quality of the information you gather depends on how well it suits the purpose for which you collected it.

Three Decision Processes

Choosing the appropriate decision process will increase the odds of making a good decision. The three processes address routine, non-routine and novel decisions. The first is characterized by relatively stable cause-effect connections. The second is more complicated in that no one has all the information required for an informed decision, but the information exists somewhere. The third is where the actual information required to make an informed decision does not exist (e.g., starting a business in an emerging market).

A key to making excellent routine decisions is to collect the facts on how the decision is currently made, evaluate its actions, and determine whether the routine can be improved. Developing a standardized checklist will help ensure that effective results are obtained consistently.

For nonroutine decisions, follow the six actions steps described above (e.g., ask lots of questions to ensure the problem has been framed correctly, take into account politics, identify stakeholders). In addition, conduct "after action reviews" to reflect on the processes that were used, the assumptions, and the implications. Denise Rousseau, an organizational psychologist, suggests answering the following four questions: (1) What did we set out to do? (2) What happened? (3) Why did it happen? (4) What are we going to do next time? Reflection typically leads to an improvement in your decisions.

Novel problems are sometimes called wicked problems not only because they are ill-defined, but because they are characterized as so confusing due to incomplete information, multiple stakeholders with conflicting values, and a lack of clarity regarding the ramifications of different solutions.[4] Solving a wicked problem requires the integration of three spheres (logic, empathy, and ethics) and syncretizing the dualities within each sphere.

Integration. The first step in tackling a wicked problem is to integrate logic, empathy, and the ethics embedded in a decision. Appeal to logic with your audience through reasoned arguments and evidence-based or hard objective data. Surface the values of your audience so as to tap into their empathy. Pay attention to ways of adding value to the human condition. Show that you are able to appreciate how your target audience thinks and feels. In other words, show that you understand the needs, motives, and interests of the different stakeholders that will be impacted by a decision. Doing so will contribute to their long-term commitment to a decision.

With regard to ethicality, tease out the ethical principles underlying a proposed decision. Sift through a decision's layers by examining it from different angles so as to recognize the different principles that come into play.

Syncretize. The second major step to solving a wicked problem is to syncretize, that is, make congruent the dualities in each of the above three spheres. The main duality in the sphere of logic is explicit versus tacit knowledge. Explicit knowledge, typified by scientific reasoning, can be codified and articulated. But integrating tacit or contextual knowledge (e.g., years of experience) with explicit knowledge increases the sense-making of a wicked problem. Another duality in the logic sphere is knowledge versus doubt. To be wise is to be aware of one's limitations and to be skeptical so as not to be overly confident that you have found the answers.

Empathy with stakeholders needs to be congruent with its opposite, detachment. Detachment is necessary in making a decision so as not to become overwhelmed by the emotions that often bubble up in a sticky situation.

Ethicality requires leaning in favor of "enlightened self-interest" that stems from a moral high ground consistent with the norms and mores of the culture or situation where the final decision will be made. Recall that Tim Cook, the CEO of Apple, in his interaction with the FBI was required to decide between two equally fundamental values for the people in the United States, namely, the value to be free versus the value to be safe.

Roadblocks to wise decisions. There are at least five roadblocks to making a wise decision: (1) thinking only about the short term, (2) an emphasis on speed in making a decision, (3) working in silos, (4) the reward system, and (5) employee turnover.

Wisdom requires taking the long-term implications of a decision into account. An axiom to keep in mind is to endure short-term pain for long-term gain. An emphasis on speed for "getting on with it" exacerbates the problem of working in silos. Speed almost always leads to ill-thought-through decisions. It is a primary cause of "groupthink" (see chapter 2). Working within silos in your organization prevents the different teams within each silo from seeing diverse points of view, let alone gaining experience in ways to reconcile them.

The scandals at Enron and Volkswagen highlight unwise decisions with regard to reward systems. Reward systems, as well as a focus on speedy decisions with little or no concern for long-term implications, facilitated unethical behavior. And as a result of employee turnover, institutional memory is often lost unless it has been codified into your organization's routines.

The role of emotions. Emotions affect the decisions we make regardless of whether they are relevant to the problem we are contemplating. There are three strategies that will help you use emotion to aid rather than detract from good decision making. Suppressing an unwanted emotion is not one of them.[5]

Suppressing an emotion is counterproductive in that it typically backfires. Attempts at suppression intensify it. Moreover, suppression comes at a cognitive cost. Our brain has a limited capacity for simultaneous processing. While trying to suppress an emotion, we distract ourselves from paying attention to the facts at hand. Hence, we are prone to making a bad decision regarding an issue we are dealing with. So, if suppression is not the answer, what should we do?

The first strategy is to use what behavioral scientists refer to as choice architecture. By that we mean create a system that minimizes the likelihood of an emotion influencing a decision. For example, many states in the United States require a delay between buying a gun or purchasing a marriage license and taking ownership of the gun or getting married. The message is for you to have a "cooling off period" before making the final decision, let alone executing it.

A second example of choice architecture is the anticipation of knowing you must justify your decision to others. Doing so will lead you to focus critically on important diagnostic information rather than dwell on your emotions, as you will want to be able to explain your reasons on rational grounds. In short, this step institutes accountability for the decision you make. Self-critical and effortful thinking occurs when the views of your audience are unknown, but you do know that the audience (a) wants accuracy, (b) is interested in hearing the decision process, (c) is reasonably well-informed of the issue, and (d) has legitimate concerns.

A second strategy for dealing with emotions is called cognitive reappraisal, that is, reframing an event or action by adopting a different mind-set. This strategy (e.g., putting yourself in another's shoes) can be effective even for resolving intergroup conflicts.

The third strategy is to harness a complementary emotion that will enable you to shift your focus to the potential long-term effects of a decision. Research has shown that writing down each day a few things for which you are grateful improves your psychological, physical, and financial outcomes.

Reducing a penchant for inaction. Sometimes the thought of having to make a decision is so overwhelming that a manager may choose inaction in order to avoid making a wrong decision. Inaction when confronting wicked problems can be appropriate if there is little or no cost for waiting and the probability is relatively high that a delay will allow for a gain in information that will reduce ambiguity. If this is not the case, inaction is dysfunctional. To minimize inaction that is dysfunctional, consider the following four steps.[6]

First, when an issue needing resolution is presented, require people to be accountable for their inactions as well as actions. Requiring people to be accountable only for the actions taken can predispose them to put off making a decision.

Second, require a discussion of the consequences of not making a decision as well as the consequences of decision alternatives. Highlighting the consequences of inaction minimizes the likelihood of not making a decision being perceived as a less harmful option than making a decision.

Third, compare and evaluate various decision possibilities without presenting "no decision" as an option. As an example, Coren and Bazerman explain how asking an HR department to compare and contrast different types of affirmative action programs and then to recommend one is preferable to asking HR to decide whether to implement such a program.

A fourth way to avoid the inclination not to make a decision is to share responsibility for the decision. This approach to making tough decisions, especially those with a moral dilemma, diffuses the anticipated burden of having chosen the wrong option. Having multiple individuals or teams accountable for a decision mitigates the focus of blame on an unfortunate few if something goes wrong.

CONCLUSION

To make good decisions, we must first take into account the context or environment where the issue calling for a decision is required. We must learn how to deal with routinized situations calling for a decision, nonroutinized situations, and wicked problems. The latter requires integration of three spheres of a problem and then making congruent the dualities within each sphere. We must also become aware of how our emotions influence our decisions and the different ways to use them to increase the likelihood of making a good decision. Finally, we must learn ways to overcome our penchant to avoid making a decision when doing so leads to harm.

QUESTIONS

1. What is the fundamental attribution error?

2. Why should you focus on the situation first and the employee second to understand performance effectiveness or ineffectiveness?

3. What are three steps you can take to improve your judgments on ways to increase your employees' performance?

4. What are six evidence-based practices that minimize bias when making decisions?

5. What are three decision-making processes that will increase your odds of making a good decision?

6. What is a wicked problem? How would you go about making decisions regarding a wicked problem?

7. How do emotions affect the decisions you make?

8. What are three strategies for using emotions to make a good decision?

9. What is the danger of inaction when a decision is required?

10. What are the ways of overcoming the desire to avoid making a decision?

APPRAISE *AND* COACH YOUR EMPLOYEES TO BE HIGH PERFORMERS

Ironically, one of the most widely used management tools of all time—the performance appraisal—often does exactly the opposite of what it's supposed to do: It often discourages rather than motivates employees. An article published in *Public Personnel Management* concluded that a performance appraisal is given by someone who doesn't want to give it to someone who doesn't want to get it.[1] A study reported in that same journal showed that poorly implemented performance appraisals increase employee burnout.[2]

Many types of appraisals, including bottom-line and trait-based measures, frequently fail to deliver desired results in employee productivity. Yet organization after organization, manager after manager, still use the performance appraisal system as the primary tool for managing employees. Unlike many of their counterparts, evidence-based managers know that performance management needs to start with the right kind of appraisal, then center on committed, ongoing coaching.

When employees feel they have been judged on the wrong criteria by the wrong people, or that their appraisal is based more on the biases of their boss than it is on what they are doing or have done on the job, their performance suffers. In contrast, coaching— ongoing performance management—paired with the right kind of appraisal instrument has a good chance of improving employee performance. Just as sports coaches give feedback many times a day from multiple sources (for example, assistant coaches), evidence-based managers know the importance of providing ongoing feedback in the workplace from multiple sources. Here are four keys to appraising and coaching:

- Choose the right appraisal tool.

- Be fair—minimize your biases.

- Get feedback about an employee from multiple sources.

- Coach, coach, coach (don't just appraise).

WHAT WORKS, IN BRIEF

Performance appraisals have two overall purposes. The first is administrative. They produce a written document for justifying who will be promoted, demoted, or laid off, and for explaining who will get no pay raise, a moderate pay raise, or a large one. The second and arguably the more important reason for performance appraisals is developmental and motivational. They are done as a means of instilling in employees the desire for continuous improvement.

Appraisals—What to Use

Appraisal instruments are not all created equal. The kind of appraisal instrument you select, and the people who do the appraisal, can dramatically affect the performance of your team. Some tools generate positive changes, while others, such as a trait scale that assesses attitudes or personality (applying labels such as "aggressive") can actually do harm.

Appraisals based on behavioral criteria linked to your organization's strategy provide the best platform for reviewing performance. Research in Israel, the Netherlands, and my own research in the United States shows that appraisal tools based on observable

FURTHER EVIDENCE

The courts dislike trait scales because traits are too vague and subjective. They don't help an employee figure out what to start, stop, or continue doing.[3] A series of studies have shown that behavioral observation scales (BOS) correlate with measures of employee productivity. They are defensible in the courtroom because they are based on a systematic job analysis and because they focus on observable behavior as opposed to personality traits.[4]

behavior, called *behavioral observation scales* (BOS), are well-liked by both coaches and the people being coached.[5] This type of appraisal conveys precisely what a person must do to be effective, and the feedback is perceived by employees as factual, objective, and unbiased. Most important, feedback based on observable behavior helps to clarify and set SMART goals. And BOS appraisals foster behavioral improvements, in part because they help employees identify and resolve their own performance problems.

Avoid bottom-line measures, trait-based scales, and electronic performance management.

There are three appraisal types to avoid: bottom-line measures, trait-based scales, and electronic performance management. These tools fall short in helping an employee understand what to start doing, keep doing, or stop doing—a key characteristic of an effective appraisal.

The Fair Manager

Whether we want to admit it or not, we all bring biases to the table. Which is why, as an evidence-based manager, you must become aware of your own biases and know how to set them aside. A massive study looked at ratings of more than 4,000 managers with self-appraisals and appraisals from at least two supervisors, two peers, and two subordinates. The results showed that the idiosyncrasies and biases of an appraiser influence the ratings that appraiser provides. The US Army too found that a person's knowledge and ability only partially explained ratings in appraisals from a supervisor and peers.[6] Another study revealed that if the supervisor held the person in high regard, it resulted in both positive leniency and "halo" errors, which occur when a person who is good at one thing is assessed as being good at everything. Other studies have found that similarities between the subordinate and the supervisor inflate appraisals.[7] Which is to say, we like people like ourselves, and then we give them high ratings. This is especially true when we perceive people to be like ourselves with regard to extroversion, conscientiousness, and emotional stability.[8]

It's important that you, as an evidence-based manager, keep an eye out for your own bias in the appraisal process (it will likely save you legal trouble later) and create a system of checks and balances that will outweigh, if not eliminate, that bias. You are more likely to be seen as fair if you base your appraisals on observable behaviors and seek feedback on an employee's performance from multiple sources. By doing so, you'll avoid the bias trap and develop employees who see you as trustworthy.

Get Feedback from Multiple Sources

An appraisal from your perspective as manager is unlikely to provide a comprehensive picture of an employee's performance. Instead, for the best appraisal results, you'll want to gather information on an employee from a range of sources: you, your employees' peers, your employees' subordinates, and the employees themselves (called self-appraisal). In this way, you will get the fullest picture of an employee's performance.

Feedback from multiple sources, known as *360-degree appraisal* (boss, peer, and subordinate ratings) correlates highly with bottom-line performance measures (for example, retail store revenue and gross margins).[9] Another study has shown that

> **FURTHER EVIDENCE**
>
> To be effective as a leader, you not only need to be fair, you must be seen by the people who report to you as fair. A key driver of fairness is perceived justice in the interactions between you and your direct reports. To earn the trust of the people on your team, you must be sincere and you must explain the logic for the actions you take. People don't have to agree with you; they do have to understand the basis of your appraisal of them. It is incumbent on you to get that understanding.[10]

managers who take action to improve their own performance based on multisource feedback see a decrease in employee turnover and an increase in the quality of service. This same study showed that 360-degree feedback accurately distinguishes between high- and low-performing managers.[11]

Coach Your Team to Success

More than periodic appraisals, though, your team needs cyclical, year-round coaching to achieve the high performance that you want and your organization demands.

A study in *Public Personnel Management* showed that providing a combination of executive coaching and training increased employee productivity by 88 percent.[12] The improvements in employee behavior occurred when managers challenged their employees daily and instilled in them the confidence that they had the ability to expand their talents to attain desired goals.

APPRAISAL AND COACHING TOOLS IN PRACTICE

So how can you use this management evidence in your own appraisal and coaching of employees? Read on.

Tools to Use: Observable Behavior

You can find good appraisal tools out there—but they may not be the kind of appraisals you're used to giving (or required by HR to give). A wide body of research has shown certain appraisal instruments to be more effective than others in improving employee performance. The first key to creating the most effective appraisal instrument for your organization lies in using appraisals based on *observable behaviors* that are directly linked to executing your organization's strategy. These behaviors are identified in a job analysis, the critical incident technique described in chapter 1.

Behavioral observation scales reduce ambiguity by making explicit what an employee should start doing, keep doing, or stop doing to be effective. By using a BOS as you appraise your employees, you as an evidence-based manager and coach can figure out what people are doing well and spot what they can do to improve their performance. It is an effective diagnostic instrument because of the way that it focuses your attention, as well as your employees' attention, on those areas that move your team's strategy from words to action. See figure 4 for an example of a behavioral observation scale.

Development of a behavioral observation scale should be embedded in the larger development of organizational strategy. It's useful to look at how this particular appraisal tool and strategy are linked. First, consider the following questions, which can be used to develop an organization's strategy:

- How can we create new and different advantages in the marketplace?

- How can we create fundamentally new and valuable customer experiences?

- How can we increase levels of credibility and trust?

- How can we leverage competencies across corporate entities or divisions?

FIGURE 4. A BEHAVIORAL OBSERVATION
SCALE FOR MANAGERS

Behavior: Team-playing

1. Invites the input of team members on issues that will directly affect them before making a decision.

Almost Never   0   1   2   3   4   Almost Always

2. Explains to employees the rationale behind directives, decisions, and policies that may or will affect other divisions.

Almost Never   0   1   2   3   4   Almost Always

3. Keeps fellow managers informed of major changes in the department regarding people, policies, projects, construction, and so on.

Almost Never   0   1   2   3   4   Almost Always

4. Continually seeks input of fellow managers as a group on capital policy and plans rather than engaging primarily in interactions with individual managers.

Almost Never   0   1   2   3   4   Almost Always

5. Is open to criticism and questioning of decisions from fellow managers.

Almost Never   0   1   2   3   4   Almost Always

Each of these questions leads to answers that dictate what employees must start doing, keep doing, or stop doing. Besides being clear about your strategy, you must be equally clear about the behavior required to implement it.

Keep these three things in mind when picking which behaviors to assess in the behavioral observation scale:

- The behaviors you assess must be observable.

- They must be within an employee's control.

- They must be critical to the implementation of your organization's strategy.

For example, there is no point in assessing an employee on a characteristic such as "thinks carefully before acting." Such behavior is not observable. Behavioral scales

> *The behaviors you appraise should be critical to strategy execution.*

should focus on behaviors such as "consults stakeholders before taking actions that affect them." Such behavior is not only observable but under an employee's control. The behaviors you appraise should also be critical to strategy execution. Performance management is capable of bringing your team and department strategy to life as long as you make sure to assess the behaviors that matter most to the implementation of that strategy.

Tools to Avoid

As noted, for a variety of reasons, I recommend you avoid three often-used appraisal types: bottom-line measures, trait-based scales, and electronic performance monitoring. Here's a brief look at the inherent weaknesses of each of these appraisal tools.

Bottom-Line Measures

Bottom-line measures often take the form of "management by objectives" (known as MBO). This approach asks, "Were goals X, Y, and Z attained? Were they done on time? Was the quality satisfactory?" The relevance of such questions is difficult to challenge. They are reasonably objective, making it likely that two or more appraisers will reach the same conclusion regarding performance. Still, bottom-line measures leave much to be desired when used as the primary appraisal on which to base coaching an employee.

To start, when receiving a "good" appraisal is contingent on attaining certain goals, a smart employee may find ingenious ways to ensure that the goals are easy. Second, bottom-line measures can be affected by factors beyond a person's control (for example, an increase or decrease in the value of the dollar), and as a result an employee may be unfairly penalized or rewarded. Bottom-line measures are also poor for assessing factors that are crucial to a team's success yet go beyond concrete numbers (for example, courteous customer service, constructive teamwork). Finally, bottom-line measures yield no information about what a person should start doing, keep doing, or stop doing to execute strategy with excellence. So while this appraisal tool can sound appealing, the drawbacks outweigh the benefits. Such measures can be appropriate for assessing the team as a whole, but not an individual on the team.[13]

Trait-Based Scales

Trait-based scales are used to assess attitude and personality variables such as commitment, creativity, loyalty, and initiative. Yet they provide little insight to the person being coached. Unless the traits are defined behaviorally, they are too vague, subjective, and ambiguous to be useful. I have seen many cases where people are appraised on "commitment"; everyone gets "good," and no one knows why. Without workable definitions of commitment and other apparently desirable traits, this appraisal tool reflects little more than the caprice of the appraiser. As the late management guru Peter Drucker said more than a quarter of a century ago: "An employer has no business with a man's personality. Management and manager development should concern themselves with changes in behavior likely to make a man more effective."[14]

Electronic Performance Monitoring

An emerging trend in performance management is to bypass appraisal formats altogether and rely instead on EPM (electronic performance monitoring), a tool used to continuously monitor employees by audio or video. EPM is used widely in call centers, where employees' every conversation is tracked by software. Another common use of EPM is for tracking speed and accuracy in data entry jobs. Many organizations praise EPM because it allegedly enforces performance standards and tracks tardiness and because data logging makes sure that appraisals are based on recorded facts.

Despite these advantages, the use of EPM usually results in an increase in job-related stress, which can lead to illness, which in turn leads to absenteeism, job dissatisfaction, and turnover.[15] In addition, EPM removes control over the type and scope of information an employee shares with others. Consequently, EPM changes the basic nature of personal relationships in your workplace, which in turn can trigger strong negative reactions among the people on your team.

Who Appraises: Information from a Range of Sources

The type of appraisal isn't all that matters; it's also important *who* provides the appraisal. The appraisal should combine reviews from *multiple sources* including you the manager, an employee's peers, subordinates, and the employees themselves. Gathering information from a range of sources—using what's called a "360-degree appraisal"—is key to producing a complete, relatively accurate picture of an employee's performance.

> *How employees interact with you is not necessarily how they behave with colleagues.*

Anyone who has seen children in action knows that how kids interact with one group of people (for example, friends) is not necessarily how they interact with another group of people (their parents, babysitters, or siblings). Moreover, how children behave on the playground is unlikely to yield clues as to how they behave in the classroom, let alone in the home. The answer to "Who is my child?" is "All of the above." The same is true for the people you manage: How they interact with you is not necessarily how they behave with their colleagues or subordinates.

For that reason, perceptions of an employee's performance often vary among subordinates, peers, and supervisors, so multisource feedback can provide an integrated, holistic view of an employee, offsetting the biases of an appraisal from any single vantage point. An article in *HR Magazine* reported that upwards of 90 percent of Fortune 1000 firms, including DuPont, General Electric, Motorola, Procter & Gamble, and United Parcel Service now use multisource feedback in employee appraisals.[16]

It's natural that in a 360-degree appraisal, the feedback from different parties will be different, because each person observes an employee in a different context. Typically, an assessment from a supervisor tends to agree with assessments by peers, whereas an employee's self-ratings and assessments from subordinates show the least agreement. In other words, your boss and your peers probably agree about your performance, but your subordinates may assess you very differently from the way you assess yourself.[17] The picture that 360-degree appraisals provide is both more complete and more accurate than relying on just your perspective. Nevertheless, each perspective in an appraisal has pros and cons that you need to be aware of.

Manager Appraisal: Watch for Your Biases

As an evidence-based manager, you need to recognize how your appraisal ratings can be affected by factors that have little or nothing to do with an employee's performance. Here are some things to watch out for:

- **Bias based on accepted social norms.** One potential area for bias relates to whether an employee conforms to mainstream social norms. Interestingly, in this new millennium, people who smoke are rated lower than nonsmokers on their professional behavior, how well they work with others, and their dependability. Smokers are viewed as wasting valuable time as a result of taking smoking breaks.[18] I don't smoke and probably share this bias, but if I'm an evidence-based manager I will not rate a person with average performance more highly than an individual with high performance just because the latter individual smokes.

- **Bias based on gender.** Even now, when women have risen to the highest levels of the corporate hierarchy, men are typically evaluated as more effective than women. Even when males and females demonstrate the same leadership behavior, women are often devalued when the appraisers are male. However, it is also true that the composition of a group of workers in terms of gender can also affect appraisal results.

  In one study of a large group of people in which there were only a few females, the appraisers reported that the men possessed the motivation and leadership qualities necessary for effective performance, whereas the women possessed feminine attitudes that impaired their performance. Yet, *there were no performance differences between men and women on any objective measure.* In another study, the performance of women was rated higher than that of men when there were more women in the group than men.[19]

- **Bias against top performers.** Many managers make the mistake of hesitating to give a top performer the top marks that person deserves. They'll give an 8 out of 10 or maybe even a 9 out of 10—but never a 10 out of 10. The underlying assumption is that people who receive high evaluations will rest on their laurels. As a psychologist, teacher, and parent, I can assure you that the assumption is not true. If someone deserves a 10 on a 10-point scale, rate the person a 10—then watch this individual sweat as there is no place to go but down. The self-imposed pressure of a high performer

An Insurance Company Ends Leniency

In the 1990s, Metropolitan Life Insurance had been showing poor returns relative to competitors for years. Performance reviews were essentially a farce because bonuses were awarded to virtually everyone regardless of their performance. When Robert Benmosche assumed the role of CEO of the organization in 1998, this leniency in appraisals and bonuses was called to a halt. Those who exceeded expectations, rated 4 or 5, received bonuses 46 percent higher than employees rated 3. Those grade-3 employees were awarded bonuses 68 percent higher than those rated 1 or 2. As Lisa Weber, the senior VP and chief administrative officer, reported, "When you treat your top performers like the stars they are, you will get their loyalty forever, and that's what it's all about. When you have their loyalty, you get the production, and that is how the organization can win from within."[20]

requires that individual to continue to work hard to ensure excellence.

Another way to violate employees' perceptions of fairness is to rate everyone's performance as high. Although a non-evidence-based manager will typically do this to be well liked, the result is often the opposite. A team will see the injustice when only a few people are truly high performers and others are definitely not.

FURTHER EVIDENCE

A study in the *Journal of Business and Psychology* reported that many managers are so uncomfortable conducting appraisals that they give all the people on their team a high rating. Consequently, employees experience dissatisfaction with the process of their performance assessment—and with the decisions made as a result of their performance assessment.[21]

Here's a look at an organization example:

Ensuring that your employees perceive the appraisal and coaching process as fair means checking your biases at the door. This isn't always easy. Research suggests the following three-step procedure is effective:[22]

1. Working in groups of five managers, define an error (for example, similar-to-me bias, halo, leniency, stereotyping).

2. Give an example of where each of you has made this error or has seen it made by others. Be specific.

3. Brainstorm concrete ways you will avoid these errors in the future.

Not doing so could result in your getting a call from the legal department. But don't despair as you consider all of these downsides. *Personnel Psychology* published a study showing that managers are helpful despite the biases they bring to a performance appraisal of the people on their teams. Performance was found to increase significantly more in those years in which managers conducted appraisals than in those years when they skipped doing them.[23]

Peer Appraisal

Peer appraisals have grown increasingly common as teams have become a way of life in organizational settings. Anonymous peer evaluations are among the best predictors of how well a given employee will perform in a training program and subsequently on the job. This is because peers often have more job-relevant information about someone than any other source, including managers. In fact, many managers spend less than 1 percent of their time observing their subordinates.[24] Consequently, another reason why appraisals can fail to improve performance is employee hostility toward the appraiser—you. Difficulty in answering satisfactorily such questions as "On what basis are you able to evaluate me?" undermines your credibility as an appraiser. Peers, on the other hand, typically see an employee's good and bad qualities daily. Peers see how well an employee accepts responsibility and seeks challenges on a day-to-day basis. Making team members responsible for appraising and coaching one another can improve group cohesion and performance, openness of communication, employee motivation, and group satisfaction.[25]

This straightforward appraisal process offers one way to use peer appraisals to bring about positive behavior changes in your team:

1. Have employees evaluate one another anonymously on each behavior.

2. Calculate the average rating.

3. Meet as a group and, focusing on one person and one behavior at a time, ask: "What is [name] doing well in this area? What is the one behavior you'd like to see [name] improve upon?"

Note that you do not ask who gave whom which rating. Your focus is solely on reinforcing behaviors that are effective and changing those that are viewed by peers as ineffective. The focus is twofold: on present positive behaviors—the current "well dones"—and on future positive changes needed for improvement. Avoid delving into the past; past behaviors can't be undone. Starting a conversation—or worse, an argument—about the past is likely to put your employee or team on the defensive.

Peers are among the most reliable and valid sources of information about a person's performance.

The peer assessment ends with each person setting three to five specific behavioral goals for changing certain behaviors on their own. Three to six months later, you should meet again with the group to assess goal attainment and then set new behavioral goals.

Although I use this process frequently with senior managers, I have also found it to be effective with hourly people and union leadership.

Subordinate Appraisal

Few of us fail to see the value of listening to our customers and anticipating their needs. So why would you fail to see the value of listening to your employees and anticipating their needs? A critical variable affecting customer relations is your treatment of your employees.[26] At Disney World the philosophy is: "Our guests [customers] will only receive the quality of service our cast members [employees] receive." To be seen as fair, you must be responsive to your employees' needs. As stressed in chapter 4 on motivation, doing so generates better performance. It's also a way to attract talented people.[27]

Collect anonymous feedback on each of your employees from their subordinates. Often called upward feedback, subordinate appraisal is shown to lead to a significant improvement in a manager's behavior.[28] Sometimes the feedback is negative, but don't worry. The research shows that those managers who receive feedback that is more negative than their own self-evaluation show the greatest level of subsequent improvement.[29] Furthermore, these positive behavior changes have been shown to last over time. This is especially true for managers who have high self-efficacy, who believe that they can change for the better.[30]

At the Weyerhaeuser Company, the hourly people and their union stewards were highly objective in providing upward feedback, especially when behavioral observation scales were used. They'd say, "Doc, we gave that *** Sandy a high score despite the fact that Sandy is an ***."

Later, the union stewards suggested, "Let's get that *** Sandy involved in this project."

I asked, "Why would you want an *** involved?" "Because he's honest," they replied.

Their vulgarity reflected the fact that Sandy often disagreed with them and said so. Consequently, Sandy was seen as trustworthy, although not always agreeable.

For managers, I recommend categorizing feedback from subordinates into four piles and then sharing the data with the raters:

Pile 1: Positive Feedback. For this pile say, "Thank you. I appreciate your recognition and support." If there are instances where you want clarification, ask for it: "You rated me higher on behavioral item No. 8 than I rated myself. Tell me what I am doing well so I will continue to do so."

Pile 2: No Action. It is unlikely that you will take action on everything that is asked of you. However, you must explain to your people why. For example, middle and senior managers who are paying top dollar to be enrolled in our executive MBA program often argue that I should dispense with the final exam. "No way," I reply. "The moment the street decides that the E in your EMBA degree stands for 'easy' rather than 'executive,' your degree becomes worthless. The exam is on Friday." The managers quickly understand this logic.

Pile 3: Done Deal. This is the feedback you will act on immediately. For example, if I get feedback suggesting that I should show up for an EMBA class 15 or 20 minutes early so the managers can talk to me, that's a done deal. I'll be there.

Pile 4: Help Needed. Some feedback requires me to ask for help: "I agree with the feedback, but I need your help in making the change." If my students ask me to give them more discussion time in class, but also to cover additional subject matter, I'll need their help since that appears to be a conflict for the same limited resource: time.

Among the many benefits of taking positive action based on input from subordinates is the social norm of reciprocity. If people see their manager making changes based on their input, they are likely to make changes based on their manager's input.

A *word of caution*. Don't seek the input of your subordinates unless you intend to take their feedback seriously. Failing to do so will worsen your relationship with them.

> **Don't seek input from subordinates unless you intend to take feedback seriously.**

And don't be afraid to toot your horn when you do make a change based on their input. Human beings are notoriously closed-minded. My wife is forever saying that I fail to take out the garbage. To get her to see otherwise, I need to let her know each time I do so, for several months, before I can hope to get her to change her mind on this issue. The same phenomenon occurs in the workplace.

Self-Appraisal

Not surprisingly, our self-appraisals are less accurate than those from other sources. Self-appraisals not only have the weakest agreement ratings from other sources (from peers and supervisors), they have the lowest ability to predict our own subsequent performance.[31] However, intriguing research has shown that if your self-appraisal is in agreement with the appraisals you receive from others, you are likely to become a high performer.[32] Such a correlation is a good indication of high self-awareness, which in turn is a good indication of your ability to see the effect of your actions on others (what the researchers call *outcome expectancies*). The problem with self-appraisals is that highly competent employees underestimate their performance and less competent employees tend to overestimate theirs. To develop an effective self-appraisal system for your employees, use the same BOS that you used in collecting information from peers and subordinates.

Coach Your Team to Success

Once you know which appraisal tools get the best marks and which to steer clear of, you can use those appraisals as the basis for coaching the people on your team.

Even the best performance appraisals have their limits. All appraisals should serve only as the starting point of performance management—and there is no substitute for ongoing coaching as the most effective way to manage a team's performance over time. You don't just want to evaluate your people, you want to develop their ability to succeed through ongoing coaching. Evidence-based managers know that to raise the performance bar, they must coach their team *every day.*

There is no substitute for ongoing coaching.

What makes a good performance coach? Among the most important characteristics are an ability to listen, clarify, and explain; an ability to empathize with the employee's thoughts and feelings; and an ability to understand the political and cultural aspects of an organization.[33] Besides these broad characteristics, you can learn three concrete steps to coach your team to success: the "GROW" method, feedback, and a guide to changing employee behavior.

The GROW Method

GROW is an acronym that stands for the four aspects of an effective coach: *goal setting* for the short and long term; *reality checking* to explore the current situation; looking at *options* or different courses of action; and organizing *what* is to be done when. The GROW method can be broken down into a set of questions to ask an employee:

- **Goal**. What do you want to accomplish? Is the goal SMART?

- **Reality**. What is now happening? Who is involved? What are the possibilities and constraints of the situation?

- **Options**. What options do you have?

- **What and when**. What changes need to be made? What support do you need? When does it need to happen?

The GROW method and these questions represent a path to action in coaching the people on your team.

Feedback for Results

A key component of the coaching process is providing feedback to your employees. But take care: Feedback can be a double-edged sword.[34] The right kind of feedback can improve your team's performance; the wrong kind can actually hurt performance. Many managers instinctively fear a negative consequence and, as a result, choose not to give feedback at all. That's a mistake. Evidence-based managers know the difference between helpful and harmful feedback. Here is a five-point checklist for ensuring that the feedback you provide your people will improve their performance:

- **Focus on the behavior rather than the person**. For example, rather than saying, "You are worthless," say, "Please double-check these reports for accuracy before submitting them." If you focus on the person instead of the behavior, your employee is likely to get defensive and become less responsive to your coaching.

- **Give feedback on one or two critical behaviors**. Do not over-whelm someone by giving too much feedback on too many behaviors at once.

- **Focus feedback on desired rather than undesired behaviors**. For example, rather than saying, "You talk too much," emphasize the behavior you want to see by saying, "Listen closely to what the customer is saying to you."

- **Focus on the future, not the past**. No matter what, the events of last week or any other earlier moment in time can't be undone, so do not waste time discussing them unless you are doing so to explain why you are removing the person from your team.

- **Never confuse honesty with hurtfulness**. If your employee feels bad after hearing feedback from you, you haven't done your job well. You've just reduced the effectiveness of both your employee and the team in which this person is a member.

There is a final point that you should keep in mind. It goes back to the goal setting that I've underscored throughout this book: Feedback in the absence of goal setting will have little or no effect on a person's behavior.

Feedback by itself is only information; its effect on an employee's behavior depends on the context in which the feedback is delivered and how it is linked to concrete goals. For feedback to improve behavior, it must be connected with specific, high goals and coupled with employee commitment to attaining those goals.[35] Otherwise feedback goes in one ear and quickly out the other.

> *Feedback in the absence of goal setting has little or no effect.*

10-Step Guide to Changing Employee Behavior

When appraisals and feedback show that change is in order, that's when you can step in to coach your employees to make improvements to their behavior. Don't expect change to come about as the result of a single conversation; real change requires ongoing coaching. Here is a 10-step guide to coaching your employees to change their behavior.

1. Explain the behavior that you have observed or that has been reported to you. Do so without hostility. Be as straightforward as possible. You don't want to put the person on the defensive. If the person does go on the defensive, you will have made your job of coaching extremely difficult.

2. Explain why a change in behavior is necessary. Is the change critical for improving teamwork, meeting a deadline, or implementing strategy? If the person understands your logic and sees you as sincere in wanting to serve as a coach, trust between the two of you is likely.

FURTHER EVIDENCE

Cyclical year-round performance management has been found to increase an organization's performance. A study of over 1,000 senior managers found that those who worked with an executive coach in an organization that used 360-degree feedback set specific, high goals and actively sought feedback on ways to improve their performance. This led to an improvement in the performance ratings they received from their subordinates as well as from their supervisors.[36]

3. Ask your employee for an explanation. For example, is there a personal or medical reason for the behavior? Were you or others wrong in your initial conclusion? If so, stop here.

4. Focus on one behavioral issue at a time. This is important to remember because someone who isn't keen to make a change may quickly try to get you off-topic, or point out other positive behaviors to distract you from the problem at hand. You want to stick to the issue.

5. Ask your employee for solutions on how to change the behavior. As soon as the person offers ideas, that is tantamount to an admission that the problem is worthy of discussion. However, if this employee does not immediately see or understand how the behavior is problematic or how the situation can be resolved, go to step 6.

6. Offer your own solutions. As manager, you may have insights that are lacking in the person you are coaching.

7. Once you've agreed on a solution or solutions, summarize the commitment you hear from your employee. This will help ensure your understanding is mutual and prevent arguments and misunderstandings down the line.

8. Set a follow-up meeting. This sends your employee the signal that there is a goal to attain that requires both commitment and accountability.

9. Document the coaching conversation if it does not go well. You don't need to document every coaching session; the records will get overwhelming. However, if you believe the session went poorly and may lead to disciplinary action, you should document it, as it will show you gave your employee a chance to solve the problem before proceeding to discipline. A note of caution: Keep this document impartial, factual, and free of your personal opinion. Doing otherwise could undermine its value and your perspective as manager.

10. Praise your employee's changed behavior. By simply saying "thank you" or "I appreciate your hard work," you signal to the individual and all those watching that you believe a leopard can change its spots—and are quick to acknowledge it. You will show that you don't carry a grudge and are able to move on; you will show you are an evidence-based manager.

UNCONVENTIONAL PERFORMANCE APPRAISALS

Two new unconventional yet effective ways of conducting performance appraisals are the feedforward interview (FFI) and the use of mystery shoppers. These two alternatives are worthy of your consideration because, as I told you earlier, traditional approaches to conducting a performance appraisal often decrease rather than increase an employee's performance. This in turn leads to a decrease in job satisfaction and organizational commitment. An employee's reaction, in many cases justified, is that the appraisal is often biased and politically motivated. This reaction is exacerbated when the discussion revolves around an employee's mistakes and shortfalls. Little wonder that an employee's subsequent motivation for making a significant contribution to the organization is diminished.

Consequently, Avi Kluger, an organizational psychologist, has developed an alternative to the traditional approaches to conducting appraisals, namely, the feedforward interview. My former doctoral student Marie-Helene Budworth, her doctoral student Laxmikant Manroop, and I conducted research that showed the FFI does indeed increase the job performance of managers over and above a traditional performance review.[37] Moreover, it is viewed by employees as a process that is fair.

Feedforward Interview

What makes the FFI so effective in the eyes of employees is its focus on the positive aspects of their job performance rather than on "what is wrong." This is because the FFI elicits success stories from an employee for the purpose of creating similar experiences in the future, hence the name feedforward.

At the core of the FFI is the fact that eliciting stories from an employee about past successes enables an employee to identify the conditions that will lead to future high performance. Thus, the intent of the FFI is to enable an employee to develop a knowledge base of his or her best practices to draw upon in the future. Research shows that a focus on the strengths, successes, and values of an employee facilitates a positive change in behavior.

The FFI is conducted similarly to the critical incident technique described in chapter 1. First, ask an employee to recall an incident in the past six to 12 months where the employee accomplished something job-related and beneficial for the team or organization. Second, ask the employee to describe exactly what he or she did as well as the outcome. This step focuses on not only a successful outcome, but the behavior, process, and procedure the employee engaged in to attain the desired outcome without compromising the employee's needs or the needs of others.

Note that this second aspect of the FFI is another factor that explains its effectiveness, namely, active listening on your part.

You, as the employee's manager, are putting your opinions aside and are instead listening to fully understand what the employee is describing to you.

A third aspect of the FFI that brings about a positive behavior change is that the employee is being probed by you to recall and describe both the context and the behavior that enabled performance accomplishments.

The third question, and arguably key question, is to ask the employee ways to create similar conditions in the upcoming quarter for accomplishing as high, if not higher, achievements. Self-discovery of what led to performance effectiveness in the past forms the basis for self-set goals to further create positive experiences that will broaden an employee's strengths. In summary, the FFI is a strength-based rather than a deficit-based technique. Employees excel when they understand their pattern of strengths and learn ways to enhance them in different job contexts. Moreover, moving you, the manager, away from the role of a judge or critic, whether real or perceived, facilitates a positive coaching relationship with an employee.

Mystery Shoppers

As previously discussed, coaching involves giving feedback on an ongoing basis, similar to how coaches of athletes give players feedback while they are preparing for or playing in a game. Based on this feedback, specific, high goals are set, the relationships between what the employee is doing and the outcomes they can expect (e.g., outcome expectancy) are clarified, and good performance is praised. But unlike athletic coaches, the feedback used for coaching by managers in the private and public sectors is often not timely. Worse, because of the number of meetings you must attend and your sundry job duties, you may rarely see your employees performing their jobs. Hence, Bob Ford, a management expert in the hospitality industry; Gwen Lennox, a marketing researcher; Danny Tzabbar, a strategy professor; and I examined the adaptation of a technique often used in the customer service industry—the mystery shopper, for appraisal/coaching purposes. It proved to be a highly effective technique for increasing the job performance of servers and the organizational performance of the restaurants that employed them.[38]

Mystery shoppers, whose identity is unknown to an employee, add two important dimensions that enhance the feedback process, namely, timeliness and unpredictability as to when the feedback will be provided. Providing feedback on a variable schedule (see chapter 4) is the most powerful advantage of using this technique for coaching and appraisal purposes.

Variable interval schedules work extremely well for gambling casinos in getting gamblers to continually put money into a slot machine where the payout is seemingly random to the gambler, but in fact the machine has been programmed to distribute money approximately every x minutes/hours. Because of the variability in time periods, it is impossible for a gambler to discern the time-length between payouts. The same is true for pop quizzes. Students must constantly study in order to be prepared for an unanticipated exam.

In our evaluation of the evidence of the effectiveness of this technique in the workplace, a mystery shopper visited a restaurant at a predetermined time and then completed an assessment form, similar to a behavioral observation scale, that detailed all aspects of an employee's performance. The use of mystery shoppers for coaching or appraisal purposes is especially applicable to assessing employees in a bank, healthcare facility, hotel, or any other organization that provides a service to the public.

The benefits of using a mystery shopper for coaching and appraisal purposes are at least five-fold. First, it requires your organization to take the time to do a job analysis to specify exactly what constitutes effective and ineffective performance on the part of your employees. Second, the resulting appraisal instrument (e.g., behavioral observation scales) is customized for your employees and can be used in a uniform, consistent manner by a mystery shopper. Third, the mystery shopper's appraisal provides you, the manager, a relatively objective basis for praising good and correcting poor employee performance. Beliefs by an employee that your coaching or appraisal is based on personality clashes between the two of you or is politically motivated are minimized because the data come from an anonymous, dispassionate source—the mystery shopper. The perceived subjectivity often inherent in a traditional appraisal is removed. Fourth, the feedback to your employee is timely, generally within 24 hours of the mystery shopper's assessment. Thus, the performance assessed is fresh in the employee's mind. Fifth, employee performance increases to and remains at a high level. Because the mystery shopper appears at variable intervals, employees do not know when their performance will be assessed. Hence, they can't engage in impression management when they know their appraisal is due. Hence, employees must continually perform at their best or risk being assessed on an "off" day. What you will likely most appreciate about the use of mystery shoppers is that you no longer have to say to an employee, "Here is what I think of your performance." It will be far less stressful for you in the coaching process to be able to say to an employee, "Here are the observations of a mystery shopper," followed by a discussion with the employee that culminates in the setting of behavioral goals on ways that performance can be improved.

CONCLUSION

Fostering high performance in your employees requires a combination of the right kind of appraisals matched with coaching that is ongoing throughout the year. By basing your appraisal process on employee behaviors that can be observed and directly linked to your organization's strategy, by collecting data on each employee's performance from multiple sources (including peers and subordinates), and by coaching your employees on an ongoing basis, you will ensure that your performance management techniques inspire performance improvement rather than discourage positive change. Once the appraisal identifies the necessary changes, you can begin to coach your team to success.

QUESTIONS

1. What are the reasons why a performance appraisal often decreases rather than increases an employee's performance?

2. What is a 360-degree appraisal?

3. Why do you want to put your emphasis on coaching your employees?

4. What is the difference between appraisals based on trait, bottom-line, and behavioral measures.

5. What are the relative advantages of self, subordinate, peer, and supervisory appraisals of an employee's performance?

6. How can performance feedback be given in a constructive manner?

7. What is the GROW method?

8. What are the advantages of the feedforward technique for appraisal purposes?

9. How would you adapt the use of mystery shoppers for appraising your employees?

TWO EVIDENCE-BASED MANAGERS IN ACTION

11

This book explains how to become an evidence-based manager by providing you with the research-based tools and techniques you need to identify high-performing applicants, inspire your employees to execute strategy, develop and train a top-notch team, and continually motivate your people to achieve success. Although each chapter presents straightforward ways to ensure success that are grounded in research, I recognize that a manager's life is never captured by a formula and is rarely tidy. You will always have a host of pressing issues to face at any one time, and each situation has its unique circumstances and subtle nuances. Even so, the evidence-based tools and techniques offered in this book provide guideposts for addressing your issues, concerns, and challenges. What remains is for you to creatively draw on and synthesize these tools and techniques to fit your particular situation. Doing so will enable you to keep your team moving in the right direction and achieve the success you desire.

The following case studies, showing two very different evidence-based managers in action, illustrate how the tools and techniques presented here can be customized to any situation. They show how two managers applied the ideas in this book to achieve remarkable results at very different companies—a logging operation in the West and a technology development center in the Middle East—both of which were mired in human resources problems when their new managers took the helm. This second case is included because in a globalized economy, people often wonder if these research-based techniques work as well in the East as they do in the Western world. The answer is a resounding yes.

These managers' turnarounds provide evidence of how an inspired manager can use the tools provided in this book to bring about significant change under differing circumstances—even in highly different cultures. One manager employed the techniques described in this book to change how his company selected, appraised, and rewarded its people, as well as how he motivated them to improve their performance and coached them to success. Another brought huge changes to his organization when he created a vision to inspire his team, set high performance goals with employee input, and fostered a highly motivating workplace. Both managers based their turnaround strategies on evidence-based research.

WOODLANDS: A TURNAROUND
IN THE WESTERN WORLD

Woodlands, a division of a forest products company with a unionized workforce of about 1,600 people, faced a human resources mess.[1] This division scored the lowest on the company's attitude survey: Employee views on job fulfillment, productivity expectations, unit and company communications, and accident prevention were rock bottom. They had wildcat strikes between legal strikes. In short, employee morale was dismal. People complained of having no vision or goals to guide them in their day-to-day actions. Consequently, few employees at any level took responsibility for errors or shortfalls; finger-pointing and blame were the norm. It was at this low point that the company appointed the new vice president of Woodlands, Pete. He was charged by senior management with getting to the root of the problems and turning the region's operations around.

Pete began by taking stock of the situation through interviews with hourly employees, union officers, and managers. Next, he initiated a series of measurable action steps based directly on the input of employees at all levels in the company:

1. Develop a vision statement.

2. Conduct a job analysis.

3. Select high-performing employees on the basis of job requirements.

4. Build behavioral appraisals based on the job analysis.

5. Coach employees based on the behavioral appraisals.

6. Increase employee motivation through goal setting.

The sixth pillar of the strategy—employee motivation—was particularly key, as it underpinned the other elements. Consistent with the vision, Pete gave his employees a voice in analyzing their own jobs and in determining the behaviors that defined their personal effectiveness. He used these behaviors, in turn, to create situational interviews for selecting new hires and to develop performance appraisals. These efforts led to an overall sense of justice in the workplace, another important component of fostering employee motivation. The approach to employee engagement also earned him employee buy-in: By seeking employee input, he inspired his employees to believe that the new division strategy was worth executing.

A Closer Look

Here's a closer look at how Pete put his evidence-based strategy into action.

Vision Statement

Pete concluded that a clearly defined vision was needed. He expected this vision to become a "Woodlands way of life" for improving employee productivity. The vision the vice president ultimately developed was "the thinking person's division."

Job Analysis

As he launched into his overhaul of the division's operations, the new vice president started at the beginning, with job analysis. The traditional Woodlands job descriptions were (at best) well-written lists of minor and major job duties. Pete wanted his employees to understand the critical job behaviors—the behaviors that were a must for attaining the desired results. He set their sights on identifying job behaviors that would define what must be done to attain SMART goals. He then aligned the metrics that would measure whether employees attained these goals. To get employees engaged and to minimize the finger-pointing due to weak management morale, he held a series of discussions with his own staff to analyze their respective jobs. These managers, in turn, met with their subordinates. To ensure integrity in the process, Pete reviewed the results of those manager–subordinate meetings to ensure that the SMART goals they set and the behaviors they agreed were critical for attaining them were not in conflict with those of another department within the division.

Under the old, ill-defined job descriptions, employees had been evaluated on outcomes that were affected by factors beyond their control. For example, the export sales manager had been evaluated on ship-loading costs; other managers were being reviewed on vaguely worded goals that were not measurable (such as loyalty). The new SMART goals clarified each employee's job and highlighted potential goal conflicts among managers so that the problems could be eliminated. The redefining of jobs in terms of SMART goals clarified responsibilities and resolved problems for

- Truck supervisors who didn't know their job priorities

- A finance department whose members couldn't agree on appropriate metrics

- Individuals who viewed themselves as having little or no responsibility for things that were, in fact, major parts of their jobs

In sum, the vision ("the thinking person's division") drove behavior. Based on employee input, goals were set and behaviors were identified for attaining them based on employee input. By soliciting input from employees, by giving employees a voice, the new division vice president won their commitment.

Employee Selection

Pete abandoned the company's traditional hiring process. In its place he mandated the use of situational interviews, a method proven to be effective at selecting high performers. Previously, Woodlands had relied primarily on informal conversations to ascertain technical skills and likeability. The situational interviews, by contrast, were based on the behavioral analyses and were designed to predict performance on effectiveness measures. In the situational interviews, applicants were asked only those questions that statistically correlated with the ways successful people were shown to behave on the job.

Pete chose this technique because of the evidence that reveals a strong relationship between a person's intentions expressed during a situational interview and subsequent behavior on the job. The result was a workforce made up of people with a can-do mind-set.

Appraisals and Performance Feedback

Based on research, Pete chose the best appraisal model: one focused on behavior and tied directly to the division's strategy. This new appraisal was based on the job analysis that had been developed with input from hourly employees, supervisors, and managers. The analyses identified behaviors that were critical to implementing the division's strategy. The appraisal, in turn, assessed personal effectiveness in terms of those observable behaviors exhibited by an

individual employee. Consistent with the evidence on the importance of participation in employee decision making, the appraisal
instrument was developed by the people for the people.

Performance feedback from Pete, coupled with anonymous
feedback from subordinates, provided Pete's managers with the
information they needed to perform their jobs effectively. This
feedback improved the performance of the Woodlands division
significantly. The feedback was perceived as fair because it came
from multiple sources. Armed with this information, people knew
exactly what they needed to start doing, stop doing, or continue
doing to be effective.

Coaching

Pete provided his managers with training on coaching and developing their employees. The training emphasized ways to focus on
behavior rather than on personalities, which had previously been
the norm. Under this new approach, managers and employees
learned to make praise specific and immediate, and to emphasize
what actions people needed to take to do things right, rather than
focusing on what they were doing wrong. The focus was placed
on the future rather than the past. In addition, it was centered on
desired behavior rather than on an employee's undesired behavior.

The new emphasis in Woodlands was on ongoing performance
management rather than the performance appraisal. The quarterly
appraisal for managers was used only to get feedback from subordinates and, on the basis of that feedback, to set new goals.

Employee Motivation

Pete's goal of motivating employees underpinned all the other
steps. His attention to goal setting, ongoing performance feedback,
and coaching all served to motivate employees to achieve higher
and higher performance. As an added step, he changed the way

Woodlands distributed money as a reward. No longer would money be tied only to seniority; instead, it would be linked to an individual's performance. The result was higher productivity levels as employees set higher and higher goals for themselves to increase their chances of receiving a greater monetary reward. To further boost money's motivating power, he also developed innovative ways to make work fun by doling out monetary rewards based on a variable reward schedule.

Money is not in and of itself a motivator for all employees; the relationship between money and worker motivation is complex, and Pete understood this. By tying bonuses directly to performance and distributing the bonuses on a variable schedule, he ensured that money motivated his workforce.

The Results: Five Years Later

The results achieved at Woodlands over the five-year period following Pete's arrival were impressive. The numbers per unit of production are part of the story: employee-hours per unit went from 1.46 to 1.34; raw materials usage per unit went from .20 to .15; lumber usage per unit went from 3.36 to 2.74.

Employee behavior changed: Hours worked per grievance increased from 7,436 to 10,950. Tellingly, work stoppages in terms of total hours lost over the five-year period went from 28,281 to 0. Voluntary turnover went from 10.6 percent to 5.6 percent. However, discharges rose from 1.0 percent to 1.7 percent. Absenteeism fell from 3.9 percent to 2.7 percent.

To further illustrate the positive results, the attitude survey taken five years later showed marked improvements in employee perceptions. On a 4-point scale, the subordinates' evaluations of supervisors went from 2.9 to 3.2; the managers' evaluations of these same supervisors went from 2.8 to 3.5. In sum, Pete's action steps engendered improvements across the board that showed up in various measures of productivity, worker turnover, and employee satisfaction.

Why It Worked

Why was Woodlands so successful? Pete based his approach on research evidence. He formulated a vision that required the involvement of his employees in the decision-making process, including defining the measures of their job effectiveness and setting SMART goals. He set up a performance appraisal system that was behavior-based. Again, the employees defined the behaviors that constituted job effectiveness. He backed up the appraisal system with ongoing coaching for employees. The combination of vision, goals, voice, and feedback served as motivators for employees to continually seek ways to improve their performance. Rewards were administered contingent upon performance; ongoing coaching was provided for continuity. Pete's vision was straightforward. It quickly permeated the organization: Take advantage of the brains of every employee; hence the phrase "the thinking person's division."

TECH-M/E: TURNAROUND IN THE MIDDLE EAST

Tech-M/E, a technology development center based in the Middle East, faced a number of troubles—not the least of which was a rigid bureaucracy stemming from the center's status as a state-run monopoly—as well as a crumbling infrastructure due to lack of government funding. Tech-M/E had no agreed-upon governance system, nor did it have current or future objectives. It was even unclear who the center's priority customers were in the public and private sectors. Thus, it was not surprising that there were no scheduled projects or action plans for upgrading the facility.

A new director, Kazem, set out to bring significant changes to this troubled place. Basing his strategy on best practices rooted in research, Kazem approached his overhaul with a five-pronged plan of action. His strategy consisted of

1. Establishing a vision

2. Setting goals

3. Reinstating a sense of organizational justice

4. Training

5. Motivating employees

As Pete did at Woodlands, Kazem made motivation the underlying driver of all other parts of his strategy. He determined that the key to turning a troubled government entity around lay in inspiring his staff to action (after years of relative inaction) and motivating them to set and commit to specific, high goals.

Kazem also began by soliciting input—by giving people a voice. Interviews with direct reports and their employees revealed that Tech-M/E lacked both a vision and a set of SMART goals. Consequently, people were frustrated and disillusioned. Managers blamed each other and their respective staff for the center's poor performance. When Kazem pointed out that it was the managers who were responsible for setting high performance goals and inspiring their people to success, they responded with more finger-pointing and excuses. Although their response was unproductive, in truth, they had been given precious little direction from previous directors. The directorship had been a revolving door, with five directors in the span of seven years. During that time, the middle managers and their staff had learned helplessness.

A key to resolving these human resource problems was establishing a vision. Kazem then decided to back his vision up with goals (and the resources to attain them), an upgraded technical governance system to ensure consistent and standardized technological and engineering processes, administrative governance to make sure people felt that they were being treated fairly, training for the employees, and new incentives—monetary and otherwise—to get people motivated. Employees needed to be engaged. They needed to believe their work was worthwhile and appreciated.

A Closer Look

Here's how Kazem executed his strategy—using an approach strikingly similar to the one Pete used at Woodlands, even though the center involved was on the other side of the world and in a Middle Eastern rather than a Western country.

Vision

The government bureaucrat who hired Kazem couldn't tell him if there was a vision for the center. As a result, Kazem's first order of business was to craft a vision for the center's future.

Kazem knew he could inspire his employees to execute his strategy if he articulated a vision with which they could connect. He involved his employees in the development of the center's vision and in setting clear goals to accompany it.

The vision, "empowered employees," was designed to galvanize people to take personal initiative, to take action to enhance the center's effectiveness.

Goals

The situation was so dire that Tech-M/E was in danger of being shut down due to disagreements between local and central government officials. Kazem knew he needed to make basic changes—and fast. He asked his management team for assistance: He explained he would need them to help him set specific, high goals and develop plans to attain them. He insisted that they clarify their roles and responsibilities, as well as those of their respective staff. He then asked that they hold themselves and their staffs accountable for executing those responsibilities. He stressed the importance of ongoing performance monitoring to achieve this end.

What were some of these performance goals, and how did this new director define them? Goals that are specific and challenging (yet attainable) will do more to motivate people to action than goals that are vague or too easy. For example, one of his goals for the engineering division was to develop capability in design, engineering, and construction support of facilities that used complex technologies in specified fields. Design and engineering capabilities would develop as complexity of the applied technologies grew. By involving his employees in the goal-setting process, Kazem ensured their understanding of and commitment to the resulting goals. He also engaged his engineering staff in all stages of project development—from conceptual and basic design to procurement engineering, through the construction, installation, and operation of developed facilities. Together, he and his team developed governance procedures for ensuring consistency, coordination among departments, and quality assurance. And even though the changes he was making shook the center to its core, he resolved to communicate all his decisions clearly, sincerely, and in a timely manner. He bent over backward to ensure that everyone knew the logic underlying his decisions. People didn't always agree with Kazem's decisions, but they couldn't say they didn't understand them. This is the bedrock for perceptions of organizational justice.

This combination of the vision and goal setting, based on employee input, served to motivate the center's employees to improve their performance, while Kazem's commitment to providing continuous feedback kept his direct reports on track to attain the goals.

Organizational Justice

Employee perceptions of their workplace were negative, to say the least, when Kazem first arrived. There was an overwhelming sense among the employees that the governance system was unfair. Orders came from the top down and were rarely backed up with the appropriate resources. Kazem knew that if he was going to motivate his employees to do anything at all, he'd have to change their perceptions of unfairness in the workplace. He did so by applying principles of organizational justice. In particular, he established processes to allocate resources in a fair manner, and he continually sought feedback from his team.

As with so many of the actions of an evidence-based manager, applying psychology gets the desired work done. As an engineer, Kazem saw engaging his staff in developing governance procedures as a way to ensure performance quality; the psychologist sees it as a way to ensure a sense of organizational justice. The outcome is a successfully led, motivated team.

Training

When Kazem first arrived, many of the center's employees were already highly trained people who had earned advanced degrees at top universities in the West. But the center still relied heavily on foreign expertise for technology development strategies and action steps, particularly from the West. The absence of an engineering team at the center was a critical impediment to empowering the center to translate its technological know-how to engineering documents that would enable application of the technology in the field. This led to a sense of disempowerment and helplessness on the part of these highly trained workers. Kazem wanted to bring technology development operations in-house, instead of leaving them under foreign contracts. He was able to do so by relying on the training principle of *enactive mastery.*

Enactive mastery is essentially the principle of setting people up to succeed. Kazem first embarked on hiring engineering graduates for the engineering team as well as injecting fresh blood into the disillusioned technology development departments. To train his employees, Kazem focused on small, attainable steps. He would assign staff to technology development projects that grew in complexity as the capability of his staff developed on the job. He allowed the owner of the technology to oversee all steps and deliverables of the basic and detail engineering, through construction and commissioning, so that the specified technological development was achieved before signing the project closure with the contracted technologist. Soon, his employees had created active technology development and engineering departments with integrated technical and administrative governance. This in turn translated technological know-how into procurement and construction documents that enabled national contractors to build the projected facility. These goals not only won the support of the government, they proved to be highly motivating for the new hires—and for the experienced staff professionals who were already highly trained.

Motivation

When Kazem arrived at the center, the employees had all but lost respect for the entire senior management team. A series of flawed decisions had taught the employees not to trust their bosses. Furthermore, the work environment was plagued by rumor and gossip. As a result, employee morale and work ethic were nonexistent. Employees hated the word *boss* and anything resembling "plans for the center's future," as all they had ever experienced were failed initiatives. There was strong consensus that the center was the trash bin of taxpayers' money.

Kazem determined that what his people wanted more than anything was to be heard after so many years of being ordered around aimlessly. He began to give them a voice by providing his staff with the professional attention they craved. He solicited their input in setting goals, and he repeatedly asked them how to attain these goals. In short, Kazem clarified outcome expectancies. He understood the research showing that people will do what they need to do to succeed only if they trust the link between those necessary actions and the desired outcomes. He helped people see the relationship between their actions and the outcomes they could expect.

Motivating his employees with evidence-based incentives that went beyond bonuses—being a government entity, the firm couldn't offer monetary bonuses—became extremely important as Kazem began to restructure the center. With the start of new projects, the volume of engineering activities swelled. Reams of drawings and data sheets now needed to be produced. Thousands of acres of land needed to be developed, and equipment weighing hundreds of thousands of tons needed to be installed and commissioned. He knew he would have to find a creative way to motivate and retain highly qualified staff. This urgency was aggravated by the fact that staffers would in many cases be interacting with more highly paid contractors (what researchers would call *comparison others*), whose presence would cause feelings of injustice.

To minimize a potential turnover problem, Kazem decided to spin off some operations into three employee-owned and operated private companies, one for engineering, one for construction, and one for support services. In that way, employees gained control and augmented their earning power. For example, an engineering company was formed and 300 employees were transferred to it. The center rented to the new unit its offices and leased it all the necessary computers, tools, and sundry equipment. Kazem helped the new companies establish performance-based compensation and bonuses according to project earnings. This created an incentive for increased efficiencies on both the personal and organizational levels. The changes also inspired performance improvements, as employees were more driven now that they were working for themselves.

Kazem drew up a "charter of unity" for the newly formed engineering company that was based on input from the employees. The charter explained why they should work as a team, how they should maintain their team, and how they would share the benefits and rewards of teamwork. Kazem found that this sense of ownership enhanced the employees' motivation more than any monetary bonus could have done.

The Results: Five Years Later

Five years after the new director began his sweeping changes, Tech-M/E is a very different organization. The center now has a government-approved long-term plan, including several technology development projects. It grew from approximately 250 staff (with fewer than 50 technical personnel) to nearly 1,000 staff, with more than 50 percent comprising the technologists and engineering staff.

It later shrunk to around 200 staff with the formation of the three private companies, when most of the center's engineering and construction projects, with associated support services, were contracted to them. The engineering team (with advanced simulation and design tools) is actively involved in the engineering and construction support of the technology development projects. Several international contracts, highly focused on training and technology transfer, have been secured. An integrated set of engineering and administration governance, supported by an information system infrastructure, is up and running. Several labs and technological development test facilities as well as a training center are established, while many full-scale technology application projects are going through various stages of basic or detail engineering, procurement, or construction, under the supervision of the contracted technologist. The center, which once was under serious threat of closure, is back on the map again and has become one of the country's top-10 priority projects.

CONCLUSION

Both the Woodlands and Tech-M/E case studies show how a manager who relies on evidence-based techniques can transform an organization and inspire employees to commit to executing strategy. How did the region vice president do it at Woodlands? How did the new director do it at the center?

- They had a vision.

- They sought employee input.

- They set specific goals.

- They hired high-performing people committed to the vision and goals.

- They built trust through integrity, using principles of organizational justice.

- They established a system of goal-setting and rewards to motivate employees.

- They provided ongoing feedback that was timely and relevant.

- They then coached their people on an ongoing basis.

This is the essence of an evidence-based manager: using proven techniques to inspire, develop, motivate, appraise, and coach a team to the highest performance possible. Whether you're managing a major manufacturing operation overseas or a corner store in Kansas, you can do the same.

NOTES

Introduction

1. P. Sweeney, "Teaching New Hires to Feel at Home," *New York Times*, February 14, 1999.

Chapter 1

1. R. C. Ford and C. P. Heaton, *Managing the Guest Experience in Hospitality* (New York: Delmar, 2000).

2. Reliability means the test yields approximately the same score when people retake it again and again (test-retest reliability), or that two or more interviewers or assessors reach the same conclusion independently regarding an applicant's suitability for the job (interobserver reliability). Validity refers to accuracy in making predictions about whether an applicant will perform well on the job. Accuracy is determined by seeing whether the score people receive on a selection test correlates with the scores on how effectively they are performing on the job. R. M. Guion, *Assessment, Measurement, and Prediction for Personnel Decisions* (New Jersey: Erlbaum, 1998).

3. W. H. Wiesner and S. F. Cronshaw, "The Moderating Impact of Interview Format and Degree of Structure on the Validity of the Employment Interview," *Journal of Occupational Psychology* 61 (1988): 275–290.

4. J. P. Wanous, *Organizational Entry: Recruitment, Selection, Orientation, and Socialization of Newcomers*, 2nd ed. (New York: Addison-Wesley, 1992).

5. G. P. Latham, L. M. Saari, E. D. Pursell, and M. Campion, "The Situational Interview," *Journal of Applied Psychology* 65 (1980): 422–427.

    G. P. Latham and C. Sue-Chan, "A Meta-Analysis of the Situational Interview: An Enumerative Review of Reasons for Its Validity," *Canadian Psychology* 40 (1999): 56–67.

    C. Sue-Chan and G. P. Latham, "The Situational Interview as a Predictor of Academic and Team Performance: A Study of the Mediating Effects of Cognitive Ability and Emotional Intelligence," *International Journal of Selection and Assessment* 12 (2004): 312–320.

    U. C. Klehe and G. P. Latham, "The Predictive and Incremental Validity of the Situational and Patterned Behavior Description Interviews for Team-playing Behavior," *International Journal of Selection and Assessment* 13 (2005): 108–115.

A.I Huffcutt, S.S. Culbertson, and W.S Weybrauch, "Employment Interview Reliability: New Estimates by Structures and Format", *International Journal of Selection and Assessment*, 21 (2013): 264–276.

G. P. Latham and D. Skarlicki, "Criterion-Related Validity of the Situational and Patterned Behavior Description Interviews with Organizational Citizenship Behavior," *Human Performance* 8 (1995): 67–80.

6. J. C. Flanagan, "The Critical Incident Technique," *Psychological Bulletin* 51 (1954): 327–358.

7. T. Janz, "Patterned Behavior Description Interviews," in *The Employment Interview: Theory, Method, and Practice*, eds. G. Ferris and R. Eder (California: Sage, 1989), 158–168.

T. Janz, "Initial Comparisons of the Patterned Behavior Description Interviews Versus Unstructured Interviews," *Journal of Applied Psychology* 67 (1982): 577–580.

T. Janz, L. Hellervik, and D. C. Gilmore, *Behavior Description Interviewing* (Massachusetts: Allyn & Bacon, 1986).

P. C. Green, *Get Talent: Interview for Actions, Select for Results* (Tennessee: Skilfast, 2007).

8. W. V. Bingham, "Halo, Invalid and Valid," *Journal of Applied Psychology* 23 (1939): 221–228.

T. M. Rand and K. N. Wexley, "Demonstration of the Effect, 'Similar to Me,' in Simulated Employment Interviews," *Psychological Reports* 36 (1975): 535–544.

K. N. Wexley, G. A. Yukl, S. Z. Kovacs, and R. E. Sanders, "Importance of Contrast Effects in Employment Interviews," *Journal of Applied Psychology* 56 (1972): 45–48.

G. P. Latham, K. N. Wexley, and E. D. Pursell, "Training Managers to Minimize Rating Errors in the Observation of Behavior," *Journal of Applied Psychology* 60 (1975): 550–555.

E. C. Webster, *Decision Making in the Employment Interview* (Montreal: McGill University Industrial Relations Center, 1964).

9. B. B. Gaugler, D. B. Rosenthal, G. C. Thorntons, and C. Bentson, "Meta-Analysis of Assessment Center Validity," *Journal of Applied Psychology* 72 (1987): 493–511.

A. Howard and D. W. Bray, *Managerial Lives in Transition: Advancing Age and Changing Times* (New York: Guilford Press, 1988).

D. W. Bray and D. W. Howard, "Predictions of Managerial Success Over Long Periods of Time: Lessons from the Management Progress Study," in

Measures of Leadership, eds. K. E. Clark and M. B. Clark (New Jersey: Leadership Library of America, 1990): 113–130.

10. P. Squires, S. J. Torkel, J. W. Smither, and M. R. Ingate, "Validity and Generalizability of a Role-Play Test to Select Telemarketing Representatives," 64 (1991): 37–47.

J. R. Schneider and N. Schmitt, "An Exercise Design Approach to Understanding Assessment Center Dimensions and Exercise Constructs," *Journal of Applied Psychology* 77 (1992): 32–41.

11. G. C. Thornton III and W. C. Byham, *Assessment Centers and Managerial Performance* (New York: Academic Press, 1982).

D. W. Bray, R. J. Campbell, and D. L. Grant, *Formative Years in Business: A Long-Term Study of Managerial Lives* (New York: Wiley, 1974).

12. J. P. Wanous, *Organizational Entry: Recruitment, Selection, and Socialization* (Massachusetts: Addison-Wesley, 1980).

P. Popovich and J. P. Wanous, "The Realistic Job Preview as a Persuasive Communication," *Academy of Management Review* 7 (1982): 570–578.

13. D. Hollander, "Creating an Onboarding Culture," *HR News Magazine*, June 2008, 6–10.

K. J. Templar, C. Tay, and N. A. Chandrasekar, "Motivational Cultural Intelligence, Realistic Job Preview, Realistic Living Condition Preview, and Cross-Cultural Adjustment," *Group and Organization Management* 31 (2006): 154–173.

J. P. Wanous and A. Colella, "Organizational Entry Research: Current Status and Future Directions," in *Research in Personnel and Human Resource Management*, eds. K. M. Rowland and G. R. Ferris (Connecticut: JAI Press, 1989): 59–120.

L. W. Porter and R. M. Steers, "Organizational, Work, and Personal Factors in Employee Turnover and Absenteeism," *Psychological Bulletin* 80 (1973): 151–176.

J. P. Wanous, T. D. Poland, S. L. Premack, and K. S. Davis, "The Effects of Met Expectations on Newcomer Attitudes and Behavior: A Review and Meta-Analysis," *Journal of Applied Psychology* 77 (1992): 288–297.

14. P. R. Sackett, M. S. Borneman, and B. S. Connelly, "High-Stakes Testing in Higher Education and Employment: Appraising the Evidence for Validity and Fairness," *American Psychologist* 63 (2008): 215–227.

15. N. R. Lockwood, "Workforce Diversity: Leveraging the Power of Difference for Competitive Advantage," *SHRM Research Quarterly* (2005): 1–13.

J. N. Matton and C. M. Hernandez, "A New Study Identifies the 'Makes and Breaks' of Diversity Initiatives," *Journal of Organizational Excellence* 23 (August 2004): 47–58.

National Urban League, *Diversity Practices That Work: The American Worker Speaks* (New York: National Urban League, 2004).

E. E. Hubbard, *The Diversity Scorecard: Evaluating the Impact of Diversity on Organizational Performance* (Massachusetts: Elsevier Butterworth-Heinemann, 2004).

M. L. Lengnick-Hall, P. H. Gaunt, and J. Collison, *Employer Incentives for Hiring Individuals with Disabilities* (Virginia: Society for Human Resource Management, April 2003).

T. Kochan et al., "The Effects of Diversity on Business Performance: Report of the Diversity Research Network," *Human Resource Management* 42, no. 1 (Spring 2003): 3–21.

M. A. Hart, *Managing Diversity for Sustained Competitiveness* (New York: Conference Board, 1997).

16. F. P. Morgeson et al., "Are We Getting Fooled Again? Coming to Terms with Limitations in the Use of Personality Tests for Personnel Selection," *Personnel Psychology* 60 (2007): 1029–1049.

17. American Educational Research Association, American Psychological Association, and National Council on Measurement in Education, *The Standards for Educational and Psychological Testing* (Washington, DC: American Educational Research Association, 1999).

18. L. R. Goldberg, "The Structure of Phenotypic Personality Traits," *American Psychologist* 48 (1993): 26–34.

O. John, "The 'Big Five' Factor Taxonomy: Dimensions of Personality in the Natural Languages and in Questionnaires," in *Handbook of Personality Theory and Research*, ed. L. Pervin (New York: Guilford Press, 1990): 66–100.

S. V. Paunonen, D. N. Jackson, J. Treblinski, and F. Forsterling, "Personality Structure Across Cultures: A Multimethod Evaluation," *Journal of Personality and Social Psychology* 62 (1992): 447–556.

19. M. R. Barrick, M. K. Mount, and T. A. Judge, "Personality and Performance at the Beginning of the New Millennium: What Do We Know and Where Do We Go Next?" *International Journal of Selection and Assessment* 9 (2001): 9–30.

20. G. D. Anderson and C. Viswesvaran, "An Update of the Validity of Personality Scales in Personnel Selection: A Meta-Analysis of Studies Published Between 1992-1997," paper presented at the 13th Annual Meeting of the Society for Industrial and Organizational Psychology, Dallas, 1998.

M. R. Barrick and M. K. Mount, "The Big Five Personality Dimensions and Job Performance: A Meta-Analysis," *Personnel Psychology* 44 (1991): 1-26.

J. F. Salgado, "The Five Factor Model of Personality and Job Performance in the European Community," *Journal of Applied Psychology* 82 (1997): 30-43.

21. Barrick, Mount, and Judge, "Personality and Performance at the Beginning of the New Millennium."

22. M. R. Barrick et al., "Relating Member Ability and Personality to Work Team Processes and Team Effectiveness," *Journal of Applied Psychology* 83 (1998): 377-391.

M. K. Mount, M. R. Barrick, and G. L. Stewart, "Five-Factor Model of Personality and Performance in Jobs Involving Interpersonal Interactions," *Human Performance* 11 (1998): 145-165.

23. Barrick and Mount, "The Big Five Personality Dimensions and Job Performance."

Mount, Barrick, and Stewart, "Five-Factor Model of Personality and Performance in Jobs Involving Interpersonal Interactions."

24. Barrick, Mount, and Judge, "Personality and Performance at the Beginning of the New Millennium."

25. L. M. Penney and P. E. Spector, "Narcissism and Counterproductive Work Behavior: Do Bigger Egos Mean Bigger Problems?" *International Journal of Selection and Assessment* 10 (2002): 126-134.

26. D. S. Ones and C. Viswesvaran, "Gender, Age and Race Differences on Overt Integrity Tests: Results from Four Large-Scale Job Applicant Datasets," *Journal of Applied Psychology* 83 (1998): 35-42.

27. S. Cote, "Enhancing Managerial Effectiveness via Four Core Facets of Emotional Intelligence: Self-Awareness, Facial Perception, Emotion Understanding, and Emotion Regulation." *Organizational Dynamics* 46 (2017): 140-147.

S. Cote, "Emotional Intelligence in Organizations," *Annual Review of Organizational Behavior* 1: 459-488.

Chapter 2

1. The axiom "that which gets measured gets done" was coined by the late Mason Haire, an organizational psychologist, formerly at the University of California, Berkeley. Later research showed that "what is measured" becomes a goal in the eyes of employees for them to attain. Thus, it is more accurate to say "that which gets measured against goals gets done," E. A. Locke and G. P. Latham, *A Theory of Goal Setting and Task Performance* (New Jersey: Prentice Hall, 1990).

2. T. R. Mitchell and D. Daniels, "Motivation," in *Handbook of Psychology, vol. 12: Industrial Organizational Psychology*, eds. W. C. Borman, D. R. Ilgen, and R. J. Klimoski (New York: Wiley, 2003): 225–254.

   C. C. Pinder, *Work Motivation in Organizational Behavior* (New Jersey: Prentice Hall, 1998).

3. G. P. Latham, T. R. Mitchell, and D. L. Dossett, "The Importance of Participative Goal Setting and Anticipated Rewards on Goal Difficulty and Job Performance," *Journal of Applied Psychology* 63 (1978): 163–171.

4. Analysis of four historical fiascoes showed them to have resulted from faulty group decision-making processes: Pearl Harbor, the invasion of North Korea, the Bay of Pigs, and the escalation of the Vietnam War. In each case, members of a small, cohesive group under pressure to make a decision began to think as one mind. They ignored dissenting opinions and alternative courses of action because of their overriding desire to reach consensus. Janis called this phenomenon groupthink. Research shows that faulty decision making can be avoided in groups with a moderate amount of collective self-efficacy, that is, a group can-do mind-set. These groups make better decisions because they take a more vigilant approach to problem solving. I. L. Janis, *Victims of Groupthink: A Psychological Study of Foreign-Policy Decisions and Fiascoes* (Oxford: Houghton Mifflin, 1972).

   K. Tasa and K. Whyte, "Collective Efficacy and Vigilant Problem Solving in Group Decision Making: A Non-Linear Model," *Organizational Behavior and Human Decision-Making Processes* 96 (2005): 119–129.

5. R. C. Ford and C. P. Heaton, *Managing the Guest Experience in Hospitality* (New York: Delmar, 2000).

6. G. P. Latham and E. A. Locke, "Enhancing the Benefits and Overcoming the Pitfalls of Goal Setting," *Organization Dynamics* 35 (2006): 332–340.

   E. A. Locke and G. P. Latham, "A Theory of Goal Setting and Task Performance."

E. A. Locke, and G. P. Latham, "Building a Practically Useful Theory of Goal Setting and Task Motivation: A 35-Year Odyssey," *American Psychologist* 57 (2002): 705-717.

G. P. Latham, *Work Motivation: History, Theory, Research and Practice* (California: Sage, 2012).

G. P. Latham and E. A. Locke, "New Developments in and Directions for Goal Setting," *European Psychologist* 12 (2007): 290-300.

7. G. P. Latham and S. B. Kinne, "Improving Job Performance Through Training in Goal Setting," *Journal of Applied Psychology* 59 (1974): 187-191.

8. Latham and Locke, "Enhancing the Benefits and Overcoming the Pitfalls of Goal Setting."

9. D. Winters and G. P. Latham, "The Effect of Learning Versus Outcome Goals on a Simple Versus a Complex Task," *Group and Organization Management* 21 (1996): 236-250.

G. H. Seijts et al., "Goal Setting and Goal Orientation: An Integration of Two Different Yet Related Literatures," *Academy of Management Journal* 47 (2004): 227-239.

G. H. Seijts and G. P. Latham, "Learning Versus Performance Goals: When Should Each Be Used?" *Academy of Management Executive* 19 (2005): 124-131.

G. H. Seijts, and G. P. Latham, "The Effect of Learning, Outcome, and Proximal Goals on a Moderately Complex Task," *Journal of Organizational Behavior* 22 (2001): 291-307.

10. The *Journal of Organizational Behavior* reported a study where people who were hired to make toys discovered that the amount of money they could make from selling a given toy changed without notice. Those who had subgoals made more money than those who only had a long-term SMART goal and more than those who were urged to make as much money as possible. G. P. Latham and G. H. Seijts, "The Effects of Proximal and Distal Goals on Performance on a Moderately Complex Task," *Journal of Organizational Behavior* 20 (1999): 421-429.

11. Ford and Heaton, *Managing the Guest Experience in Hospitality.*

12. Ibid.

13. Ibid.

14. B. Bass and F. J. Yammarino, "Congruence of Self and Others' Leadership

Ratings of Naval Officers for Understanding Successful Performance," *Applied Psychology: An International Review* 40 (1991): 437–454.

15. N. R. F. Maier, *Psychology in Industry* (Massachusetts: Houghton Mifflin, 1955).

16. J. Greenberg, "A Taxonomy of Organizational Justice Theories," *Academy of Management Review* 12 (1987): 9–22.

    J. Greenberg, "The Social Side of Fairness: Interpersonal and Informational Classes of Organizational Justice," in "Justice in the Workplace: Approaching Fairness in Human Resource Management," ed. R. Cropanzano, *Applied Psychology* (New Jersey: Erlbaum, 1993): 79–103.

    J. Greenberg, "Losing Sleep Over Organizational Injustice: Attenuating Insomniac Reactions to Underpayment Inequity with Supervisory Training in Interactional Justice," *Journal of Applied Psychology* 91 (2006): 58–69.

    R. Folger and R. Cropanzano, *Foundations for Organizational Science: Organizational Justice and Human Resource Management* (California: Sage, 1998).

17. Personal communication, September 12, 2005.

Chapter 3

1. C. Argyris, "Teaching Smart People How to Learn," in *Organization Development: A Jossey-Bass Reader*, ed. J. Y. Galls (California: Jossey-Bass, 2006): 267–285.

2. D. C. Meichenbaum, "Enhancing Creativity by Modifying What Subjects Say to Themselves," *American Educational Research Journal* 12 (1975): 129–145.

    D. C. Meichenbaum, *Cognitive Behavior Modification: An Integrative Approach* (New York: Plenum Press, 1977).

3. A. Bandura, "Self-Efficacy: Toward a Unifying Theory of Behavioral Change," *Psychological Review* 84 (1977): 191–215.

    A. Bandura, "Self-Efficacy Mechanism in Human Agency," *American Psychologist* 37 (1982): 122–147.

    A. Bandura, *Self-Efficacy: The Exercise of Control* (New York: Freeman, 1977).

    A. Bandura, "Social Cognitive Theory: An Agentic Perspective," *Annual Review of Psychology* 52 (2001): 1–26.

4. Z. Millman and G. P. Latham, "Increasing Re-employment Through Training in Verbal Self-Guidance," in *Work Interventions in the Context of*

a Globalizing Economy, eds. M. Erez, U. Kleinbleck, and H. Thierry (New Jersey: Erlbaum, 2001), 87–97.

5. T. C. Brown and G. P. Latham, "The Effect of Training in Verbal Self-Guidance on Performance Effectiveness in a MBA Program," *Canadian Journal of Behavioral Science* 38 (2006): 1–11.

G. P. Latham and M. H. Budworth, "The Effect of Training in Verbal Self-Guidance on the Self-Efficacy and Performance of Native North Americans in the Selection Interview," *Journal of Vocational Behavior* 68 (2006): 516–523.

B. Yanar, M. H. Budworth, and G. P. Latham, "The Effect of Verbal Self-Guidance Training for Overcoming Employment Barriers: A Study of Muslim Women," *Applied Psychology: An International Review* (2009, 58, 586-601).

6. R. D. Marx, "Relapse Prevention for Managerial Training: A Model for Maintenance of Behavioral Change," *Academy of Management Review* 7 (1982): 433–441.

L. A. Burke and T. T. Baldwin, "Workforce Training Transfer: A Study of the Effect of Relapse Prevention Training and Transfer Climate," *Human Resource Management* 38 (1999): 227–242.

7. Accounting for the remaining 5 percent of the managers who participated in the training, one decided to return to school and another chose to retire. Five did not find employment, and four could not be located.

8. J. T. E. Richardson, "Vividness and Unvividness: Reliability, Consistency, and Validity of Subjective Imagery Ratings," *Journal of Mental Imagery* 12 (1988): 115–122.

A. Richardson, *Individual Differences in Imaging: Their Measurement, Origins, and Consequences* (New York: Baywood, 1994).

C. P. Neck and C. C. Manz, "Thought Self-Leadership: The Influence of Self-Talk and Mental Imagery on Performance," *Journal of Organizational Behavior* 13 (1992): 681–699.

S. M. Murphy, "Models of Imagery in Sport Psychology: A Review," *Journal of Mental Imagery* 14 (1990): 153–172.

J. E. Driskell, C. Copper, and A. Moran, "Does Mental Practice Enhance Performance?" *Journal of Applied Psychology* 79 (1994): 481–492.

G. Fontani et al., "Effect of Mental Imagery on the Development of Skilled Motor Actions," *Perceptual and Motor Skills* 105 (2007): 803–826.

9. L. Morin and G. P. Latham, "Effect of Mental Practice and Goal Setting as a

Transfer of Training Intervention on Supervisors' Self-Efficacy and Communication Skills: An Exploratory Study," *Applied Psychology: An International Review* 49 (2000): 566–578.

10. This technique too has its origins in clinical psychology. The late Fred Kanfer of the University of Illinois developed this methodology and used it successfully to help people stop smoking and overcome drug addiction. F. H. Kanfer, "Self-Regulation: Research, Issues, and Speculations," in *Behavior Modification in Clinical Psychology*, eds. C. Neuringer and J. Michael (New York: Appleton-Century-Crofts, 1974), 178–220.

   F. H. Kanfer, "Self-Management Methods," in *Helping People Change*, ed. F. H. Kanfer (New York: Wiley, 1975), 309–355.

   F. H. Kanfer, "Self-Management Methods," in *Helping People Change: A Textbook of Methods*, 2nd ed., eds. F. H. Kanfer and A. P. Goldstein (New York: Pergamon Press, 1980), 334–389.

11. C. A. Frayne and G. P. Latham, "Application of Social Learning Theory to Employee Self-Management of Attendance," *Journal of Applied Psychology* 72 (1987): 387–392. Nine months after training the employees in self-management to increase their job attendance, Collette trained a human resource manager to teach this technique to the employees who were in the control group. Within three months those people increased their job attendance to the high level attained by those who were in the original training group. G. P. Latham and C. A. Frayne, "Self-Management Training for Increasing Job Attendance: A Follow-up and a Replication," *Journal of Applied Psychology* 74 (1989): 411–416.

12. Bandura, the psychologist at Stanford University I refer to in note 3, has performed countless experiments showing that behavioral modeling increases self-efficacy, a can-do mind-set. If you align your organization's vision, goals, and strategy you will find you'll make believers out of your employees.

13. R. C. Ford and C. P. Heaton, *Managing the Guest Experience in Hospitality* (New York: Delmar, 2000).

14. Ibid.

15. Ibid.

16. J. A. Chatham, "Matching People and Organizations: Selection and Socialization in Public Accounting Firms," *Administrative Science Quarterly* 36 (1991): 459–484.

   M. Rokeach, *The Nature of Human Values* (New York: Free Press, 1973).

   S. H. Schwartz and G. Sagie, "Value Consensus and Importance: A

Cross-National Study," *Journal of Cross-Cultural Psychology* 31 (2000): 465–497.

J. E. Sheridan, "Organizational Culture and Employee Retention," *Academy of Management Journal* 35 (1992): 1036–1056.

S. A. Goodman and D. J. Svyantek, "Person–Organization Fit and Contextual Performance: Do Shared Values Matter?" *Journal of Vocational Behavior* 55 (1999): 254–275.

17. C. S. Dweck, "Motivational Processes Affecting Learning," *American Psychologist* 41 (1986): 1040–1048.

C. S. Dweck, *Self-Theories: Their Role in Motivation, Personality, and Development* (Pennsylvania: Psychology Press, 1999).

C. S. Dweck and E. L. A. Leggett, "A Social-Cognitive Approach to Motivation and Personality," *Psychological Review* 95 (1988): 256–273.

18. Ford and Heaton, *Managing the Guest Experience in Hospitality.*

19. N. Keith and M. Frese, "Self-Regulation in Error Management Training: Emotion Control and Metacognition as Mediators of Performance Effects," *Journal of Applied Psychology* 90 (2005): 677–691.

N. Keith and M. Frese, "Effectiveness of Error Management Training: A Meta-Analysis," *Journal of Applied Psychology* 93 (2008): 59–69.

C. van Dyck et al., "Organizational Error Management Culture and Its Impact on Performance: A Two-Study Replication," *Journal of Applied Psychology* Special Section: Theoretical Models and Conceptual Analyses 90, no. 2 (2005): 1228–1240.

20. P. A. Heslin, G. P. Latham, and D. VandeWalle, "The Effect of Implicit Person Theory on Performance Appraisals," *Journal of Applied Psychology* 90 (2005): 842–856.

P. A. Heslin, D. VandeWalle, and G. P. Latham, "Keen to Help? Managers' Implicit Person Theories and Their Subsequent Employee Coaching," *Personnel Psychology* 59 (2005): 871–902.

Chapter 4

1. R. C. Ford and C. P. Heaton, *Managing the Guest Experience in Hospitality* (New York: Delmar, 2000).

2. N. R. F. Maier, *Psychology in Industry* (Massachusetts: Houghton Mifflin, 1955).

3. E. L. Deci, *Intrinsic Motivation* (New York: Plenum, 1975).

E. L. Deci and R. M. Ryan, "The General Causality Orientation Scale:

Self-Determination in Personality," *Journal of Research in Personality* 19 (1985): 109–137.

E. L. Deci and R. M. Ryan, "A Motivational Approach to Self: Integration in Personality," in *Nebraska Symposium on Motivation* vol. 328, ed. R. Dienstbier (Nebraska: University of Nebraska Press, 1990), 237–288.

4. G. P. Latham, *Work Motivation: History, Theory, Research and Practice* (California: Sage, 2012).

   E. Lawler, *Talent: Making People Your Competitive Advantage* (California: Jossey-Bass, 2008).

5. F. W. Wicker et al., "On Reconsidering Maslow: An Examination of the Deprivation/Domination Proposition," *Journal of Research in Personality* 27 (1993): 118–199.

   Rosen, S. "Self-Actualization Versus Collectualization: Implications for Motivation Theories," in *Work Motivation in the Context of a Globalizing Economy*, eds. M. Erez, U. Klenbeck, and H. K. Thierry (New Jersey: Erlbaum, 2001), 341–368.

   A. N. Kluger and J. Tikochinsky, "The Error of Accepting the 'Theoretical' Null Hypothesis: The Rise, Fall, and Resurrection of Commonsense Hypotheses in Psychology," *Psychological Bulletin* 127 (2001): 408–423.

   D. Van-Dijk and A. N. Kluger, "Feedback Sign Effect on Motivation: Is It Moderated by Regulatory Focus?" *Applied Psychology: An International Review* 53 (2004): 113–135.

6. E. A. Locke and G. P. Latham, *A Theory of Goal Setting and Task Performance* (New Jersey: Prentice Hall, 1990).

   E. A. Locke and G. P. Latham, "Building a Practically Useful Theory of Goal Setting and Task Motivation: A 35-Year Odyssey," *American Psychologist* 57 (2002): 705–717.

   E. A. Locke, "Motivation, Cognition, and Action: An Analysis of Studies of Task Goals and Knowledge," *Applied Psychology: An International Review* 49 (2000): 408–429.

   G.P. Latham and E.A. Locke, "Goal Setting Theory: Controverises and Resolutions," in *Handbook of Industrial, Work and Organizational Psychology*, eds. D. Ones, N. Anderson, V. Viswesvaran, and H. Handan (Los Angeles, Sage, 2018), 145–166.

7. G. P. Latham and T. C. Brown, "The Effect of Learning vs. Outcome Goals on Self-Efficacy, Satisfaction and Performance in an MBA Program," *Applied Psychology: An International Review* 55, no. 4 (2006): 606–623.

L. T. Eby et al., "Motivational Bases of Affective Organizational Commitment: A Partial Test of an Integrative Theoretical Model," *Journal of Occupational and Organizational Psychology* 72 (1999): 463–483.

8. B. S. Wiese and A. M. Freund, "Goal Progress Makes One Happy, or Does It? Longitudinal Findings from the Work Domain," *Journal of Occupational and Organizational Psychology* 78 (2005): 1–19.

9. G. P. Latham, *Work Motivation: History, Theory, Research and Practice.*

J. P. Meyer, T. E. Becker, and C. Vandenberghe, "Employee Commitment and Motivation: A Conceptual Analysis and Interpretative Model," *Journal of Applied Psychology* 89 (2004): 991–1007.

J. P. Meyer and L. Herscovitch, "Commitment in the Workplace: Toward a General Model," *Human Resource Management Review* 11 (2001): 299–326.

10. W. W. Ronan, G. P. Latham, and S. B. Kinne, "The Effects of Goal Setting and Supervision on Worker Behavior in an Industrial Situation," *Journal of Applied Psychology* 58 (1973): 302–307.

G. P. Latham and S. B. Kinne, "Improving Job Performance Through Training in Goal Setting," *Journal of Applied Psychology* 59 (1974): 187–191.

G. P. Latham and E. A. Locke, "Increasing Productivity with Decreasing Time Limits: A Field Replication of Parkinsons' Law," *Journal of Applied Psychology* 60 (1975): 524–526.

G. P. Latham and G. A. Yukl, "Assigned Versus Participative Goal Setting with Educated and Uneducated Wood Workers," *Journal of Applied Psychology* 60 (1975): 299–302.

11. G. P. Latham, T. R. Mitchell, and D. L. Dossett, "The Importance of Participative Goal Setting and Anticipated Rewards on Goal Difficulty and Job Performance," *Journal of Applied Psychology* 63 (1978): 163–171.

12. G. P. Latham and K. N. Wexley, *Increasing Productivity Through Performance Appraisal* (Massachusetts: Addison-Wesley, 1994).

13. G. P. Latham and L. M. Saari, "The Effects of Holding Goal Difficulty Constant on Assigned and Participatively Set Goals," *Academy of Management Journal* 22 (1979): 163–168.

G. P. Latham, T. P. Steele, and L. M. Saari, "The Effects of Participation and Goal Difficulty on Performance," *Personnel Psychology* 35 (1982): 677–686.

G. P. Latham, M. Erez, and E. A. Locke, "Resolving Scientific Disputes by the Joint Design of Crucial Experiments by the Antagonists: Application of the Erez-Latham Dispute Regarding Participation in Goal Setting," *Journal of Applied Psychology Monograph* 73 (1988): 753–772.

14. A. H. Brayfield and W. H. Crockett, "Employee Attitudes and Employee Performance," *Psychological Bulletin* 52 (1955): 396–424.

V. H. Vroom, *Work Motivation* (New York: Wiley, 1964).

E. E. Lawler and L. W. Porter, "The Effect of Performance on Job Satisfaction," *Industrial Relations* 7 (1967): 20–28.

A. Bandura, "Self-Regulation of Motivation and Action Through Internal Standards and External Goal Systems," in *Goal Concepts in Personality and Social Psychology*, ed. L. A. Pervin (New Jersey: Erlbaum, 1989), 19–85.

D. Cervone, N. Jiwani, and R. Wood, "Goal Setting and the Differential Influence of Self-Regulatory Processes on Complex Decision-Making Performance," *Journal of Personality and Social Psychology* 61 (1991): 257–266.

15. F. Herzberg, *Work and the Nature of Man* (New York: Word Publishing Company, 1966).

J. R. Hackman and G. R. Oldham, "Development of the Job Diagnostic Survey," *Journal of Applied Psychology* 60 (1975): 159–170.

J. R. Hackman and G. R. Oldham, "Motivation Through the Design of Work: Test of a Theory," *Organizational Behavior and Human Performance* 16 (1976): 250–279.

16. S. K. Parker, "Longitudinal Effects of Lean Production on Employee Outcomes and Mediating Role of Work Characteristics," *Journal of Applied Psychology* 88 (2003): 620–634.

S. K. Parker and T. D. Wall, *Job and Work Design: Organizing Work to Promote Well-Being and Effectiveness* (California: Sage, 1998).

T. Theorell and R. A. Karasek, "Current Issues to the Psychosocial Job Strain and Cardiovascular Disease Research," *Journal of Occupational Health Psychology* 1 (1996): 9–26.

C. Argyris, *Personality and Organization* (New York: HarperCollins, 1957).

17. H. Aguinis and C. A. Henle, "The Search for Universals in Cross-Cultural Organizational Behavior," in *Organizational Behavior: The State of Science*, ed. J. Greenberg (New Jersey: Erlbaum, 2003), 373–419.

C. D. Silverthorne, "Motivation and Management Styles in the Public and Private Sectors in Taiwan and a Comparison with the United States," *Journal of Applied Social Psychology* 26 (1992): 1827–1837.

R. A. Roe et al., "A Comparison of Work Motivation in Bulgaria, Hungary, and the Netherlands: Test of a Model," *Applied Psychology: An International Review* 49 (2000): 658–687.

G. E. Popp, H. J. Davis, and T. T. Herbert, "Those Things Yonder Are No Giants, but Decision Makers in International Teams," in *New Perspectives* on *International Industrial/Organizational Psychology*, eds. P. C. Earley and M. Erez (California: Jossey-Bass, 1986), 410–455.

G. G. Alpander and K. D. Carter, "Strategic Multinational Intra-Company Differences in Employee Motivation," *Journal of Managerial Psychology* 6 (1991): 25–32.

18. P. M. Wright and J. L. Cordery, "Production Uncertainty as a Contextual Moderator of Employee Reactions to Job Design," *Journal of Applied Psychology* 84 (1999): 456–463.

19. M. A. Campion and P. W. Thayer, "Development and Field Evaluation of an Interdisciplinary Measure of Job Design," *Journal of Applied Psychology* 70 (1985): 29–43.

    M. Frese et al., "Personal Initiative at Work: Differences Between East and West Germany," *Academy of Management Journal* 39 (1996): 37–63.

20. C. B. Ferster and B. F. Skinner, *Schedules of Reinforcement* (Connecticut: Appleton-Century-Crofts, 1957).

    B. F. Skinner, *Science and Human Behavior* (New York: Macmillan, 1953).

    B. F. Skinner, *About Behaviorism* (Oxford: Knopf, 1974).

21. G. P. Latham and D. L. Dossett, "Designing Incentive Plans for Unionized Employees: A Comparison of Continuous and Variable Ratio Reinforcement Schedules," *Personnel Psychology* 31 (1978): 47–61.

22. L. M. Saari and G. P. Latham, "Employee Reactions to Continuous and Variable Ratio Reinforcement Schedules Involving a Monetary Incentive," *Journal of Applied Psychology* 67 (1982): 506–508.

23. The effect of society on an employee's values was shown in a landmark study by Geert Hofstede. He analyzed the questionnaire responses of 116,000 employees in 50 countries and found that each country could be described in terms of four values—power distance, individualism, masculinity, and uncertainty avoidance. Power distance defines the extent to which a less powerful person in a given society accepts and considers inequality in power as normal. An individualist culture emphasizes enlightened self-interest whereas a collectivist culture values ways of enhancing a group's interests. Masculine cultures value such personality traits as assertiveness, ambitiousness, and competitiveness, especially in regard to material success. A feminine culture emphasizes quality of life, interpersonal relationships, and a value for taking care of the weak. Uncertainty avoidance refers to the extent to which people are made nervous by situations that are unstructured, unclear, or unpredictable. Strict codes of behavior and

a belief in absolute truths typify this society. G. Hofstede, *Culture's Consequences: International Differences in Work-Related Values* (California: Sage, 1980).

G. Hofstede, "The Cultural Relativity of the Quality of Life Concept," *Academy of Management Review* 9 (1984): 389–398.

G. Hofstede, *Culture's Consequences* (California: Sage, 2001).

24. M. Erez, "Make Management Practice Fit the National Culture," in *Handbook of Principles of Organizational Behavior*, ed. E. A. Locke (Oxford: Blackwell, 2000), 418–434.

M. Erez and P. C. Earley, *Culture, Self-Identity, and Work* (New York: Oxford University Press, 1993).

P. C. Earley, "Redefining Interactions Across Cultures and Organizations: Moving Forward with Cultural Intelligence," in *Research in Organizational Behavior: An Annual Series of Analytical Essays and Critical Reviews*, eds. B. M. Staw and R. M. Kramer (Pennsylvania: Elsevier, 2002), 271–299.

25. K. T. Dirks and J. Mclean-Parks, "Conflicting Stories: The State of the Science of Conflict," in *Organizational Behavior: The State of the Science*, ed. J. Greenberg (New Jersey: Erlbaum, 2003), 283–324.

26. F. Herzberg, *Work and the Nature of Man* (New York: Word Publishing Company, 1966).

F. Herzberg, "One More Time: How Do You Motivate Employees?" *Harvard Business Review* 46 (1968): 53–62.

27. R. Folger and R. Cropanzano, *Foundations for Organizational Science: Organizational Justice and Human Resource Management* (California: Sage, 1998).

J. Greenberg, "A Taxonomy of Organizational Justice Theories," *Academy of Management Review* 12 (1987): 9–22.

J. Greenberg, "Looking Fair vs. Being Fair: Managing Impressions of Organizational Justice," in *Research in Organizational Behavior*, vol. 12, eds. B. M. Staw and L. L. Cummings (Connecticut: JAI Press, 1990), 111–158.

J. Greenberg, "Promote Procedural Justice to Enhance the Acceptance of Work Outcomes," in *A Handbook of Principles of Organizational Behavior*, ed. E. A. Locke (Oxford: Blackwell, 2000). 181–196.

28. T. A. Judge and J. A. Colquitt, "Organizational Justice and Stress: The Mediating Role of Work Family Conflict," *Journal of Applied Psychology* 89 (2004): 395–404.

M. Inness, J. Barling, and N. Turner, "Understanding Supervisor-Targeted

Aggression: A Within-Person, Between-Jobs Design," *Journal of Applied Psychology* 90 (2005): 731–739.

29. S. S. Masterson, "A Trickle-Down Model of Organizational Justice: Relating Employees' and Customers' Perceptions and Reactions to Fairness," *Journal of Applied Psychology* 86 (2001): 594–604.

30. D. M. Rousseau, "Schema, Promise and Mutuality: The Building Blocks of the Psychological Contract," *Journal of Occupational and Organizational Psychology* 74 (2001): 511–541.

   D. M. Rousseau, *Idiosyncratic Deals: When Workers Bargain for Themselves* (New York: Sharp, 2005).

31. E. W. Morrison and S. L. Robinson, "When Employees Feel Betrayed: A Model of How Psychological Contract Violation Develops," *Academy of Management Review* 22 (1997): 226–256.

   S. L. Robinson and E. W. Morrison, "The Development of Psychological Contract Breach and Violation: A Longitudinal Study," *Journal of Organizational Behavior* 21 (2000): 525–546.

32. S. W. Gilliland, L. Benson, and D. H. Schepers, "A Rejection Threshold in Justice Evaluation: Effects in Judgment and Decision-Making," *Organizational Behavior and Human Decision Processes* 76 (1998): 113–131.

   S. W. Gilliland and D. Chan, "Justice in Organizations," in *Handbook of Industrial, Work, and Organizational Psychology*, vol. 2, eds. N. Anderson et al. (London: Sage, 2001), 143–165.

Chapter 5

1. Among the leading researchers on what increases job satisfaction is Greg Oldman, a behavioral scientist at Tulane University in New Orleans.

2. John Meyer, *Handbook of Employee Commitment* (Northampton: Edward Elgar Publishing, 2016).

3. A. B. Bakker, E. Demerouti, and A. I. Sanz-Vergel, "Burnout and Work Engagement: The JD-R Approach," *Annual Review of Organizational Psychology and Organizational Behavior*, no. 1: 389–441.

4. J. M. Byrne and A. Camato, "It's Been a Hard Day's Night: Work Family Interface and Employee Engagement," *Organizational Dynamics*, no. 46: 104–112.

5. W. B. Schaufeli, "Engaging Leadership in the Job Demands-Resources Model," *Career Development International*, no. 20: 446–463. For more information on the Energy Compass, see W.B. Schaufel; "The Job

Demands–Resources Model: A 'how to guide' to increase work engagement and prevent burnout," *Organizational Dynamics*, in-press.

6. K. Alfes and N. Langer, "Paradoxical Leadership: Understanding and Managing Conflicting Tensions to Foster Volunteer Engagement," *Organizational Dynamics*, no. 46: 96–103.

7. A. M. Saks, "Translating Employee Engagement Research into Practice," *Organizational Dynamics*, no. 46: 76–86.

Chapter 6

1. Among the privileges of serving as the editor of *Organizational Dynamics* is that I am among the first to read the results of leading-edge research. The primary audience of this journal is managers and MBA students. This chapter is based on a series of articles edited by Peter Heslin and Daniel Turban. The title of their opening editorial is "Enabling Career Success as an Emergent Process," *Organizational Dynamics* (2016): 155–164.

2. E. H. Schein and J. Van Maanen, "Career Anchors and Job/Role Planning: Tools for Career and Talent Management," *Organizational Dynamics* (2016): 165–173.

3. D. T. Hall and J. Yip, "Discerning Career Cultures at Work," *Organizational Dynamics* (2016): 174–184.

4. M. Wolfgang et al., "Career Success Across the Globe: Insights from the 5C Project," *Organizational Dynamics* (2016): 197–205.

5. S. K. Parker and J. Liao, "Wise Proactivity: How to be Proactive and Wise in Building Your Career," *Organizational Dynamics* (2016): 217–227.

6. S. E. Seibert, M. L. Kraimer, and P. A. Heslin, "Developing Career Resilience and Adaptivity," *Organizational Dynamics* (2016): 245–257.

7. D. Rousseau, M. Tomprou, and M. Simosi, "Negotiating Flexible and Fair Idiosyncratic Deals (I-deals)," *Organizational Dynamics* (2016): 185–196.

8. B. R. Ragins, "From the Ordinary to the Extraordinary: High Quality Mentoring Relationships at Work," *Organizational Dynamics* (2016): 228–244.

Chapter 7

1. G. Tinline and C. Cooper, "Work-Related Stress: The Solution Is Management Not Mindfulness," *Organizational Dynamics*, in-press.

2. A. Day, S. Penney, and N. Hartling, "The Psychology, Potential Perils, and Practice of Leading Healthy Workplaces," *Organizational Dynamics*, in press.

E. K. Kelloway and A. Day, "Building Healthy Workplaces: What We Know So Far," *Canadian Journal of Behavioural Science* 37: 223–235.

D. Montano, A. Reeske, F. Franke, and J. Huffmeier, "Leadership, Followers' Mental Health and Job Performance in Organizations: A Comprehensive Meta-Analysis from an Occupational Perspective," *Journal of Organizational Behavior* 38 (2017): 327–350.

3. F. St-Hilaire and H. H. Gilbert, "What Do Leaders Need to Know About Managers' Mental Health," *Organizational Dynamics*, in-press.

F. St-Hilaire, H. H. Gilbert, and J. Brun, "What If Subordinates Took Care of Managers' Mental Health at Work?" *International Journal of Human Resource Management.*

4. J. K. Dimoff and E. K. Kelloway, "Mental Health Problems Are Management Problems: Exploring the Critical Role of Managers in Supporting Employee Mental Health." *Organizational Dynamics*, in-press.

J. K. Dimoff and E. K. Kelloway, "The Development and Evaluation of an Intervention for Workplace Leaders," *International Journal of Stress Management* (2016): 167–189.

5. S. Bonaccio, L. Lapierre, and J. O'Reilly, "Creating Work Climates that Facilitate and Maximize the Benefits of Disclosing Mental Health Problems in the Workplace," *Organizational Dynamics*, in-press.

A. Santuzzi and P. Waltz, "Disability in the Workplace: A Unique and Variable Identity," *Journal of Management* 43 (2016): 1111–1135.

P. E. Fournier, A. A. Sisitsky, C. T. Pike, and R. C. Kessler, "The Economic Burden of Adults with Major Depression Disorder," *Journal of Clinical Psychology* 76 (2015): 155–162.

Chapter 8

1. A. Bandura, *Social Foundations of Thought and Action* (New Jersey: Prentice Hall, 1986).

A. Bandura, "Social Cognitive Theory: An Agentic Perspective," *Annual Review of Psychology* 52 (2001): 1–26.

A. Bandura, "Self-Efficacy: Toward a Unifying Theory of Behavioral Change," *Psychological Review* 84 (1977): 191–215.

2. G. P. Latham, "The Importance of Understanding and Changing Employee Outcome Expectancies for Gaining Commitment to an Organizational Goal," *Personnel Psychology* 54 (2001): 707–716.

3. A. Bandura, *Self-Efficacy: The Exercise of Control* (New York: Freeman, 1997).

4. K. Weick, "Small Wins: Redefining the Scale of Social Problems," *American Psychologist* 39 (1984): 40–49.

5. M. E. P. Seligman, *Learned Optimism: How to Change Your Mind and Your Life* (New York: Pocket Books, 1998).

Chapter 9

1. J. Mark Weber, "Individuals Matter, but the Situation's the Thing: The Case for a Habitual Situational Lens in Leadership and Organizational Decision-Making," *Organizational Dynamics*, in-press.

2. Denise Rousseau, "Making Evidence-Based Organizational Decisions in an Uncertain World," *Organizational Dynamics*, in-press.

3. A.R. Elangovan and Roy Suddaby, "Solomons for Our Times: Wisdom in Decision Making," *Organizational Dynamics*, in-press.

4. C. A. Darison, J. Kim, and J. S. Lerner, "The Role of Emotion in Managerial Judgment and Decision Making," *Organizational Dynamics*, in-press.

5. N. Barak-Corren and M. H. Bazerman, "Inaction and Decision Making in Moral Contexts," *Organizational Dynamics*, in-press.

Chapter 10

1. J. S. Bowman, "Performance Appraisal: Verisimilitude Trumps Veracity," *Public Personnel Management*, Ethics Special Issue 28 (1999): 557–594.

2. G. T. Gabris and D. M. Ihrke, "Does Performance Appraisal Contribute to Heightened Levels of Employee Burnout? The Results of One Study," *Public Personnel Management* 30 (2001): 157–172.

3. J. M. Werner and M. C. Bolino, "Explaining U.S. Courts of Appeals Decisions Involving Performance Appraisal: Accuracy, Fairness, and Validation," *Personnel Psychology* 50 (1997): 1–24.

   H. S. Field and W. H. Holley, "The Relationship of Performance Appraisal System Characteristics to Verdicts in Selected Employment Discrimination Cases," *Academy of Management Journal* 25 (1982): 392–406.

4. G. P. Latham and K. N. Wexley, "Behavioral Observation Scales for Performance Appraisal Purposes," *Personnel Psychology* 30 (1977): 255–268.

   G. P. Latham and K. N. Wexley, *Increasing Productivity Through Performance Appraisal*, 2nd ed. (Massachusetts: Addison-Wesley, 1994).

5. A. Tziner and K. R. Murphy, "Additional Evidence of Attitudinal Influences in Performance Appraisal," *Journal of Business and Psychology* 13 (1999): 407–419.

A. Tziner and R. E. Kopelman, "Is There a Preferred Performance Rating Format? A Non-Psychometric Perspective," *Applied Psychology: An International Review* 51 (2002): 479–503.

A. Tziner, C. Joannis, and K. R. Murphy, "A Comparison of Three Models of Performance Appraisal with Regard to Goal Properties, Goal Perception and Ratee Satisfaction," *Group & Organization Management* 25 (2000): 175–190.

U. Wiersma and G. P. Latham, "The Practicality of Behavioral Observation Scales, Behavioral Expectation Scales, and Trait Scales," *Personnel Psychology* 39 (1986): 619–628.

U. J. Wiersma, P. Van Den Berg, and G. P. Latham, "Dutch Reactions to Behavioral Observation, Behavioral Expectation, and Trait Scales," *Group and Organization Management* 20 (1995): 297–309.

A. Erikson and T. Allen, "Linking 360-Degree Feedback to Business Outcome Measures," paper presented at the annual meeting of the Society for Industrial and Organizational Psychology, Orlando, FL, 2003.

6. S. E. Scullen, M. K. Mount, and M. Goff, "Understanding the Latent Structure of Job Performance Ratings," *Journal of Applied Psychology* 85 (2000): 956–970.

7. S. J. Wayne and R. C. Liden, "Effects of Impression Management on Performance Ratings: A Longitudinal Study," *Academy of Management Journal* 38 (1995): 232–260.

W. V. Bingham, "Halo, Invalid and Valid," *Journal of Applied Psychology* 23 (1939): 221–228.

J. Lefkowitz, "The Role of Interpersonal Affective Regard in Supervisory Performance Ratings: A Literature Review and Proposed Causal Model," *Journal of Occupational and Organizational Psychology* 73 (2000): 67–85.

8. J. P. Strauss, M. Barrick, and M. Connerley, "An Investigation of Personality Similarity Effects (Relational and Perceived) on Peer and Supervisor Ratings and the Role of Familiarity and Liking," *Journal of Occupational and Organizational Psychology* 74 (2001): 637–657.

9. Erikson and Allen, "Linking 360-Degree Feedback to Business Outcome Measures."

10. J. Greenberg, "A Taxonomy of Organizational Justice Theories," *Academy of Management Review* 12 (1987): 9–22.

J. Greenberg, "The Social Side of Fairness: Interpersonal and Informational Classes of Organizational Justice," in *Justice in the Workplace: Approaching*

Fairness in Human Resource Management, ed. R. Cropanzano (New Jersey: Erlbaum, 1993): 79–103.

R. Folger and R. Cropanzano, *Foundations for Organizational Science: Organizational Justice and Human Resource Management* (California: Sage, 1998).

R. Folger, M. Konovsky, and R. Cropanzano, "A Due Process Metaphor for Performance Appraisal," *Research in Organizational Behavior* 14 (1992): 129–177.

11. A. H. Church, "Do Higher Performing Managers Actually Receive Better Ratings? A Validation of Multirater Assessment Methodology," *Consulting Psychology Journal: Practice and Research* 52 (2000): 99–116.

12. G. Olivero, K. D. Bane, and R. E. Kopelman, "Executive Coaching as a Transfer of Training Tool: Effects on Productivity in a Public Agency," *Public Personnel Management* 26 (1997): 461–469.

13. A meta-analysis published in *Personnel Psychology* showed the interchangeability of bottom-line and behavioral measures of employee performance. This is because behavior identified through a job analysis specifies what a person must do to impact the bottom line. W. H. Bommer et al., "On the Interchangeability of Objective and Subjective Measures of Employee Performance: A Meta-Analysis," *Personnel Psychology* 48 (1995): 587.

14. P. Drucker, *Management: Tasks, Responsibilities, and Practices* (New York: HarperCollins, 1973).

15. D. Zweig and K. Scott, "When Unfairness Matters Most: Supervisory Violations of Electronic Monitoring Practices," *Human Resource Management Journal* 17 (2007): 227–247.

D. Zweig and J. Webster, "Where Is the Line Between Benign and Invasive? An Examination of Psychological Barriers to the Acceptance of Awareness Monitoring Systems," *Journal of Organizational Behavior* 23 (2002): 605–633.

16. L. E. Atwater and D. A. Waldman, "Accountability in 360 Degree Feedback," *HR Magazine* (May 1998): 96–104.

17. A study published in the *Journal of Applied Psychology* showed that an effective way to get agreement between self- and supervisory accounts of job performance is to use a behavioral appraisal instrument. B. W. Schrader and D. D. Steiner, "Common Comparison Standards: An Approach to Improving Agreement Between Self and Supervisory Performance," *Journal of Applied Psychology* 81 (1996): 813–820.

18. G. R. Gilbert, E. L. Hannan, and K. B. Lowe, "Is Smoking Stigma Clouding

the Objectivity of Employee Performance Appraisal?" *Public Personnel Management* 27 (1998): 285–300.

19. A. H. Eagly, S. J. Karau, and M. G. Makhijani, "Gender and the Effectiveness of Leaders: A Meta-Analysis," *Psychological Bulletin* 117 (1995): 125–145.

    A. H. Eagly, M. G. Makhijani, and B. G. Klonsky, "Gender and the Evaluation of Leaders: A Meta-Analysis," *Psychological Bulletin* 111 (1992): 3–22.

    J. Boldry, W. Wood, and D. A. Kashy, "Gender Stereotypes and the Evaluation of Men and Women in Military Training," *Journal of Social Issues* 57 (2001): 689–705.

    A. Pazy and I. Oron, "Sex Proportion and Performance Evaluation Among High-Ranking Military Officers," *Journal of Organizational Behavior* 22 (2001): 689–702.

20. R. C. Ford and C. P. Heaton, *Managing the Guest Experience in Hospitality* (New York: Delmar, 2000).

21. A. Tziner and K. R. Murphy, "Additional Evidence of Attitudinal Influences in Performance Appraisal," *Journal of Business and Psychology* 13 (1999): 407–419.

22. G. P. Latham, K. N. Wexley, and E. D. Pursell, "Training Managers to Minimize Rating Errors in the Observation of Behavior," *Journal of Applied Psychology* 60 (1975): 550–555.

23. A. G. Walker and J. W. Smither, "A Five-Year Study of Upward Feedback: What Managers Do with Their Results Matters," *Personnel Psychology* 52 (1999): 393–423.

24. J. L. Komaki and M. L. Desselles, *Supervision Reexamined: The Role of Monitors and Consequences* (Massachusetts: Allyn & Unwin, 1994).

25. P. G. Dominick, R. R. Reilly, and J. W. McGourty, "The Effects of Peer Feedback on Team Member Behavior," *Group and Organization Management* 22 (1997): 508–520.

    V. U. Druskat and S. B. Wolff, "Effects and Timing of Developmental Peer Appraisals in Self-Managing Work Groups," *Journal of Applied Psychology* 84 (1999): 58–74.

26. B. Schneider and D. E. Bowen, *Winning the Service Game* (Massachusetts: Harvard Business School Press, 1995).

27. Ford and Heaton, *Managing the Guest Experience in Hospitality.*

28. L. Atwater, P. Roush, and A. Fischthal, "The Influence of Upward Feedback on Self- and Follower Ratings of Leadership," *Personnel Psychology* 48 (1995): 35–59.

29. C. Bailey and C. Fletcher, "The Impact of Multiple Source Feedback on

Management Development: Findings from a Longitudinal Study," *Journal of Organizational Behavior* 23 (2002): 853–867.

P. W. B. Atkins and R. E. Wood, "Self- Versus Others' Ratings as Predictors of Assessment Center Ratings: Validation Evidence for 360-Degree Feedback Programs," *Personnel Psychology* 55 (2002): 871–904.

30. P. Heslin and G. P. Latham, "The Effect of Upward Feedback on Managerial Behavior," *Applied Psychology: An International Review* 53 (2004): 23–38.

31. T. A. Beehr et al., "Evaluation of 360-Degree Feedback Ratings: Relationships with Each Other and with Performance and Selection Predictors," *Journal of Organizational Behavior* 22 (2001): 775–788.

32. C. Fletcher, "Self-Awareness: A Neglected Attribute in Selection and Assessment?" *International Journal of Selection and Assessment* 5 (1997): 183–187.

33. L. Richardson, "Five-Minute Sales Coaching," *Training and Development* 52 (1998): 53–57.

K. Tyler, "Prepare Managers to Become Career Coaches," *HR Magazine* 42, 1997, 98–101.

34. A. N. Kluger and A. DeNisi, "The Effects of Feedback Interventions on Performance: A Historical Review, a Meta-Analysis, and a Preliminary Feedback Intervention Theory," *Psychological Bulletin* 119 (1996): 254–284.

35. E. A. Locke and G. P. Latham, *A Theory of Goal Setting and Task Performance* (New Jersey: Prentice Hall, 1990).

G. P. Latham and E. A. Locke, "New Developments in and Directions for Goal Setting," *European Psychologist* 12 (2007): 290–300.

36. J. D. Campbell, R. B. Garfinkel, and L. Moses, "Strategies for Success in Measuring Performance," *HR Magazine* 41, 1996, 98.

J. W. Smither et al., "Can Working with an Executive Coach Improve Multisource Feedback Ratings Over Time? A Quasi-Experimental Field Study," *Personnel Psychology* 56 (2003): 23–44.

37. M. H. Budworth, G. P. Latham, and L. Manroop "Looking Forward to Performance Improvement," *Human Resource Management* 54 (2015): 45–54.

38. R. C. Ford, G. P. Latham, and G. Lennox, "Mystery Shopper: A New Tool for Coaching Employee Performance Improvement," *Organizational Dynamics* 40 (2015): 157–164.

Chapter 11

1. The names of the companies and people in this chapter are fictional. The case information and results are factual.

REFERENCES

Aguinis, H., and Henle, C. A. "The Search for Universals in Cross-Cultural Organizational Behavior." In *Organizational Behavior: The State of Science*, edited by J. Greenberg, 373–419. New Jersey: Erlbaum, 2003.

Alpander, G. G., and Carter, K. D. "Strategic Multinational Intra-Company Differences in Employee Motivation." *Journal of Managerial Psychology* 6 (1991): 25–32.

American Educational Research Association, American Psychological Association, and National Council on Measurement in Education. *The Standards for Educational and Psychological Testing*. Washington, DC: American Educational Research Association, 1999.

Anderson, G. D., and Viswesvaran, C. "An Update of the Validity of Personality Scales in Personnel Selection: A Meta-Analysis of Studies Published Between 1992-1997." Paper presented at the 13th Annual Meeting of the Society for Industrial and Organizational Psychology, Dallas, 1998.

Argyris, C. *Personality and Organization*. New York: HarperCollins, 1957.

———. "Teaching Smart People How to Learn." In *Organization Development: A Jossey-Bass Reader*, edited by J. Y. Galls, 267–285. San Francisco: Jossey-Bass, 2006.

Atkins, P. W. B., and Wood, R. E. "Self- Versus Others' Ratings as Predictors of Assessment Center Ratings: Validation Evidence for 360-Degree Feedback Programs." *Personnel Psychology* 55 (2002): 871–904.

Atwater, L., Roush, P., and Fischthal, A. "The Influence of Upward Feedback on Self- and Follower Ratings of Leadership." *Personnel Psychology* 48 (1995): 35–59.

Atwater, L. E., and Waldman, D. A. "Accountability in 360-Degree Feedback." *HR Magazine*, May 1998.

Bailey, C., and Fletcher, C. "The Impact of Multiple Source Feedback on Management Development: Findings from a Longitudinal Study." *Journal of Organizational Behavior* 23 (2002): 853–867.

Bandura, A. *Self-Efficacy: The Exercise of Control*. New York: Freeman, 1997.

———. "Self-Efficacy: Toward a Unifying Theory of Behavioral Change." *Psychological Review* 84 (1977): 191–215.

———. "Self-Efficacy Mechanism in Human Agency." *American Psychologist* 37 (1982): 122–147.

———. "Self-Regulation of Motivation and Action Through Internal Standards and External Goal Systems." In *Goal Concepts in Personality and Social Psychology*, edited by L. A. Pervin, 19–85. New Jersey: Erlbaum, 1989.

———. "Social Cognitive Theory: An Agentic Perspective." *Annual Review of Psychology* 52 (2001): 1–26.

———. *Social Foundations of Thought and Action.* New Jersey: Prentice Hall, 1986.

Barak-Corren, N., and Bazerman, M.H. "Inaction and Decision Making in Moral Contexts." *Organizational Dynamics*, in press.

Barrick, M. R., and Mount, M. K. "The Big Five Personality Dimensions and Job Performance: A Meta-Analysis." *Personnel Psychology* 44 (1991): 1–26.

Barrick, M. R., Mount, M. K., and Judge, T. A. "Personality and Performance at the Beginning of the New Millennium: What Do We Know and Where Do We Go Next?" *International Journal of Selection and Assessment* 9 (2001): 9–30.

Barrick, M. R., Stewart, G. L., Neubert, M., and Mount, M. K. "Relating Member Ability and Personality to Work Team Processes and Team Effectiveness." *Journal of Applied Psychology* 83 (1998): 377–391.

Bass, B., and Yammarino, F. J. "Congruence of Self and Others' Leadership Ratings of Naval Officers for Understanding Successful Performance." *Applied Psychology: An International Review* 40 (1991): 437–454.

Beehr, T. A., Ivanitskaya, L., Hansen, C. P., Erofeev, D., and Gudanowski, D. M. "Evaluation of 360 Degree Feedback Ratings: Relationships with Each Other and with Performance and Selection Predictors." *Journal of Organizational Behavior* 22 (2001): 775–788.

Bingham, W. V. "Halo, Invalid and Valid." *Journal of Applied Psychology* 23 (1939): 221–228.

Boldry, J., Wood, W., and Kashy, D. A. "Gender Stereotypes and the Evaluation of Men and Women in Military Training." *Journal of Social Issues* 57 (2001): 689–705.

Bommer, W. H., Johnson, J. L., Rich, G. A., Podsakoff, P. M., and Mackenzie, S. B. "On the Interchangeability of Objective and Subjective Measures of Employee Performance: A Meta-Analysis." *Personnel Psychology* 48 (1995): 587.

Bonaccio, S., Lapierre, L., and O'Reilly, J. "Creating Work Climates that Facilitate and Maximize the Benefits of Disclosing Mental Health Problems in the Workplace." *Organizational Dynamics.*

Bowman, J. S. "Performance Appraisal: Verisimilitude Trumps Veracity." *Public Personnel Management* 28 (1999): 557–594.

Bray, D. W., Campbell, R. J., and Grant, D. L. *Formative Years in Business: A Long-Term Study of Managerial Lives.* New York: Wiley, 1974.

Bray, D. W., and Howard, D. W. "Predictions of Managerial Success Over Long Periods of Time: Lessons from the Management Progress Study." In *Measures of Leadership*, edited by K. E. Clark and M. B. Clark, 113–130. New Jersey: Leadership Library of America, 1990.

Brayfield, A. H., and Crockett, W. H. "Employee Attitudes and Employee Performance." *Psychological Bulletin* 52 (1955): 396–424.

Brown, T. C., and Latham, G. P. "The Effect of Training in Verbal Self-Guidance on Performance Effectiveness in a MBA Program." *Canadian Journal of Behavioural Science* 38 (2006): 1–11.

Budworth, M. H., Latham, G. P. and Manroop, L. "Looking Forward to Performance Improvement." Human Resource Management 54 (2015): 45–54.

Burke, L. A., and Baldwin, T. T. "Workforce Training Transfer: A Study of the Effect of Relapse Prevention Training and Transfer Climate." *Human Resource Management* 38 (1999): 227–242.

Campbell, J. D., Garfinkel, R. B., and Moses, L. "Strategies for Success in Measuring Performance." *HR Magazine*, 1996.

Campion, M. A., and Thayer, P. W. "Development and Field Evaluation of an Interdisciplinary Measure of Job Design." *Journal of Applied Psychology* 70 (1985): 29–43.

Cervone, D., Jiwani, N., and Wood, R. "Goal Setting and the Differential Influence of Self-Regulatory Processes on Complex Decision-Making Performance." *Journal of Personality and Social Psychology* 61 (1991): 257–266.

Chatham, J. A. "Matching People and Organizations: Selection and Socialization in Public Accounting Firms." *Administrative Science Quarterly* 36 (1991): 459–484.

Church, A. H. "Do Higher Performing Managers Actually Receive Better Ratings? A Validation of Multirater Assessment Methodology." *Consulting Psychology Journal: Practice and Research* 52 (2000): 99–116.

Cote, S. "Emotional Intelligence in Organizations." *Annual Review of Organizational Behavior* 1: 459–488.

Cote, S. "Enhancing Managerial Effectiveness via Four Core Facets of Emotional Intelligence: Self-Awareness, Facial Perception, Emotion Understanding, and Emotion Regulation." *Organizational Dynamics* 46 (2017): 140–147.

Darison, C. A., Kim, J., and Lerner, J. S. "The Role of Emotion in Managerial Judgment and Decision Making." *Organizational Dynamics.*

Day, A., Penney, S., and Hartling, N. "The Psychology, Potential Perils, and Practice of Leading Healthy Workplaces." *Organizational Dynamics.*

Deci, E. L. *Intrinsic Motivation.* New York: Plenum, 1975.

Deci, E. L., and Ryan, R. M. "The General Causality Orientation Scale: Self-Determination in Personality." *Journal of Research in Personality* 19 (1985): 109–137.

———. "A Motivational Approach to Self: Integration in Personality." In *Nebraska Symposium on Motivation,* edited by R. Dienstbier, 237–288. Nebraska: University of Nebraska Press, 1990.

Dimoff J. K., and Kelloway, E. K. "The Development and Evaluation of an Intervention for Workplace Leaders." *International Journal of Stress Management* (2016): 167–189.

Dimoff, J. K., and Kelloway, E. K. "Mental Health Problems Are Management Problems: Exploring the Critical Role of Managers in Supporting Employee Mental Health." *Organizational Dynamics,* in-press.

Dirks, K. T., and Mclean-Parks, J. "Conflicting Stories: The State of the Science of Conflict." In *Organizational Behavior: The State of the Science,* edited by J. Greenberg, 283–324. New Jersey: Erlbaum, 2003.

Dominick, P. G., Reilly, R. R., and McGourty, J. W. "The Effects of Peer Feedback on Team Member Behavior." *Group and Organization Management* 22 (1997): 508–520.

Driskell, J. E., Copper, C., and Moran, A. "Does Mental Practice Enhance Performance?" *Journal of Applied Psychology* 79 (1994): 481–492.

Drucker, P. *Management: Tasks, Responsibilities, and Practices.* New York: HarperCollins, 1973.

Druskat, V. U., and Wolff, S. B. "Effects and Timing of Developmental Peer Appraisals in Self-Managing Work Groups." *Journal of Applied Psychology* 84 (1999): 58–74.

Dweck, C. S. "Motivational Processes Affecting Learning." *American Psychologist* 41 (1986): 1040–1048.

———. *Self-Theories: Their Role in Motivation, Personality, and Development.* Pennsylvania: Psychology Press, 1999.

Dweck, C. S., and Leggett, E. L. A. "A Social-Cognitive Approach to Motivation and Personality." *Psychological Review* 95 (1988): 256–273.

Eagly, A. H., Karau, S. J., and Makhijani, M. G. "Gender and the Effectiveness of Leaders: A Meta-Analysis." *Psychological Bulletin* 117 (1995):125–145.

Eagly, A. H., Makhijani, M. G., and Klonsky, B. G. "Gender and the Evaluation of Leaders: A Meta-Analysis." *Psychological Bulletin* 111 (1992): 3–22.

Earley, P. C. "Redefining Interactions Across Cultures and Organizations: Moving Forward with Cultural Intelligence." In *Research in Organizational Behavior: An Annual Series of Analytical Essays and Critical Reviews*, edited by B. M. Staw and R. M. Kramer, 271–299. Pennsylvania: Elsevier, 2002.

Eby, L. T., Freeman, D. M., Rush, M. C., and Lance, C. E. "Motivational Bases of Affective Organizational Commitment: A Partial Test of an Integrative Theoretical Model." *Journal of Occupational and Organizational Psychology* 72 (1999): 463–483.

Elangovan, A. R., and Suddaby, R. Solomons. "For Our Times: Wisdom in Decision Making." *Organizational Dynamics.*

Erez, M. "Make Management Practice Fit the National Culture." In *Handbook of Principles of Organizational Behavior*, edited by E. A. Locke, 418–434. Oxford: Blackwell, 2000.

Erez, M., and Earley, P. C. *Culture, Self-Identity, and Work.* New York: Oxford University Press, 1993.

Erikson, A., and Allen, T. "Linking 360-Degree Feedback to Business Outcome Measures." Paper presented at the annual meeting of the Society for Industrial and Organizational Psychology, Orlando, FL, 2003.

Ferster, C. B., and Skinner, B. F. *Schedules of Reinforcement.* Connecticut: Appleton-Century-Crofts, 1957.

Field, H. S., and Holley, W. H. "The Relationship of Performance Appraisal System Characteristics to Verdicts in Selected Employment Discrimination Cases." *Academy of Management Journal* 25 (1982): 392–406.

Flanagan, J. C. "The Critical Incident Technique." *Psychological Bulletin* 51 (1954): 327–358.

Fletcher, C. "Self-Awareness: A Neglected Attribute in Selection and Assessment?" *International Journal of Selection and Assessment* 5 (1997): 183–187.

Folger, R., and Cropanzano, R. *Foundations for Organizational Science: Organizational Justice and Human Resource Management.* California: Sage, 1998.

Folger, R., Konovsky, M., and Cropanzano, R. "A Due Process Metaphor for Performance Appraisal." *Research in Organizational Behavior* 14 (1992): 129–177.

Fontani, G., Migliorini, S., Benocci, R., Facchini, A., Casini, M., and Corradeschi,

F. "Effect of Mental Imagery on the Development of Skilled Motor Actions." *Perceptual and Motor Skills* 105 (2007): 803–826.

Ford, R. C., and Heaton, C. P. *Managing the Guest Experience in Hospitality.* New York: Delmar, 2000.

Ford, R. C., Latham, G. P., and Lennox, G. "Mystery Shopper: A New Tool for Coaching Employee Performance Improvement." *Organizational Dynamics* 40 (2015): 157–164.

Fournier, P. E., Sisitsky, A. A., Pike, C. T., and Kessler, R. C. "The Economic Burden of Adults with Major Depression Disorder." *Journal of Clinical Psychology* 76 (2015): 155–162.

Frayne, C. A., and Latham, G. P. "Application of Social Learning Theory to Employee Self-Management of Attendance." *Journal of Applied Psychology* 72 (1987): 387–392.

Frese, M., Kring, W., Soose, A., and Zempel, J. "Personal Initiative at Work: Differences Between East and West Germany." *Academy of Management Journal* 39 (1996): 37–63.

Gabris, G. T., and Ihrke, D. M. "Does Performance Appraisal Contribute to Heightened Levels of Employee Burnout? The Results of One Study." *Public Personnel Management* 30 (2001): 157–172.

Gaugler B. B., Rosenthal, D. B., Thorntons, G. C., and Bentson, C. "Meta-Analysis of Assessment Center Validity." *Journal of Applied Psychology* 72 (1987): 493–511.

Gilbert, G. R., Hannan, E. L., and Lowe, K. B. "Is Smoking Stigma Clouding the Objectivity of Employee Performance Appraisal?" *Public Personnel Management* 27 (1998): 285–300.

Gilliland, S. W., Benson, L., and Schepers, D. H. "A Rejection Threshold in Justice Evaluation: Effects in Judgment and Decision-Making." *Organizational Behavior and Human Decision Processes* 76 (1998): 113–131.

Gilliland, S. W., and Chan, D. "Justice in Organizations." In *Handbook of Industrial, Work and Organizational Psychology*, edited by N. Anderson, D. Ones, H. Sinangil, and C. Viswesvaran, 143–165. London: Sage, 2001.

Goldberg, L. R. "The Structure of Phenotypic Personality Traits." *American Psychologist* 48 (1993): 26–34.

Goodman, S. A., and Svyantek, D. J. "Person–Organization Fit and Contextual Performance: Do Shared Values Matter?" *Journal of Vocational Behavior* 55 (1999): 254–275.

Green, P. C. *Get Talent: Interview for Actions, Select for Results.* Tennessee: Skilfast, 2007.

Greenberg, J. "Looking Fair vs. Being Fair: Managing Impressions of Organizational Justice." In *Research in Organizational Behavior*, edited by B. M. Staw and L. L. Cummings, 111–158. Greenwich, CT: JAI Press, 1990.

———. "Losing Sleep Over Organizational Injustice: Attenuating Insomniac Reactions to Underpayment Inequity with Supervisory Training in Interactional Justice." *Journal of Applied Psychology* 91 (2006): 58–69.

———. "Promote Procedural Justice to Enhance the Acceptance of Work Outcomes." In A *Handbook of Principles of Organizational Behavior*, edited by E. A. Locke, 181–196. Oxford: Blackwell, 2000.

———. "The Social Side of Fairness: Interpersonal and Informational Classes of Organizational Justice." In *Justice in the Workplace: Approaching Fairness in Human Resource Management*, edited by R. Cropanzano, 79–103. New Jersey: Erlbaum, 1993.

———. "A Taxonomy of Organizational Justice Theories." *Academy of Management Review* 12 (1987): 9–22.

Guion, R. M. *Assessment, Measurement, and Prediction for Personnel Decisions*. New Jersey: Erlbaum, 1998.

Hackman, J. R., and Oldham, G. R. "Development of the Job Diagnostic Survey." *Journal of Applied Psychology* 60 (1975): 159–170.

———. "Motivation Through the Design of Work: Test of a Theory." *Organizational Behavior and Human Performance* 16 (1976): 250–279.

Hart, M. A. *Managing Diversity for Sustained Competitiveness*. New York: Conference Board, 1997.

Herzberg, F. "One More Time: How Do You Motivate Employees?" *Harvard Business Review* 46 (1968): 53–62.

———. *Work and the Nature of Man*. New York: Word Publishing Company, 1966.

Heslin, P., and Latham, G. P. "The Effect of Upward Feedback on Managerial Behavior." *Applied Psychology: An International Review* 53 (2004): 23–38.

Heslin, P. A., Latham, G. P., and VandeWalle, D. "The Effect of Implicit Person Theory on Performance Appraisals." *Journal of Applied Psychology* 90 (2005): 842–856.

Heslin, P. A., VandeWalle, D., and Latham, G. P. "Keen to Help? Managers' Implicit Person Theories and Their Subsequent Employee Coaching." *Personnel Psychology* 59 (2005): 871–902.

Hofstede, G. "The Cultural Relativity of the Quality of Life Concept." *Academy of Management Review* 9 (1984): 389–398.

———. *Culture's Consequences*. California: Sage, 2001.

———. *Culture's Consequences: International Differences in Work-Related Values*. California: Sage, 1980.

Hollander, D. C. "Creating an Onboarding Culture." *HR News Magazine*, June 2008.

Howard, A., and Bray, D. W. *Managerial Lives in Transition: Advancing Age and Changing Times*. New York: Guilford Press, 1988.

Hubbard, E. E. *The Diversity Scorecard: Evaluating the Impact of Diversity on Organizational Performance*. Massachusetts: Elsevier Butterworth-Heinemann, 2004.

Huffcutt A.I., Culbertson, S.S., and Weybrauch, W.S. "Employment Interview Reliability: New Estimates by Structures and Format", *International Journal of Selection and Assessment*, 21 (2013): 264–276.

Inness, M., Barling, J., and Turner, N. "Understanding Supervisor-Targeted Aggression: A Within-Person, Between-Jobs Design." *Journal of Applied Psychology* 90 (2005): 731–739.

Janis, I. L. *Victims of Groupthink: A Psychological Study of Foreign-Policy Decisions and Fiascoes*. Oxford: Houghton Mifflin, 1972.

Janz, J. T. "Initial Comparisons of the Patterned Behavior Description Interviews Versus Unstructured Interviews." *Journal of Applied Psychology* 67 (1982): 577–580.

Janz, J. T., Hellervik, L., and Gilmore, D. C. *Behavior Description Interviewing*. Massachusetts: Allyn & Bacon, 1986.

Janz, T. "Patterned Behavior Description Interviews." In *The Employment Interview: Theory, Research, and Practice*, edited by G. Ferris and R. Eder, 158–168. California: Sage, 1989.

John, O. "The 'Big Five' Factor Taxonomy: Dimensions of Personality in the Natural Languages and in Questionnaires." In *Handbook of Personality Theory and Research*, edited by L. Pervin, 66–100. New York: Guilford Press, 1990.

Judge, T. A., and Colquitt, J. A. "Organizational Justice and Stress: The Mediating Role of Work Family Conflict." *Journal of Applied Psychology* 89 (2004): 395–404.

Kanfer, F. H. "Self-Management Methods." In *Helping People Change*, edited by F. H. Kanfer, 309–355. New York: Wiley, 1975.

———. "Self-Management Methods." In *Helping People Change: A Textbook of Methods* 2nd ed., edited by F. H. Kanfer and A. P. Goldstein, 334–389. New York: Pergamon Press, 1980.

———. "Self-Regulation: Research, Issues, and Speculations." In *Behavior*

Modification in Clinical Psychology, edited by C. Neuringer and J. Michael, 178–220. New York: Appleton-Century-Crofts, 1974.

Keith, N., and Frese, M. "Effectiveness of Error Management Training: A Meta-Analysis." *Journal of Applied Psychology* 93 (2008): 59–69.

——. "Self-Regulation in Error Management Training: Emotion Control and Metacognition as Mediators of Performance Effects." *Journal of Applied Psychology* 90 (2005): 677–691.

Kelloway, E. K., and Day, A. "Building Healthy Workplaces: What We Know So Far." *Canadian Journal of Behavioural Science* 37: 223–235.

Klehe, U. C., and Latham, G. P. "The Predictive and Incremental Validity of the Situational and Patterned Behavior Description Interviews for Teamplaying Behavior." *International Journal of Selection and Assessment* 13 (2005): 108–115.

Kluger, A. N., and DeNisi, A. "The Effects of Feedback Interventions on Performance: A Historical Review, a Meta-Analysis, and a Preliminary Feedback Intervention Theory." *Psychological Bulletin* 119 (1996): 254–284.

Kluger, A. N., and Tikochinsky, J. "The Error of Accepting the 'Theoretical' Null Hypothesis: The Rise, Fall, and Resurrection of Commonsense Hypotheses in Psychology." *Psychological Bulletin* 127 (2001): 408–423.

Kochan, T., Bezrukova, K., Ely, R., Jackson, S., Joshi, A., Jen, K., et al. "The Effects of Diversity on Business Performance: Report of the Diversity Research Network." *Building Opportunities for Leadership Development Initiative*, Alfred P. Sloan Foundation and the Society for Human Resource Management, October 2002.

Komaki, J. L., and Desselles, M. L. *Supervision Reexamined: The Role of Monitors and Consequences*. Massachusetts: Allyn & Unwin, 1994.

Latham, G. P. "The Importance of Understanding and Changing Employee Outcome Expectancies for Gaining Commitment to an Organizational Goal." *Personnel Psychology* 54 (2001): 707–716.

——. *Work Motivation: History, Theory, Research and Practice*. California: Sage, 2012.

Latham, G. P., and Brown, T. C. "The Effect of Learning vs. Outcome Goals on Self-Efficacy, Satisfaction and Performance in an MBA Program." *Applied Psychology: An International Review* 55, no. 4 (2006): 606–623.

Latham, G. P., and Budworth, M. H. "The Effect of Training in Verbal Self-Guidance on the Self-Efficacy and Performance of Native North Americans in the Selection Interview." *Journal of Vocational Behavior* 68 (2006): 516–523.

Latham, G. P., and Dossett, D. L. "Designing Incentive Plans for Unionized

Employees: A Comparison of Continuous and Variable Ratio Reinforcement Schedules." *Personnel Psychology* 31 (1978): 47–61.

Latham, G. P., Erez, M., and Locke, E. A. "Resolving Scientific Disputes by the Joint Design of Crucial Experiments by the Antagonists: Application of the Erez-Latham Dispute Regarding Participation in Goal Setting." *Journal of Applied Psychology Monograph* 73 (1988): 753–772.

Latham, G. P., and Frayne, C. A. "Self-Management Training for Increasing Job Attendance: A Follow-up and a Replication." *Journal of Applied Psychology* 74 (1989): 411–416.

Latham, G. P., and Kinne, S. B. "Improving Job Performance Through Training in Goal Setting." *Journal of Applied Psychology* 59 (1974): 187–191.

Latham, G. P., and Locke, E. A. "Enhancing the Benefits and Overcoming the Pitfalls of Goal Setting." *Organization Dynamics* 35 (2006): 332–340.

———. "Increasing Productivity with Decreasing Time Limits: A Field Replication of Parkinsons' Law." *Journal of Applied Psychology* 60 (1975): 524–526.

———. "New Developments in and Directions for Goal Setting." *European Psychologist* 12 (2007): 290–300.

Latham, G. P., & Locke, E. A. (2018). Goal setting theory: Controversies and resolutions. In D. Ones, N. Anderson, C. Viswesvaran, & H. Sinangil (Eds.) *Handbook of Industrial, Work & Organizational Psychology*, Vol 1., 103-124 Sage.

Latham, G. P., Mitchell, T. R., and Dossett, D. L. "The Importance of Participative Goal Setting and Anticipated Rewards on Goal Difficulty and Job Performance." *Journal of Applied Psychology* 63 (1978): 163–171.

Latham, G. P., and Saari, L. M. "The Effects of Holding Goal Difficulty Constant on Assigned and Participatively Set Goals." *Academy of Management Journal* 22 (1979): 163–168.

Latham, G. P., Saari, L. M., Pursell, E. D., and Campion, M. "The Situational Interview." *Journal of Applied Psychology* 65 (1980): 422–427.

Latham, G. P., and Seijts, G. H. "The Effects of Proximal and Distal Goals on Performance on a Moderately Complex Task." *Journal of Organizational Behavior* 20 (1999): 421–429.

Latham, G. P., and Skarlicki, D. "Criterion-Related Validity of the Situational and Patterned Behavior Description Interviews with Organizational Citizenship Behavior." *Human Performance* 8 (1995): 67–80.

Latham, G. P., Steele, T. P., and Saari, L. M. "The Effects of Participation and Goal Difficulty on Performance." *Personnel Psychology* 35 (1982): 677–686.

Latham, G. P., and Sue-Chan, C. "A Meta-Analysis of the Situational Interview:

An Enumerative Review of Reasons for Its Validity." *Canadian Psychology* 40 (1999): 56-67.

Latham, G. P., and Wexley, K. N. "Behavioral Observation Scales for Performance Appraisal Purposes." *Personnel Psychology* 30 (1977): 255-268.

———. *Increasing Productivity Through Performance Appraisal*, 2nd ed. Massachusetts: Addison-Wesley, 1994.

Latham, G. P., Wexley, K. N., and Pursell, E. D. "Training Managers to Minimize Rating Errors in the Observation of Behavior." *Journal of Applied Psychology* 60 (1975): 550-555.

Latham, G. P., and Yukl, G. A. "Assigned Versus Participative Goal Setting with Educated and Uneducated Wood Workers." *Journal of Applied Psychology* 60 (1975): 299-302.

Lawler, E. *Talent: Making People Your Competitive Advantage*. California: Jossey-Bass, 2008.

Lawler, E. E., and Porter, L. W. "The Effect of Performance on Job Satisfaction." *Industrial Relations* 7 (1967): 20-28.

Lefkowitz, J. "The Role of Interpersonal Affective Regard in Supervisory Performance Ratings: A Literature Review and Proposed Causal Model." *Journal of Occupational and Organizational Psychology* 73 (2000): 67-85.

Lengnick-Hall, M. L., Gaunt, P. H., and Collison, J. *Employer Incentives for Hiring Individuals with Disabilities*. Virginia: Society for Human Resource Management, 2003.

Locke, E. A. "Motivation, Cognition, and Action: An Analysis of Studies of Task Goals and Knowledge." *Applied Psychology: An International Review* 49 (2000): 408-429.

Locke, E. A., and Latham, G. P. "Building a Practically Useful Theory of Goal Setting and Task Motivation: A 35-Year Odyssey." *American Psychologist* 57 (2002): 705-717.

———. *A Theory of Goal Setting and Task Performance*. New Jersey: Prentice Hall, 1990.

Locke, E. A., & Latham, G. P. (2013). *New developments in goal setting and task performance*. New York: Routledge.

Lockwood, N. R. "Workforce Diversity: Leveraging the Power of Difference for Competitive Advantage." *SHRM Research Quarterly* (2005): 1-13.

Maier, N. R. F. *Psychology in Industry*. Massachusetts: Houghton Mifflin, 1955.

Marx, R. D. "Relapse Prevention for Managerial Training: A Model for Maintenance of Behavioral Change." *Academy of Management Review* 7 (1982): 433-441.

Masterson, S. S. "A Trickle-Down Model of Organizational Justice: Relating Employees' and Customers' Perceptions and Reactions to Fairness." *Journal of Applied Psychology* 86 (2001): 594–604.

Matton, J. N., and Hernandez, C. M. "A New Study Identifies the 'Makes and Breaks' of Diversity Initiatives." *Journal of Organizational Excellence* 23 (August 2004): 47–58.

Meichenbaum, D. C. *Cognitive Behavior Modification: An Integrative Approach.* New York: Plenum Press, 1977.

——. "Enhancing Creativity by Modifying What Subjects Say to Themselves." *American Educational Research Journal* 12 (1975): 129–145.

Meyer, J. P., Becker, T. E., and Vandenberghe, C. "Employee Commitment and Motivation: A Conceptual Analysis and Interpretative Model." *Journal of Applied Psychology* 89 (2004): 991–1007.

Meyer, J. P., and Herscovitch, L. "Commitment in the Workplace: Toward a General Model." *Human Resource Management Review* 11 (2001): 299–326.

Millman, Z., and Latham, G. P. "Increasing Re-employment Through Training in Verbal Self-Guidance." In *Work Interventions in the Context of a Globalizing Economy*, edited by M. Erez, U. Kleinbleck, and H. Thierry, 87–97. New Jersey: Erlbaum, 2001.

Mitchell, T. R., and Daniels, D. "Motivation." In *Handbook of Psychology, vol. 12: Industrial Organizational Psychology*, edited by W. C. Borman, D. R. Ilgen, and R. J. Klimoski, 225–254. New York: Wiley, 2003.

Montano, D., Reeske, A., Franke, F., and Huffmeier. "Leadership, Followers' Mental Health and Job Performance in Organizations: A Comprehensive Meta-Analysis from an Occupational Perspective." *Journal of Organizational Behavior* 38 (2017): 327–350.

Morgeson, F. P., Campion, M. A., Dipboye, R. L., Hollenbeck, J. R., Murphy, K., and Schmitt, N. "Are We Getting Fooled Again? Coming to Terms with Limitations in the Use of Personality Tests for Personnel Selection." *Personnel Psychology* 60 (2007): 1029–1049.

Morin, L., and Latham, G. P. "Effect of Mental Practice and Goal Setting as a Transfer of Training Intervention on Supervisors' Self-Efficacy and Communication Skills: An Exploratory Study." *Applied Psychology: An International Review* 49 (2000): 566–578.

Morrison, E. W., and Robinson, S. L. "When Employees Feel Betrayed: A Model of How Psychological Contract Violation Develops." *Academy of Management Review* 22 (1997): 226–256.

Mount, M. K., Barrick, M. R., and Stewart, G. L. "Five-Factor Model of

Personality and Performance in Jobs Involving Interpersonal Interactions." *Human Performance* 11 (1998): 145–165.

Murphy, S. M. "Models of Imagery in Sport Psychology: A Review." *Journal of Mental Imagery* 14 (1990): 153–172.

National Urban League. *Diversity Practices That Work: The American Worker Speaks.* New York: National Urban League, 2004.

Neck, C. P., and Manz, C. C. "Thought Self-Leadership: The Influence of Self-Talk and Mental Imagery on Performance." *Journal of Organizational Behavior* 13 (1992): 681–699.

Olivero, G., Bane, K. D., and Kopelman, R. E. "Executive Coaching as a Transfer of Training Tool: Effects on Productivity in a Public Agency." *Public Personnel Management* 26 (1997): 461–469.

Ones, D. S., and Viswesvaran, C. "Gender, Age and Race Differences on Overt Integrity Tests: Results from Four Large-Scale Job Applicant Datasets." *Journal of Applied Psychology* 83 (1998): 35–42.

Parker, S. K. "Longitudinal Effects of Lean Production on Employee Outcomes and Mediating Role of Work Characteristics." *Journal of Applied Psychology* 88 (2003): 620–634.

Parker, S. K., and Wall, T. D. *Job and Work Design: Organizing Work to Promote Well-Being and Effectiveness.* California: Sage, 1998.

Paunonen, S. V., Jackson, D. N., Treblinski, J., and Forsterling, F. "Personality Structure Across Cultures: A Multimethod Evaluation." *Journal of Personality and Social Psychology* 62 (1992): 447–556.

Pazy, A., and Oron, I. "Sex Proportion and Performance Evaluation Among High-Ranking Military Officers." *Journal of Organizational Behavior* 22 (2001): 689–702.

Penney, L. M., and Spector, P. E. "Narcissism and Counterproductive Work Behavior: Do Bigger Egos Mean Bigger Problems?" *International Journal of Selection and Assessment* 10 (2002): 126–134.

Pinder, C. C. *Work Motivation in Organizational Behavior.* New Jersey: Prentice Hall, 1998.

Popovich, P., and Wanous, J. P. "The Realistic Job Preview as a Persuasive Communication." *Academy of Management Review* 7 (1982): 570–578.

Popp, G. E., Davis, H. J., and Herbert, T. T. "Those Things Yonder Are No Giants, but Decision Makers in International Teams." In *New Perspectives on International Industrial/Organizational Psychology,* edited by P. C. Earley and M. Erez, 410–455. California: Jossey-Bass, 1986.

Porter, L. W., and Steers, R. M. "Organizational, Work, and Personal Factors in Employee Turnover and Absenteeism." *Psychological Bulletin* 80 (1973): 151–176.

Rand, T. M., and Wexley, K. N. "Demonstration of the Effect, 'Similar to Me,' in Simulated Employment Interviews." *Psychological Reports* 36 (1975): 535–544.

Richardson, A. *Individual Differences in Imaging: Their Measurement, Origins, and Consequences.* New York: Baywood, 1994.

Richardson, J. T. E. "Vividness and Unvividness: Reliability, Consistency, and Validity of Subjective Imagery Ratings." *Journal of Mental Imagery* 12 (1988): 115–122.

Richardson, L. "Five-Minute Sales Coaching." *Training and Development* 52 (1998): 53–57.

Robinson, S. L., and Morrison, E. W. "The Development of Psychological Contract Breach and Violation: A Longitudinal Study." *Journal of Organizational Behavior* 21 (2000): 525–546.

Roe, R. A., Zinovieva, I. L., Diebes, E., and Ten Horn, L. A. "A Comparison of Work Motivation in Bulgaria, Hungary, and the Netherlands: Test of a Model." *Applied Psychology: An International Review* 49 (2000): 658–687.

Rokeach, M. *The Nature of Human Values.* New York: Free Press, 1973.

Ronan, W. W., Latham, G. P., and Kinne, S. B. "The Effects of Goal Setting and Supervision on Worker Behavior in an Industrial Situation." *Journal of Applied Psychology* 58 (1973): 302–307.

Rosen, S. "Self-Actualization Versus Collectualization: Implications for Motivation Theories." In *Work Motivation in the Context of a Globalizing Economy,* edited by M. Erez, U. Klenbeck, and H. K. Thierry, 341–368. New Jersey: Erlbaum, 2001.

Rousseau, D. "Making Evidence-Based Organizational Decisions in an Uncertain World." *Organizational Dynamics.*

Rousseau, D. M. *Idiosyncratic Deals: When Workers Bargain for Themselves.* New York: Sharp, 2005.

———. "Schema, Promise and Mutuality: The Building Blocks of the Psychological Contract." *Journal of Occupational and Organizational Psychology* 74 (2001): 511–541.

Saari, L. M., and Latham, G. P. "Employee Reactions to Continuous and Variable Ratio Reinforcement Schedules Involving a Monetary Incentive." *Journal of Applied Psychology* 67 (1982): 506–508.

Sackett, P. R., Borneman, M. S., and Connelly, B. S. "High-Stakes Testing in

Higher Education and Employment: Appraising the Evidence for Validity and Fairness." *American Psychologist* 63 (2008): 215–227.

Salgado, J. F. "The Five Factor Model of Personality and Job Performance in the European Community." *Journal of Applied Psychology* 82 (1997): 30–43.

Santuzzi, A. and Waltz, P. "Disability in the Workplace: A Unique and Variable Identity." *Journal of Management* 43 (2016): 1111–1135.

Schneider, B., and Bowen, D. E. *Winning the Service Game.* Massachusetts: Harvard Business School Press, 1995.

Schneider, J. R., and Schmitt, N. "An Exercise Design Approach to Understanding Assessment Center Dimension and Exercise Constructs." *Journal of Applied Psychology* 77 (1992): 32–41.

Schrader, B. W., and Steiner, D. D. "Common Comparison Standards: An Approach to Improving Agreement Between Self and Supervisory Performance." *Journal of Applied Psychology* 81 (1996): 813–820.

Schwartz, S. H., and Sagie, G. "Value Consensus and Importance: A Cross-National Study." *Journal of Cross-Cultural Psychology* 31 (2000): 465–497.

Scullen, S. E., Mount, M. K., and Goff, M. "Understanding the Latent Structure of Job Performance Ratings." *Journal of Applied Psychology* 85 (2000): 956–970.

Seijts, G. H., and Latham, G. P. "The Effect of Learning, Outcome, and Proximal Goals on a Moderately Complex Task." *Journal of Organizational Behavior* 22 (2001): 291–307.

———. "Learning Versus Performance Goals: When Should Each Be Used?" *Academy of Management Executive* 19 (2005): 124–131.

Seijts, G. H., Latham, G. P., Tasa, K., and Latham, B. W. "Goal Setting and Goal Orientation: An Integration of Two Different Yet Related Literatures." *Academy of Management Journal* 47 (2004): 227–239.

Seligman, M. E. P. *Learned Optimism: How to Change Your Mind and Your Life.* New York: Pocket Books, 1998.

Sheridan, J. E. "Organizational Culture and Employee Retention." *Academy of Management Journal* 35 (1992): 1036–1056.

Silverthorne, C. D. "Motivation and Management Styles in the Public and Private Sectors in Taiwan and a Comparison with the United States." *Journal of Applied Social Psychology* 26 (1992): 1827–1837.

Skinner, B. F. *About Behaviorism.* Oxford: Knopf, 1974.

———. *Science and Human Behavior.* New York: Macmillan, 1953.

Smither, J. W., London, M., Flautt, R., Vargas, Y., and Kucine, I. "Can Working with an Executive Coach Improve Multisource Feedback Ratings Over Time?

A Quasi-Experimental Field Study." *Personnel Psychology* 56 (2003): 23–44.

Squires, P., Torkel, S. J., Smither, J. W., and Ingate, M. R. "Validity and Generalizability of a Role-Play Test to Select Telemarketing Representatives." *Journal of Occupational Psychology* 64 (1991): 37–47.

St-Hilaire, F., and Gilbert, H. H., "What Do Leaders Need to Know About Managers' Mental Health?" *Organizational Dynamics.*

St-Hilaire F., Gilbert, H. H., and Brun, J. "What If Subordinates Took Care of Managers' Mental Health at Work?" *International Journal of Human Resource Management*: doc.org10.1080/09585192.2016.1276090.

Strauss, J. P., Barrick, M., and Connerley, M. "An Investigation of Personality Similarity Effects (Relational and Perceived) on Peer and Supervisor Ratings and the Role of Familiarity and Liking." *Journal of Occupational and Organizational Psychology* 74 (2001): 637–657.

Sue-Chan, C., and Latham, G. P. "The Situational Interview as a Predictor of Academic and Team Performance: A Study of the Mediating Effects of Cognitive Ability and Emotional Intelligence." *International Journal of Selection and Assessment* 12 (2004): 312–320.

Sweeney, P. "Teaching New Hires to Feel at Home." *New York Times*, February 14, 1999.

Tasa, K., and Whyte, K. "Collective Efficacy and Vigilant Problem Solving in Group Decision Making: A Non-Linear Model." *Organizational Behavior and Human Decision Making Processes* 96 (2005): 119–129.

Templar, K. J., Tay, C., and Chandrasekar, N. A. "Motivational Cultural Intelligence, Realistic Job Preview, Realistic Living Condition Preview, and Cross-Cultural Adjustment." *Group and Organization Management* 31 (2006): 154–173.

Theorell, T., and Karasek, R. A. "Current Issues to the Psychosocial Job Strain and Cardiovascular Disease Research." *Journal of Occupational Health Psychology* 1 (1996): 9–26.

Thornton, G. C., III, and Byham, W. C. *Assessment Centers and Managerial Performance.* New York: Academic Press, 1982.

Tinline, G., and Cooper, C. "Work-Related Stress: The Solution is Management, Not Mindfulness." *Organizational Dynamics.*

Tyler, K. "Prepare Managers to Become Career Coaches." *HR Magazine*, 1997.

Tziner, A., Joannis, C., and Murphy, K. R. "A Comparison of Three Models of Performance Appraisal with Regard to Goal Properties, Goal Perception and Ratee Satisfaction." *Group & Organization Management* 25 (2000): 175–190.

Tziner, A., and Kopelman, R. E. "Is There a Preferred Performance Rating Format? A Non-Psychometric Perspective." *Applied Psychology: An International Review* 51 (2002): 479–503.

Tziner, A., and Murphy, K. R. "Additional Evidence of Attitudinal Influences in Performance Appraisal." *Journal of Business and Psychology* 13 (1999): 407–419.

Van Dyck, C., Frese, M., Baer, M., and Sonnentag, S. "Organizational Error Management Culture and Its Impact on Performance: A Two-Study Replication." *Journal of Applied Psychology Special Section: Theoretical Models and Conceptual Analyses—Second Installment* 90 (2005): 1228–1240.

Van-Dijk, D., and Kluger, A. N. "Feedback Sign Effect on Motivation: Is It Moderated by Regulatory Focus?" *Applied Psychology: An International Review* 53 (2004): 113–135.

Vroom, V. H. *Work Motivation.* New York: Wiley, 1964.

Walker, A. G., and Smither, J. W. "A Five-Year Study of Upward Feedback: What Managers Do with Their Results Matters." *Personnel Psychology* 52 (1999): 393–423.

Wanous, J. P. *Organizational Entry: Recruitment, Selection, Orientation, and Socialization of Newcomers,* 2nd ed. New York: Addison-Wesley, 1992.

———. *Organizational Entry: Recruitment, Selection, and Socialization.* Massachusetts: Addison-Wesley, 1980.

Wanous, J. P., and Colella, A. "Organizational Entry Research: Current Status and Future Directions." In *Research in Personnel and Human Resource Management,* edited by K. M. Rowland and G. R. Ferris, 59–120. Connecticut: JAI Press, 1989.

Wanous, J. P., Poland, T. D., Premack, S. L., and Davis, K. S. "The Effects of Met Expectations on Newcomer Attitudes and Behavior: A Review and Meta-Analysis." *Journal of Applied Psychology* 77 (1992): 288–297.

Wayne, S. J., and Liden, R. C. "Effects of Impression Management on Performance Ratings: A Longitudinal Study." *Academy of Management Journal* 38 (1995): 232–260.

Weber, J. M. "Individuals Matter, but the Situation's the Thing: The Case for a Habitual Situational Lens in Leadership and Organizational Decision-Making." *Organizational Dynamics,* in-press.

Webster, E. C. *Decision Making in the Employment Interview.* Montreal: McGill University Industrial Relations Center, 1964.

Weick, K. "Small Wins: Redefining the Scale of Social Problems." *American Psychologist* 39 (1984): 40–49.

Werner, J. M., and Bolino, M. C. "Explaining U.S. Courts of Appeals Decisions Involving Performance Appraisal: Accuracy, Fairness, and Validation." *Personnel Psychology* 50 (1997): 1–24.

Wexley, K. N., Yukl, G. A., Kovacs, S. Z., and Sanders, R. E. "Importance of Contrast Effects in Employment Interviews." *Journal of Applied Psychology* 56 (1972): 45–48.

Wicker, F. W., Brown, G., Wiehe, J. A., Hagen, A. S., and Reed, J. L. "On Reconsidering Maslow: An Examination of the Deprivation/Domination Proposition." *Journal of Research in Personality* 27 (1993): 118–199.

Wiersma, U., and Latham, G. P. "The Practicality of Behavioral Observation Scales, Behavioral Expectation Scales, and Trait Scales." *Personnel Psychology* 39 (1986): 619–628.

Wiersma, U. J., Van Den Berg, P., and Latham, G. P. "Dutch Reactions to Behavioral Observation, Behavioral Expectation, and Trait Scales." *Group and Organization Management* 20 (1995): 297–309.

Wiese, B. S., and Freund, A. M. "Goal Progress Makes One Happy, or Does It? Longitudinal Findings from the Work Domain." *Journal of Occupational and Organizational Psychology* 78 (2005): 1–19.

Wiesner, W. H., and Cronshaw, S. F. "The Moderating Impact of Interview Format and Degree of Structure on the Validity of the Employment Interview." *Journal of Occupational Psychology* 61 (1988): 275–290.

Winters, D., and Latham, G. P. "The Effect of Learning Versus Outcome Goals on a Simple Versus a Complex Task." *Group and Organization Management* 21 (1996): 236–250.

Wright, P. M., and Cordery, J. L. "Production Uncertainty as a Contextual Moderator of Employee Reactions to Job Design." *Journal of Applied Psychology* 84 (1999): 456–463.

Yanar, B., Budworth, M. H., and Latham, G. P. "The Effect of Verbal Self-Guidance Training for Overcoming Employment Barriers: A Study of Turkish Women." *Applied Psychology: An International Review* (2008): 1–16.

Zweig, D., and Scott, K. "When Unfairness Matters Most: Supervisory Violations of Electronic Monitoring Practices." *Human Resource Management Journal* 17 (2007): 227–247.

Zweig, D., and Webster, J. "Where Is the Line Between Benign and Invasive? An Examination of Psychological Barriers to the Acceptance of Awareness Monitoring Systems." *Journal of Organizational Behavior* 23 (2002): 605–633.

ABOUT THE AUTHOR

Gary P. Latham, PhD, is an award-winning researcher, a well-respected organizational psychologist, and Secretary of State Professor of Organizational Effectiveness at the Rotman School of Management, University of Toronto. The practical significance of his research discoveries for managers led SHRM to award him the coveted Michael R. Losey Human Resource Research Award, the "Nobel Prize" in the behavioral sciences. The Academy of Management gave him the Scholar-Practitioner Award as well as awards for Lifetime Achievement in the fields of Human Resources Management and Organizational Behavior. He is the first person to receive the awards for distinguished contributions to both science and to practice from the Society for Industrial and Organizational Psychology.

As a consultant and an academic, Latham has worked and lectured throughout Asia, Australia, Europe, and North America. A former member of the Board of Directors of SHRM and past President of both the Canadian Psychological Association and the Society for Industrial and Organizational Psychology, he has researched and published more than six books and 100 journal articles. Latham's personal motto is "no research without action, no action without research." He currently serves on the Boards of the International Association of Applied Psychology and the SHRM Foundation. He has been elected to the status of Fellow of the Academy of Management, the American Psychological Association, Association for Psychological Science, Canadian Psychological Association, International Association of Applied Psychology, National Academy of Human Resources, Society for Industrial-Organizational Psychology, and the Royal Society of Canada.

About SHRM

 The Society for Human Resource Management (SHRM) is the world's largest HR professional society, representing 285,000 members in more than 165 countries. For nearly seven decades, the Society has been the leading provider of resources serving the needs of HR professionals and advancing the practice of human resource management. SHRM has more than 575 affiliated chapters within the United States and subsidiary offices in China, India and United Arab Emirates.

About SHRM Certification

For more than 65 years, SHRM has served the human resources profession. HR professionals worldwide look to SHRM for comprehensive resources to enhance their effectiveness on the job, to develop their careers, and to partner strategically with business leaders and stakeholders.

SHRM also works to advance the HR profession as a whole, ensuring that as business evolves, HR evolves to meet business needs. Businesses increasingly understand that effective people management is a strategic imperative. As a result, business leaders expect that HR professionals will demonstrate, in addition to a thorough knowledge of HR concepts and requirements, the behavioral competencies required to effectively apply knowledge in the modern workplace in support of organizational goals.

To meet business needs, SHRM has established two behavioral competency-based certifications, the SHRM Certified Professional (SHRM-CP®) for early- and mid-career professionals and the SHRM Senior Certified Professional (SHRM-SCP®) for senior-level practitioners. SHRM regards the SHRM-CP and SHRM-SCP as the new global standard in certification for the HR profession.

The SHRM Body of Competency and Knowledge (SHRM BoCK™) is the foundation for these certifications. The SHRM BoCK is the product of rigorous research involving thousands of HR professionals organizes eight behavioral competencies into three clusters: Leadership (Leadership & Navigation, Ethical Practice), Interpersonal (Relationship Management, Communication, Global & Cultural Effectiveness), and Business (Business Acumen, Consultation, Critical Evaluation). Additionally there are 15 HR knowledge areas that are critical to the success of any HR professional.

By incorporating key HR competencies and knowledge into the SHRM-CP and SHRM-SCP exams, SHRM's certifications demonstrate to the global business community that the credential-holder has strong capabilities in both aspects of HR practice—competency and knowledge—that are required for effective job performance.

INDEX